Facing China

To John,

With my warmest regards,

Jean Pierre

Hong Kong, 23 Sept 2024

Facing China

The Prospect for War and Peace

Jean-Pierre Cabestan

Translated by N. Jayaram

ROWMAN & LITTLEFIELD
Lanham • Boulder • New York • London

Executive Acquisitions Editor: Michael Kerns
Assistant Editor: Elizabeth Von Buhr
Sales and Marketing Inquiries: textbooks@rowman.com

Credits and acknowledgments for material borrowed from other sources, and reproduced with permission, appear on the appropriate pages within the text.

Published by Rowman & Littlefield
An imprint of The Rowman & Littlefield Publishing Group, Inc.
4501 Forbes Boulevard, Suite 200, Lanham, Maryland 20706
www.rowman.com

86-90 Paul Street, London EC2A 4NE

Originally published in French as *Demain la Chine: Guerre ou Paix?* by Edition GALLIMARD

Copyright © Editions GALLIMARD, Paris, 2021

British Library Cataloguing in Publication Information Available

Library of Congress Cataloging-in-Publication Data

Names: Cabestan, Jean-Pierre, author.
  Title: Facing China: the prospect for war and peace / Jean-Pierre Cabestan; translated by N. Jayaram.
  Other titles: Demain la Chine, guerre ou paix? English
  Description: Lanham, Maryland: Rowman & Littlefield, 2023. | Includes bibliographical references and index.
  Identifiers: LCCN 2022060328 (print) | LCCN 2022060329 (ebook) | ISBN 9781538169889 (cloth) | ISBN 9781538169896 (paperback) | ISBN 9781538169902 (epub)
  Subjects: LCSH: China—Military policy—21st century. | China—Foreign relations—21st century. | China—Strategic aspects. | World politics—21st century. | Geopolitics—China—History—21st century.
  Classification: LCC UA835 .C23313 2023 (print) | LCC UA835 (ebook) | DDC 355/.033051—dc23/eng/20230206
  LC record available at https://lccn.loc.gov/2022060328
  LC ebook record available at https://lccn.loc.gov/2022060329

To Etienne and Bastienne,
hoping that the China they will see
will have remained at peace

"There have been as many plagues as wars in history;

yet always plagues and wars take people equally by surprise."

Albert Camus, *The Plague*

Contents

Map 1

China and Its Borders

Borders delineation

Borders delineated in the 1960s, 1990s—2000s

——— 1960s ▬▬▬ 1990s and 2000s

⬜ Non-delineated or contested borders

▨ Territories claimed by China

⬛ Territories claimed by India

▨ Kashmir, territory disputed by India and Pakistan

------- China's autonomous regions

▨ "Historical Tibet": Tibetan-populated territory, claimed by the Tibetans in exile

1 Arunachal Pradesh
2 Aksai Chin

0 500 km

Sources: www.globalsecurity.org: Thierry Sanjuan (dir.), (Dictionary of Contemporary China), Paris, Armand Colin, 2006.

Map 2

Territorial and maritime disputes
in the South China Sea

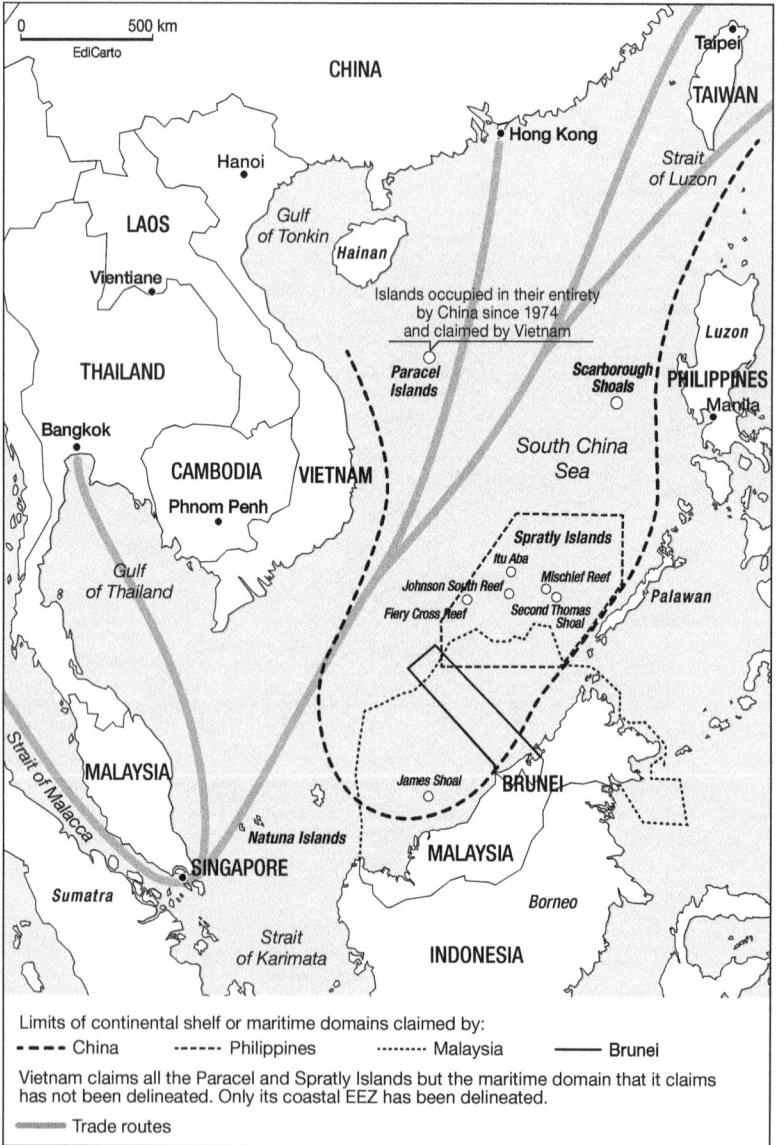

0   500 km
EdiCarto

CHINA

TAIWAN
Taipei

Hanoi

Hong Kong

Strait
of Luzon

LAOS

Gulf
of Tonkin

Hainan

Vientiane

Islands occupied in their entirety
by China since 1974
and claimed by Vietnam

Luzon

THAILAND

Paracel
Islands

Scarborough
Shoals

PHILIPPINES

Manila

Bangkok

South China
Sea

CAMBODIA   VIETNAM

Phnom Penh

Spratly Islands

Itu Aba

Gulf
of Thailand

Johnson South Reef

Mischief Reef

Fiery Cross Reef

Second Thomas
Shoal

Palawan

MALAYSIA

James Shoal

BRUNEI

Strait of Malacca

Natuna Islands

MALAYSIA

SINGAPORE

Sumatra

Borneo

Strait
of Karimata

INDONESIA

Limits of continental shelf or maritime domains claimed by:

- - - China   ------ Philippines   .... Malaysia   ——— Brunei

Vietnam claims all the Paracel and Spratly Islands but the maritime domain that it claims
has not been delineated. Only its coastal EEZ has been delineated.

▓▓▓ Trade routes

Map 3

Air Defense Identification Zones
in Northeast Asia

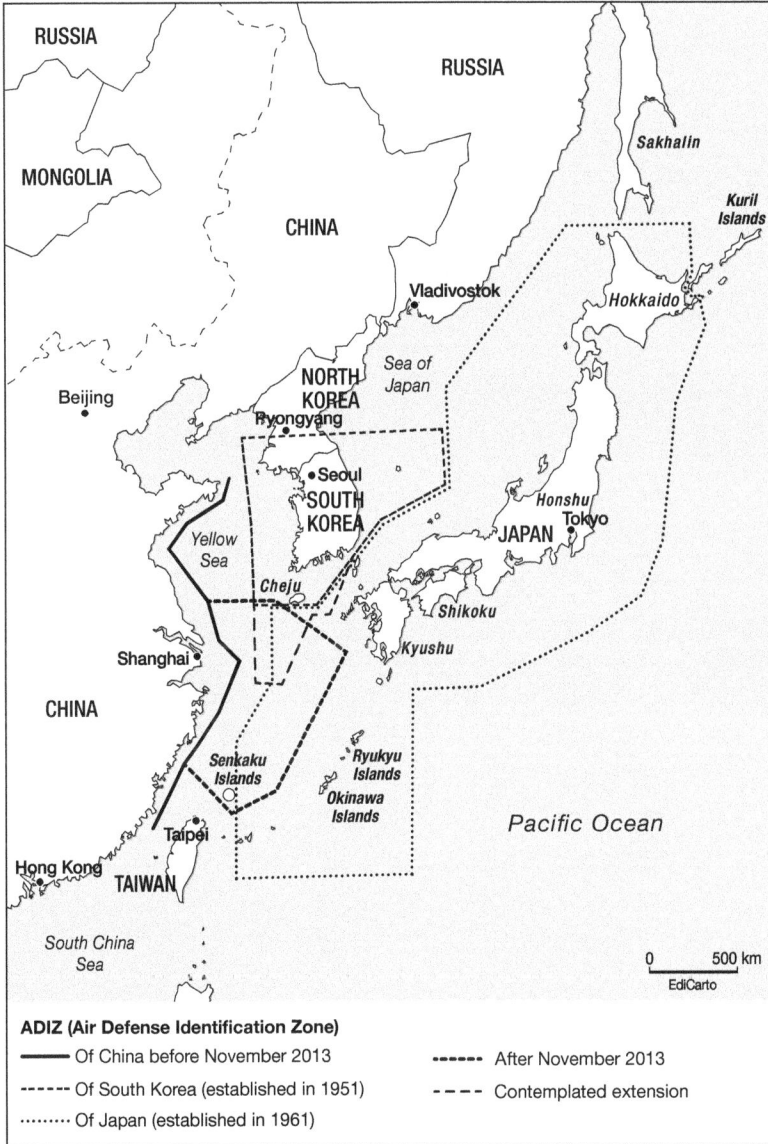

RUSSIA

RUSSIA

Sakhalin

MONGOLIA

Kuril
Islands

CHINA

Vladivostok

Hokkaido

Beijing

NORTH
KOREA

Sea of
Japan

Pyongyang

Seoul
SOUTH
KOREA

Honshu
Tokyo

JAPAN

Yellow
Sea

Cheju

Shikoku

Shanghai

Kyushu

CHINA

Senkaku
Islands

Ryukyu
Islands

Okinawa
Islands

Pacific Ocean

0   500 km

EdiCarto

Taipei

Hong Kong
TAIWAN

South China
Sea

ADIZ (Air Defense Identification Zone)

——— Of China before November 2013

------ Of South Korea (established in 1951)

·········· Of Japan (established in 1961)

---·--- After November 2013

--- --- Contemplated extension

Introduction

THE THUCYDIDES TRAP REVISITED

The China–United States rivalry is now well known. Since Xi Jinping took power in 2012, it has only become more obvious. During Donald Trump's presidency (2017–2021), this rivalry clearly deepened and since Joe Biden took office in January 2021, it has hardly diminished. Beijing's plans are getting clearer by the day: become the world's leading power and eject Washington from the pedestal; dominate East Asia and oust the United States from the Western Pacific.

Historically, this confrontation has long seemed to be strategic and centered in China's neighborhood: Taiwan and Japan, the South China Sea and the Korean peninsula. Today it encompasses the whole world. Moreover, this competition is not only strategic. It also extends to economic and technological domains as the spring 2018 Beijing–Washington trade war and the restrictions to exports of dual technologies to China imposed by the Biden Administration have showed. While it has always been ideological, this dimension has asserted itself since Xi succeeded Hu Jintao as Party leader and head of state. China has increasingly become openly anti-democratic and anti-West worldwide, especially among developing countries. Further, at the United Nations and elsewhere, it seeks to overturn international norms such that they serve its own interests. Simply put, China has become the world's main revisionist power: China–US confrontation is thus total.

Thucydides's Trap

Could this multi-dimensional confrontation presage war? Obviously, the China–US mistrust has escalated, raising risks of miscalculations over adversarial actions. But have the world's top two economies fallen into the "Thucydides Trap," the idea that Athens's rise in the fifth century BC fueled Sparta's fear, leading to an inevitable war?

Right from 2012, noted US political scientist Graham Allison began pointing to the risk of China and the United States falling into this trap. In his 2017

1

book, he elaborated the hypothesis that peace might not last: China, the rising power, could instill in the United States, the current superpower, fears that render a war inevitable, like the Athens–Sparta one.[1]

Of course, Allison does not think a China–US war is inevitable; he merely considers it more probable than is generally believed. Drawing several historical comparisons, he notes the major power transitions over the past five centuries, only four, including the Britain–US and US–Soviet Union ones, have not led to a war between an established and a rising power.[2]

But Allison's intent was to send a stern warning to Chinese and US leaders to avoid the trap and "bend the arc of history."[3]

Is Allison right to sound a warning? China's economy might overtake the United States' by 2030 or a bit later. With a modern and impressive armed force and steeped in unfailing nationalism, might China not be tempted to use its military strength to achieve its grand aims, especially reunification with Taiwan, control of the entire South China Sea, and annexation of the Diaoyu (Senkaku) islands under Japanese control since 1895, just to realize Xi's "China Dream"?

More broadly, beyond these major but risky aims, the People's Liberation Army's (PLA) rapid modernization and rising might only boost the desire and even the need of political and military leaders to test its real capabilities outside the country's borders.

China–US War Debate

The China–US war hypothesis is not new. Apart from the Cold War—the two sides faced off in Korea 1950–1953—it dates back to the mid-1990s Taiwan crisis. To show its discontent over the then Taiwanese president Lee Teng-hui's unofficial US visit in 1995 and the first democratic presidential election on the island in March 1996, China tested missiles in the Taiwan Strait, provoking the deployment of US aircraft carriers in the region. Since that crisis, several scare-mongering books predicting an inevitable Sino–US war appeared, especially in Taiwan. In the West, *The Coming Conflict with China* by Richard Bernstein and Ross H. Munro, which defends the thesis that China was bound to defy by all means, including military, US domination of the Western Pacific, enjoyed great success.[4] But such works soon turned rather irrelevant given the Beijing–Washington power imbalance and their mutual engagement policies. Moreover, they were dealing with other pressing challenges: Beijing with the painful state sector reform and Washington with rising Islamic terrorism.[5]

Chinese military brass had by then begun seriously considering asymmetrical war methods to achieve their aims against the United States. A well-known 1999 work by two PLA colonels sought precisely to exploit the American enemy's weaknesses.[6] More generally since, Sino–US rivalry has gradually been asserted. The Chinese economy's unprecedented rise and globalization, its 2001 World Trade Organization (WTO) accession and emergence as top trading power in 2012, rising influence in Asia, Africa, and Latin America, and increase in asymmetric warfare capacity recall fears of an America bogged down in Iraq and Afghanistan, struck by the 2008 financial crisis, and increasingly unsure of its technological advance and even *soft power*.

Such that some like John Mearsheimer, noted exponent of a realist approach to international relations, began right from 2004 to question the "peaceful" nature of China's "rise" under Hu Jintao.[7] China's increasingly evident assertiveness on the world scene post-2008 has also led an increasing number of US analysts to question the soundness of the engagement policy Washington adopted since Richard Nixon's 1972 Beijing trip.[8] Of course, not all believed a China–US war was inevitable or even probable. Some strategic experts like Aaron Friedberg rightly held, adopting Sun Zi's phrase, that Hu Jintao's China intended to "win without fighting" (*bu zhan er sheng*). But these realist experts also played a role in Washington's realization of new challenges posed by the rising power.[9] Since then, even liberal analysts or those from the British school of international relations like Barry Buzan have held that it would be harder for China to pursue its peaceful rise strategy and avoid war, especially with Taiwan or Japan.[10]

Since early last decade, China's growing ambition and the perceived US decline have led to comparisons with the pre-1914 international situation when Germany increasingly directly defied British might, eventually plunging the Western world into World War I. Henry Kissinger had begun to wonder whether history was repeating itself.[11] In East Asia, don't the United States, China, and Japan now occupy the positions that prevailed in early twentieth-century Europe respectively of Britain, the then dominant power, then rising power Germany, and a relatively declining power, France?[12] Now as before, these great powers are economically and humanly interdependent, something that didn't prevent the 1914 conflict. Moreover, neither London, Berlin, nor Paris wanted war and several leaders sought to prevent it. But nothing worked. Now too, no one wants war. Despite major differences between 1914 and now, World War I's lessons continue to inform discussions over the risks of a China–US war.[13]

This pre-1914 comparison has buttressed realist theses and thus weakened those of constructivist approaches to international relations. As will be discussed, in academic milieux and even governmental circles, realists have long dominated in China, gaining ground in the United States, stoking, while also seeking to prevent, the risks of armed conflict between the two. This comparison is also a reminder that passions, individual decisions, and incorrect calculations, in short, the irrational, could play a decisive role in wars erupting. Here, one of the inspirations for this book, Christopher Coker's *The Improbable War*, merits mention.[14]

On the ground, the policy of rebalancing—the pivot—toward the Asia-Pacific decided by then-president Barack Obama in 2011 and the launching by his successor Donald Trump of the Indo-Pacific strategy in 2017 showed that the United States was not about to yield. In fact, it decided to acquire the means to prevent Chinese hegemonism emerging in East Asia. Moreover, the two countries' militaries adopted increasingly offensive strategies and highly sophisticated armaments such as the AirSea Battle the Pentagon developed in 2010 and new panoplies of hypersonic missiles the PLA unveiled in the same period.

Xi's ascent to power in 2012 obviously intensified Chinese assertion of power and the resulting Sino–US rivalry. Economic and trade rivalry, obviously, with Beijing launching new Silk Roads in 2013 (officially called the Belt and Road Initiative or BRI after 2015); technological rivalry too with the 2015 announcement of the "Made in China 2025" program envisaging the country's gradual mastery over the most advanced technologies; ideological rivalry marked by the Chinese Communist Party's (CCP) ambition to advance its development and governance model against what it calls "western liberalism" and "western democracy"; military rivalry between the two countries' navies and air forces especially around Taiwan, in the East China Sea with Beijing in 2013 establishing the Air Defense Identification Zone (ADIZ) over the Senkaku (Diaoyu) Islands and in the South China Sea following the PLA's construction starting in 2015 artificial islands in the Spratlys zone; and finally, diplomatic rivalry, with China relentlessly expanding its influence among developing countries and in the UN, while ignoring the Hague tribunal's 2016 verdict declaring Beijing's claims of "historic rights" in the South China Sea lacked "legal foundation."

Such intensified Sino–US rivalry linked to the PLA's unprecedented rise—its aim now being "ready for war"—fueled discussions on China's global ambitions and on an eventual US–China armed conflict. Some American analysts such as Michael Pillsbury hold that China, having decided to keep its one-party system and defy the West, is seeking to wrest global leadership from the United States by arming itself to the teeth but stopping short of open war.[15] He believes Xi will remain as attached to Sun Zi's precept as his predecessor. Nevertheless, this intensified rivalry has also spurred more Chinese and American studies over the eventuality of armed conflict.[16]

Two Western studies which have come out after the publication of the French edition of this book deserve attention. The first, by China expert and former Australian prime minister Kevin Rudd and rightly titled "The Avoidable War," clearly demonstrates how much the world has entered a "danger zone"; hence his wise advice, in order to prevent a terrible armed confrontation, to carefully manage the growing Sino–US competition.[17] But can both sides agree upon mutually accepted "red lines" if Xi's ambition is to unify with Taiwan and take control of the whole South China Sea?

"Danger Zone: The Coming Conflict with China" is the title of the second analysis. Authored by two American strategists, Hal Brands and Michael Beckley, it is even more challenging: it predicts that China's growing economic and social difficulties will persuade Xi to launch a war to annex Taiwan before the end of this decade. Adopting another approach to Thucydides's Trap, it argues that Athens, then an already risen power, fought against Sparta to avert decline.[18] This prediction may turn right but, as we will see, it would contradict a long-entrenched CCP strategic culture, according to which when domestic problems accumulate, it is not the time to embark on an external military adventure.

Allison published his articles and his book, mentioned above, in the context of an already intensive American debate about the meaning and the direction of US–China deepening competition. He forecasts several scenarios that could lead to a US–China war, such as a collision between US and Chinese navies, a Taiwan independence declaration, a Sino–Japanese incident over Senkaku, a North Korea crisis, an escalation following a cyberattack or even what he calls "a spiraling economic dispute."[19] The book discusses most of these scenarios.

As noted, Allison does not believe war is inevitable. "Destiny dealt the hands, but men played the cards," he writes.[20] And Pierre Mélandri rightly notes: "awareness of the Thucydides' trap helps avoid it."[21]

Allison's thesis provoked many responses and refutations.[22] In fact, the 1914 analogy confronts many differences. Now too, like more than a century ago, there is the same accumulation of passions and firepower: a touchy and militant nationalism, and the Chinese military's unprecedented modernization. However, differences abound. China is more engaged with internal problems than Germany then and in general glorifies war less than the latter did a century ago; it belongs to no coalition of powers or alliances that could trigger a conflict with the United States (barring perhaps North Korea); its geographic situation too is less favorable: it is constrained by several island chains and suspicious neighbors; despite spectacularly catching up, it remains significantly less powerful militarily than the United States. Moreover, since 1945 we are in the nuclear era and starting in the late twentieth century, that of space and cybernetic wars—so many factors that fundamentally modify, albeit in different ways, the threshold and stakes of any armed conflict.[23] Finally, are we really witnessing a power transition? Or rather the emergence of a new asymmetric bipolarity tempered by a greater number of more autonomous poles than during the Cold War between the Soviet Union and the West?[24]

Allison's and others' hypotheses forces us to consider the nature of twenty-first-century war. The current era seems to be dominated by internationalized civil wars (former Yugoslavia, Libya, Syria), asymmetric wars against a weak but elusive enemy (Afghanistan, Iraq, Mali, Islamic State), and recrudescent conflicts (Abkhazia, Donbas, Nagorno Karabakh). In general, professional armies indulge in them. And they are less lethal although Afghanistan shows there are exceptions.[25] While indirect wars among great powers have not completely ceased (Libya, Syria, Yemen), they have lost their edge and especially strategic importance.

At least until the Russian invasion of Ukraine in February 2022—in other words after the publication of the French edition of this book—the bloody war between Russia and Ukraine which is going on as this book comes out has been a turning point: it has heralded the return of a major armed conflict in Europe; it involves the West through its financial and military support to the latter although neither the United States nor the United Kingdom and the European Union have declared war against the former; it has compelled many countries to take sides or, like China, remain in highly ambiguous neutrality; and it has demonstrated how easy the world can move from peace to war. Yet not being a NATO member, Ukraine could not be protected as Poland or Lithuania by NATO. It has been on its own, at least in armed conflict if not financially, confirming the strategic reality according to which nuclear powers cannot get into a direct armed confrontation.

In other words, the nuclear era's advent has precipitated the end of direct and symmetric wars between great powers and states (like North Korea but unlike India-Pakistan) possessing atomic weapons. More recently, the prospects of a space war have helped raise the stakes.

More importantly for this book, state and non-state actors now have access to a much wider range of tools to attain their political aims without getting into direct military confrontation.[26] These are the famous "gray zones" that may be defined as "an operational space between peace and war, involving coercive actions to change the status quo below a threshold that, in most cases, would prompt a conventional military response, often by blurring the line between military and nonmilitary actions and the attribution for events."[27] These actions include cyberattacks, online propaganda, remote or difficult to pinpoint operations especially against vital infrastructures or aimed at demoralizing target populations. They may also include deliberate acts backed by a heavy legal and political arsenal, aimed at intimidating or changing the status quo, the military, para-military, and civil actors being perfectly identifiable. Russia and, as shall be seen, China have over a decade been busy adopting such actions to defend their interests or push their advantage. But this large-scale recourse to gray zones carries risks. It pushed the United States to change its modus operandi in order to retrieve by military, diplomatic, informational, and economic means strategic advantage where these powers have made progress.[28]

Might China question the thesis that nuclear powers do not go to war against each other? Are Beijing and Washington capable of triggering hostilities without risking nuclearizing or even "spatializing" the conflict? Or are they doomed to take their clashes to other areas, such as technological competition or cyberwar?

Does Beijing intend to start an armed conflict with its neighbors, notably Taiwan, the countries that claim parts or the whole of the South China Sea or with Japan over the Senkaku (Diaoyu)? Or does China prefer to stay in the gray zones where it has thus far excelled?

Is Beijing ready to use force to defend what it deems national security, impose its own rules on the world, or to protect its citizens or interests abroad? Is it more likely to lead, like other major and middle powers, what are now called "overseas operations"?[29]

This book will deal with these issues.

Readers might have already noted the author's "realist" or even Aronist bent, a perspective developed from having been a French student familiar with international relations and the old Cold War through Raymond Aron's work. The subject demands it. But there are many war-like factors and any realist must consider the ambitions of states, their political leaders, and of the societies they lead, their priorities, internal problems, perceptions, passions, and their share of the irrational, of dreams.[30] In my book on China's international politics, I sought to examine its hesitations between plans to integrate with the international community—rather reintegrate after the 1949 break—inspired by constructivist theses and an increasingly obvious desire for power, which only vindicates the realist camp. China would like to be both constructivist and realist, pro–status quo and revisionist.[31] My method too will be mixed, mainly realistic or rather defending Randal Schweller's "neoclassical realism" which, while recognizing the structural character of the Sino–American strategic rivalry, takes into account the internal and therefore ideological dimension of the regimes involved, but also Robert Jervis's constructivism, in the sense that I will try to take into account the perceptions but above all *misperceptions* at play. I will also try to take into account the "defensive realism" proposed by Kenneth Waltz, according to which the world's anarchist structure encourages nation-states to favor security over adventure, balance of power over expansionism.[32]

Allison's book inspired this one, as did Christopher Coker's and others. The deeper reason for this book is my growing concern as a European of China's ambitions, the means it is equipping itself with to achieve its ends, and its growing threats to the international order, especially in its neighbor-hood. As also Gallimard Publishing House's Pierre Nora's friendly and kind invitation for me to write this book after having written, along with US expert Mélandri, an article for the French journal *Le Débat* on Beijing's view of the Thucydides Trap.[33]

This work develops that article.

It has seven chapters. Considered first are what I call an "accumulation of passions and ammunition," especially on China's part. The next chapter discusses debates over the risks of war in China. I then explore in chapters 3, 4, and 5 the most probable scenarios of a Beijing–Washington conflict: Over Taiwan, the South China Seas, and over the Senkaku islands. I then analyze Sino–Indian tensions along their mutual border that revived in 2020, so as to assess whether they might turn into a real lethal confrontation. However, I believe these scenarios are less likely to materialize than a swift operation aimed at securing the borders or defending Chinese interests or nationals (chapter 7). In the foreseeable future (conclusion), disregarding the unde-clared and ongoing cyberwar, we are above all witnessing the emergence of a new type of China–US Cold War or Cold Peace, one that the world over needs to be aware of and face the consequences of.

Notes

1. "Thucydides's Trap Has Been Sprung in the Pacific," *Financial Times*, August 22, 2012; "Obama and Xi Must Think Broadly to Avoid a Classic Trap," *The New York Times*, June 6, 2013; "The Thucydides Trap: Are the US and China Headed for War?" *Atlantic Review*, 2015; *Destined for War: Can America and China Escape Thucydides's Trap?*, Boston, New York: Houghton Mifflin Harcourt, 2017, p. xvii.
2. Ibid., cf. table of 16 cases and their analyses pp. 42, 244, and 245–86.
3. Ibid., p. xx.
4. New York: Knopf, 1998.
5. On the China-US war risk over Taiwan then, see my own book, *Chine-Taiwan: La guerre est-elle concevable?* (China-Taiwan: Is war conceivable?), Paris: Economica, 2004.
6. Qiao Liang and Wang Xiangsui, *Unrestricted Warfare: China's Master Plan to Destroy America*, Echo Point Books and Media, 2015.
7. John Mearsheimer, *The Tragedy of Great Power Politics*, New York: Norton, 2001; "Why China's Rise Will Not Be Peaceful," September 17, 2004. https://fliphtml5 .com/yhnd/otda/basic; "China's Unpeaceful Rise," *Current History*, April 2006: 160–62.
8. Among the first works, James Mann, *The Chinese Fantasy: How Our Leaders Explain Away Chinese Repression*, New York: Viking, 2007.
9. Aaron L. Friedberg, *A Contest for Supremacy: China, America, and the Struggle for Mastery in Asia*, New York: Norton, 2011.

10. Barry Buzan, "China in International Society: Is Peaceful Rise Possible?" *The Chinese Journal of International Politics*, Vol. 3, 2010, pp. 5–36.

11. Henry Kissinger, *On China*, New York: Penguin Books, 2012, pp. 518–23.

12. Norihiro Kato, "Japan's Break with Peace," *The New York Times*, July 16, 2014, cited by Pierre Mélandri, "Etats-Unis—Chine: un jour la guerre?" (US-China: War someday?), *Le Débat*, No. 202, November–December 2018, p. 30.

13. Richard N. Rosecrance and Steven E. Miller, *The Next Great War? The Roots of World War I and the Risk of U.S.-China Conflict*, Boston: MIT Press, 2014.

14. Subtitled: *China, The United States and the Logic of Great Power Conflict*, Oxford University Press, 2015. Christopher Coker is professor of international relations, London School of Economics.

15. *The Hundred-Year Marathon: China's Secret Strategy to Replace America as the Global Superpower*, Washington, DC: St. Martin's Griffin, 2016. Donald Trump's adviser on China, Pillsbury was among those who favored US hardening toward China.

16. For instance, David C. Gompert, Astrid Stuth Cevallos, and Christina L. Garafola, *War with China: Thinking the Unthinkable*, Washington, DC: Rand, 2016.

17. Kevin Rudd, *The Avoidable War: The Dangers of a Catastrophic Conflict between the US and Xi Jinping's China*, New York: Public Affairs, 2022.

18. Hal Brands and Michael Beckley, *Danger Zone: The Coming Conflict with China*, New York: W.W. Norton, 2022.

19. Allison, *Destined for War*, op. cit., p. 155.

20. Ibid., p. 233.

21. Mélandri, "US-China," op. cit., p. 32.

22. A more recent argument, against the very idea of power transition is from Steve Chan, *Thucydides's Trap? Historical Interpretation, Logic of Inquiry, and the Future of Sino-American Relations*, Ann Arbor: University of Michigan Press, 2020.

23. Rosecrance and Miller, *The Next Great War?* op. cit., pp. xviii–xx.

24. Øystein Tunsjø, *The Return of Bipolarity in World Politics: China, the United States and Geostructural Realism*, New York: Columbia University Press, 2018.

25. Benoît Durieux, Jean-Baptiste Jeangène Vilmer, and Frédéric Ramel (eds). *Dictionnaire de la guerre et de la paix* (War and peace dictionary), Paris: PUF, 2017.

26. Republic of France, *Defence and National Security Strategic Review 2017—Key Points*, Paris, 2017, p. 47.

27. Lyle J. Morris, Michael J. Mazarr, Jeffrey W. Hornung, Stephanie Pezard, Anika Binnendijk, and Marta Kepe, *Gaining Competitive Advantage in the Gray Zone: Response Options to Coercive Aggressions Below the Threshold of Major Wars*, Washington, DC: Rand Corporation, 2019, p. 8. See also Kathleen H. Hicks, Alice Hunt Friend, Joseph Federici, et al., "By Other Means: Part 1: Campaigning in the Gray Zone," Washington, DC: Center for Strategic & International Studies, 2019, https://www.csis.org/analysis/other-means-part-i-campaigning-gray -zone?utm_source=CSIS+All&utm_campaign=9aafc87f34-EMAIL_CAMPAIGN _2019_07_08_02_48&utm_medium=email&utm_term=0_f326fc46b6-9aafc87f34 -161801969.

28. Op. cit., pp. 129–87.
29. Julian Fernandez and Jean-Baptiste Jeangène Vilmer, eds., *Les opérations exté-rieures de la France* (France's overseas operations), Paris: CNRS Editions, 2020.
30. Pierre Hassner, *La revanche des passions: métamorphoses de la violence et crises du politique* (Revenge of passions: The political arena's metamorphoses of violence and crises), Paris: Fayard, 2015.
31. *La politique internationale de la Chine. Entre intégration et volonté de puissance* (China's international policies: Between integration and desire for power), revised third edition, Paris Presses de Sciences Po, 2022. See also my introduction to the special dossier, "What Kind of International Order Does China Want?" *China Perspectives*, 2016/2, pp. 3–6.
32. Randall Schweller, *Unanswered Threats: Political Constraints on the Balance of Power*, Princeton, NJ: Princeton University Press, 2006. Robert Jervis, *Perceptions and Misperception in International Relations*, Princeton, NJ: Princeton University Press, 1976. Kenneth Waltz, *Realism and International Politics*, London: Routledge, 2008.
33. "Le piège de Thucydide vu de Pékin. Affirmer son *leadership*, éviter la guerre" (Beijing's view of the Thucydides Trap: Asserting leadership, avoiding war), *Le Débat*, No. 202, November–December 2018, pp. 4–15.

1

An Accumulation of Passions and Ammunition

Wars are often unforeseen. The Ukraine war offers the most recent illustration of this precept. But what almost always characterizes prewar periods are rising passions and arms-amassment: nationalist passions and rapid modernization of war machines.

As shall be discussed, the rise or recrudescence of nationalism is ubiquitous, especially in East Asia. The end of the Cold War, globalization as well as the social, economic, and financial tensions it has engendered explain for a good part nationalisms' resurgence. The proliferation of trade frictions, especially Sino–US trade war, and the start of de-globalization they have provoked best illustrate this phenomenon. While the COVID-19 health crisis did not cause these trends, it has accentuated them. So many conflicting developments and tensions are likely to rekindle passions whose role international relations experts too often ignore.

As the Russian invasion of Ukraine has shown, China has no monopoly on the factors and risks of war, but its pursuits of power and grandeur account for both its military's unprecedented modernization and the reactions it has provoked, starting from its region. China aims to have Asia's strongest army and be able to impose an unfavorable balance of power on the United States starting in the Western Pacific and later in the Asia-Pacific region.

China's ambition directly challenges the interests not only of the United States, the established power and guarantor of Indo-Pacific allies' security (Japan, South Korea, Australia, Philippines, and Thailand), but also of others such as India and any weaker state perceiving a Chinese threat, such as Vietnam. Therefore, these actors have adapted to this new strategic environment through both military and diplomatic means, while seeking to protect their economic interests as much as possible.

Without openly rejecting globalization, their adaptation effort has mainly sought a new power balance with China to safeguard both their security and peace, in a way validating classical realist theories of international relations.

Apart from China and the United States, this chapter considers the actions of three countries that could most likely be drawn into an armed conflict: Japan, India, and Australia.

CHINA

Over the past few years, Xi's China has amassed more passion and ammunition than any other country. Its quest for power is obvious: its nationalism is increasingly finicky and vindictive, especially toward Taiwan, its foreign policy too increasingly aggressive and dominating. Its military modernization, and especially of its Navy and Air Force, is dangerously narrowing the gap between the People's Liberation Army (PLA) and US forces. Feeling ideologically challenged, it persistently seeks to protect its authoritarian system by promoting it openly and seeking to export its governance recipes. This section focuses on analyzing Chinese official statements and plans, the next chapter dealing with discussions on conflict within China's society and elites.

Unprecedented Power Quest

To start with General Secretary Xi's report to the 19th Party Congress in October 2017, in which he declared:[1]

> This new era will be an era of building on past successes to further advance our cause, and of continuing in a new historical context to strive for the success of socialism with Chinese characteristics. . . . It will be an era for all of us, the sons and daughters of the Chinese nation, to strive with one heart to realize the Chinese Dream of national rejuvenation. *It will be an era that sees China moving closer to center stage* and making greater contributions to mankind.

> [By mid-twenty-first century] China [will have] *become a global leader in terms of composite national strength and international influence.*

> . . . The Party's goal of building a strong military in the new era is *to build the people's forces into world-class forces* that obey the Party's command, can fight and win, and maintain excellent conduct. . . . [The] major country diplomacy with Chinese characteristics aims to foster a *new type of international relations and build a community with a shared future for mankind.*

A military is built to fight. Our military must regard combat capability as the criterion to meet in all its work and focus on *how to win when it is called on.*[2]

These extracts speak volumes. China wants to be the world's number one power, overtaking the United States. That will take time. By the mid-twenty-first century, or the 2049 centenary of the People's Republic's founding, China should be equipped with the world's mightiest armed forces. Its global economic, technological, cultural, and military might will be unrivaled. As of now, the Party-State intends to gradually modify international norms and unite humanity around a project in which it would play a central role, hoping that in the long run socialism triumphs over capitalism.

As Central Party School vice-president He Yiting said in May 2020:

The new period of socialism with Chinese characteristics under Xi Jinping is 21st century Marxism. . . . China's development transcends national borders and has acquired global importance, signifying China's qualification to occupy the ideological and theoretical summit guiding innovative development of global Marxism.[3]

Can China attain all these aims? Doubtful, as shall be explained later. For now, noting and wagering that by 2050 China could be the top economic power (in GDP terms), top military power in manpower and armaments strength, number three nuclear power after the United States and Russia, and number two technological power after the United States. But will this help it become the top global power and prevail in a possible war against the United States?

China's ambitions should be borne in mind: already exposed through Xi's abandoning of Deng Xiaoping's low-profile diplomacy (*taoguang yanghui*) and adoption of a more active, even aggressive foreign policy, often called "Wolf Warrior diplomacy" (see chapter 2), and a much more overt power assertion strategy. "Striving to contribute" (*fenfa youwei*) to humanity has been Chinese diplomacy's motto since Xi took office in 2012.[4]

Intense Nationalism

Chinese nationalism's evident increasing intensity is worrisome. Fueled by propaganda and an educational system that rehashes ad nauseam the nineteenth-century humiliations, this nationalism leaves little room for debate or nuance. Originally state-centered, nationalism has secreted in China a popular nationalism which often breaches the wishes of the Party, but which nevertheless exploits it. Thus, uniting society around the Party-state, it has of late become a direct factor in leaning toward war.

It should be noted that heightened nationalism is not, or no longer, shared by what I call "external China"—Hong Kong, albeit recently vanquished by Beijing, and Taiwan. Some overseas Chinese might show a real attachment to the "mainland" (*Dalu*), which they see as the motherland, and some of them identify with the communist regime. But since the early 2010s, especially Xi's ascendence, a rising number of Hong Kong residents no longer feel Chinese but rather, that they are Hongkongers. This mostly affects young people and it is still unclear whether the national security law's introduction in July 2020 and the relaunch of the "patriotic education campaign" have reversed the trend. As for the Taiwanese, after the late 1980s democratization, they have affirmed their own identity and national narrative which, while for some it may still have a Chinese cultural dimension, politically it is now completely centered around the past and the future of the island on which they live.

Note also that unlike the Kuomintang (Nationalist Party), the Chinese Communist Party (CCP) upholds not nationalism (*minzuzhuyi*) but "patriotism" (*aiguozhuyi*): a Lenin–Stalin era term long since decoupled from "proletarian internationalism," a long-discarded Marxist-Leninist one. The regime nurtures "patriotism" pervasively, even obsessively. I have previously posited that most Chinese were not nationalistic in daily life, unlike, for instance the Koreans or the Japanese.[5] Witness the many Chinese buying foreign products (especially branded ones), seeking foreign passports, opening bank accounts, or acquiring real estate should they have the means in the United States, Canada, Australia, or elsewhere, many countries where their children go to study in. Thus, many Chinese play the game of economic globalization and making the most of it. They are pragmatic and cautious and derive the best individual or family benefit from what the Americans call *hedging*, or protecting themselves against any possible risk.

However, as China gains power, makes its voice heard more widely, and strengthens its role on the world stage, nationalist passion keeps growing. Encouraged by the authorities, this passion is fueled by large segments of intellectual and media elites, reinforcing popular nationalism to the point of making it virulent and intolerant, even warmongering.

To be sure, this nationalism will keep growing as long as it presents no cost to Chinese society. If its material interests were directly affected, nationalist fervor could fade. But such reasoning ignores the passionate and thus irrational nature of the nationalist sentiments of many in China.

What are the bases and wellsprings of Chinese nationalism? They are well known and well exploited by the Party: on the one hand, the "century of humiliations," Opium Wars, "unequal treaties," "gunboat diplomacy," the foreign concessions and the reparations to be paid to the eight countries whose armies (*baguo lianjun*: expression mainly used for foreigners' crimes) invaded the Manchu Empire to quell the Boxer Rebellion in 1900;

on the other hand, Japanese invasion and war crimes in China between 1931 (Manchuria's occupation) and 1945. Such nationalism has long been shared with the KMT of Sun Yat-sen and Chiang Kai-shek. It was Chiang who ended foreign concessions in 1943 and led much of the anti-Japanese resistance, while the Communists, contrary to the myth they managed to spread, were mainly occupied with extending their "red zones" and preparing for the post-war period.

These events, which are not being contested here, helped Chinese revolutionaries in 1911 to try to build a modern state and propagate a national feeling, or nationalism, which hardly existed earlier. Imperial China was a civilization, not a nation. Traditional Chinese society identified itself first with the clan, the village, and then the province, rarely the empire.[6]

This need to build a nation-state capable of resisting Western powers' or Japanese encroachments partly explains the importance the Party attaches to patriotic education. But since the 1989 massacre, such education has sought to boost allegiance to the Party, by equating more directly and openly national interest with the Party-state's. The endless reminders to Western or Japanese interlocutors of past humiliations are only aimed at strengthening China's hand in its negotiations with them.

What matters here is the dominant influence, and in a way, effectiveness of the Party's patriotic propaganda. For many mainland Chinese, criticizing the government or the Party, especially abroad, is tantamount to criticizing the country—unacceptable and akin to "betrayal of the Han race" (*Hanjian*). Simply put, Chinese society has largely internalized the Party's discourse, and this since 1949, that is, for more than seventy years, despite many upheavals and political crises, especially until the 1989 one.

China's unprecedented development and rise have boosted such identification and fueled the rise of a popular nationalism that often exceeds the authorities' needs and seeks to influence them. China's rise also helped calibrate the patriotism message, the Party ably spreading a feeling of pride (*jiao'ao*) it knows to exploit. Often perceived by foreigners as arrogance, this pride has helped unite most people around the authorities' plans. It has engendered visceral revulsion toward the slightest objection from abroad, especially on sensitive issues such as human rights, Tibet, Xinjiang, or Taiwan. It is difficult to find critical voices on them and *a fortiori* anyone backing freedom for Taiwan, Tibet, or East Turkestan. Similarly, while there are no reliable polls, it is clear that most Chinese support their government's widespread repression of the Uyghurs, the arbitrary administrative detention of more than a million of them, ostensibly for educational purposes, and this in spite of the August 2022 devastating UN Human Rights Report on the issue. As for the South China Sea or the Diaoyu (Senkaku), *vox populi* repeats and amplifies official discourse without much reflection: that these islands have always been China's.

A rare opinion poll published in recent years showed the rise of nationalism especially "supremacism" among Chinese students, that is, in those born after 1990 and even post-1995. Admittedly, a majority adheres to "moderate nationalism" (64.5% in 2017 against 72% in 2015). But a growing minority believes the Chinese are "superior" (*youyue*) to other peoples (19.4% vs. 12.9%), their culture superior to others' (14.1% vs. 9.2%). Those favoring resort to war (literally "all means") to defend national interests rose from 13 percent to 21.3 percent.[7] So much data contradicting the trend toward a relative decline in nationalism some observed after the 2008 Beijing Olympics.[8]

Bluntly put, such blind nationalism can lead to war. On the one hand, it gives the Party-state latitude to undertake a military adventure in pursuit of its reunification or annexation plans. On the other, it has unleashed extremist currents constantly spurring nationalist sentiment and pushing the authorities to go further than they wish.

For example, support for a military adventure against Taiwan is strong and has been growing since the 2016 election of Tsai Ing-wen, a sovereignist rather than independentist, as president. Same goes for the Diaoyu (Senkaku), islets annexed by Japan in 1895, occupied by the US military in 1945–1972, and administered by Japan and Okinawa prefecture since.[9] Increasing incursions from 2010 by fishing boats and then the Chinese coast guard in waters around the Senkaku and subsequent incidents fueled nationalist discourse in the media, rallying public opinion. Nationalist media such as the *Global Times* (*Huanqiu shibao*), website *Qiangguo* (strong nation), or social networks stoke the desire for warlike adventures and vengeful passions against Japan or the West. To unleash nationalism, some sites even spread fake news that complicates China's relations with neighbors. In April 2020, a WeChat public account (*weixin gongconghao pingtai*) claimed that Kazakhstan wanted to merge with China given the latter's rise, forcing Beijing to offer reassurances that this was inaccurate.[10] Moreover, Chinese authorities' hardening on these issues has narrowed the gap between state nationalism and popular nationalism, prompting such media to abide by official discourse.[11]

Outside events too may affect and boost warmongering. After Russia annexed Crimea in 2014, many Chinese pressed for using the same methods to seize the South China Sea islets and atolls occupied by Vietnam, the Philippines, or Malaysia. This pressure is attributable to Xi himself, having declared in 2015 his admiration for Putin, who managed to acquire a "large territory and many resources" provoking little Western resistance.[12] And Putin's invasion of Ukraine in February 2022, despite the difficulties the Russian military has faced, has also intensified the debate in China about what lessons can be learned from it to annex Taiwan, a number of analysts and hordes of netizens criticizing Beijing for being too soft toward Taipei and Washington.[13]

China's government has thus far resisted such "popular" pressures and annexation temptations. While they reflect a part of the society's views, they are willingly shared by the more nationalist currents within the Party and elites. That said, all popular nationalist shows since the early 1990s have been both stoked and instrumentalized as also channeled and controlled by the Party-state. This was so in the 1999 protests over NATO planes' accidental bombing of China's Embassy in Belgrade. In 2005 with anti-Japanese protests sparked by a Tokyo–Washington strategic rapprochement over Taiwan's security or the 2012 ones after the Japanese government decided to "nationalize" three Senkaku islands, although some protesters sought to target the regime, deeming it too weak and unable to accommodate their opinions.[14]

Such emotional nationalist bursts, which I call "nationalist moments," serve the government's interests, helping it exert greater pressure on countries the protesters target.[15] Nationalist protests and fervor present a risk. Thus, since Xi rose to power, they have been mostly discouraged, the new leader not wanting his latitude curtailed by popular feelings.[16] Opinion polls on nationalism have become rare. After the 2020 Sino–Indian border incidents, Chinese social networks were dissuaded from using them for nationalist ends.

However, when needed, in cases of crisis or armed conflict, the authorities can easily mobilize nationalist resources they have themselves built and reinforced. Bearing in mind other equally blind and virulent nationalisms, the Chinese one is plainly warmongering.

Unprecedented Amassing of Arms and Ammunition

China wants to acquire a great power military machine, not only to win local wars but eventually, by mid-century, also vanquish the United States. The PLA seeks parity with US forces by 2035 and superiority to be able to defeat it by 2050.[17] This ambitious objective gives a fairly accurate idea of the unprecedented PLA modernization effort since 1979 and early this century, an effort that accelerated with Xi's rise to power in 2012.

Based on an "active defense" strategy (*jiji fangyu*), China's policy prioritizes gaining control of the maritime domain it claims—Taiwan, the South China Sea, and the Diaoyu—and safeguarding territorial integrity against forces that threaten it, especially in Xinjiang and Tibet. But its objectives have grown and diversified, now including protecting its security interests in extraterrestrial, electromagnetic, and cyber spaces as well as Chinese companies and citizens abroad.[18]

For the PLA, any future war must rely on powerful and rapid projection capabilities. It thus prioritizes the navy, air force, and marine troops capable of intervening in crises overseas. It depends on an online communication network, largely satellite-based, which must be protected or backed up permanently. It is preceded or accompanied by a silent war that has proceeded for a long time: computer warfare and the need for cybersecurity. In this new context, nuclear weapons continue to play a deterrent role, even if states possessing them are more and more tempted to develop tactical nuclear ones, known as battlefield weapons, risking lowering the threshold of any conflict's nuclearization.

The PLA modernization aims to adapt to all of these exigencies.

China's armed forces are now second only to the US ones. In sheer numbers China leads in those of its ships though not yet in those of planes. According to SIPRI, with an annual budget of 293 billion US dollars in 2021 (officially $230 billion in 2022), against $801 billion for the United States, the PLA's is Asia's highest, far ahead of India ($77 billion), Russia ($66 billion), or Japan ($54 billion).[19] In a way, the PLA is unique: a rising great power military primarily concerned with land borders, notably with India, and maritime ones but increasingly eager to project force beyond its perimeter, especially the Malacca Strait, to better protect its maritime routes, its oil supplies from the Middle East and Africa, and its interests abroad. The Djibouti naval base opened in 2017 should help the PLA better meet these needs.

This first overseas PLA base would also help China take a more active part in collective and global security. The Chinese Navy's participation in anti-piracy operations in the Gulf of Aden, the rising Chinese commitments to UN peacekeeping operations, particularly in Africa (Mali, South Sudan), and China's desire to play a greater role in Africa's security and humanitarian operations were among the official reasons for opening the base.[20] The development of what Beijing calls "military operations other than war" (*feizhangzheng junshi xingdong*) easily justifies selling PLA modernization projects as they help highlight Chinese military might's peaceful and "consensual" nature. Although in the absence of armed conflict these new missions help boost the PLA's projection and logistical capabilities, they are only part of the reality, not the main one (see chapter 7).

If China is acquiring great power military might, it is mainly to better confront the United States and impose a power balance increasingly unfavorable to US advanced deployment in the Western Pacific. It aims not only to retake Taiwan and its claimed maritime domain, but also to become the area's hegemon. When in 2014, Xi declared "Asia for Asians" at the Shanghai Conference on Interaction and Confidence-building Measures in Asia (CICA), he meant just this. China does not intend to fall into the same trap as the Soviet Union or prewar Japan: it is not yet seeking military parity with the United States in all areas nor will challenge it militarily before being sure of winning. In the near term, the PLA will keep relying partly on asymmetric methods to achieve its goals.

Thus, its nuclear strategy remains, like France's, that of deterrence "of the strong by the weak" and acquisition of second-strike capability. While Beijing declares continued adherence to no-first-use doctrine, China's military has in recent years turned more ambiguous on this subject.[21] Some PLA brass comments suggest China wanted to do what French nuclear strategists would call "sanctuarize" Taiwan: US military engagement in a conflict around Taiwan could provoke Chinese nuclear response, Major General Zhu Chenghu, then a dean at China's National Defense University, suggested in 2005.[22] Moreover, the PLA has not ruled out using tactical weapons (neutron bombs) against US military deployment in the Western Pacific, thus blurring the threshold for possible conflict nuclearization.

Although numbers are officially secret, the PLA has far fewer strategic nuclear missiles than the United States or Russia: 350 to 400 against 5,428 and 5,977 respectively in 2022 (France: 290).[23] Mainly ground-based but mobile, its nuclear missiles can reach Asian targets (DF-26 type intermediate missiles) or elsewhere, especially the United States (DF-31AG, DF-41 type ones).[24] Some opinionators, including the ultra-nationalist *Global Times*'s then-editor Hu Xijin, have recently been calling for a substantial increase, up to 1,000 nuclear warheads (including 100 DF-41s) to better evade US anti-missile defense.[25] According to American projections, Hu seems to have been listened to by the Chinese leadership: The PLA's nuclear arsenal should double by 2027 (700 warheads), triple by 2030 (at least 1,000 warheads) and probably reach 1,500 warheads by 2035.[26] This will boost Washington's pressure on Beijing to join in future talks to renew the 2011 US-Russia New START (Strategic Arms Reduction Treaty) which limits the number of strategic nuclear warheads (i.e., intercontinental) at 1,550.[27] (The current treaty was extended for five years [until February 2026] by the Biden Administration and Moscow in February 2021, but Putin decided to withdraw from it in February 2023.) Washington will also increase pressure for China to join talks on a new Intermediate-Range Nuclear Forces (INF) Treaty, if it starts, the 1987 US–Soviet missile treaty, nuclear or conventional, having been denounced by Trump in 2018 (Biden has not reversed this decision). The PLA now boasts the largest arsenal of conventional ballistic or cruise missiles (more than 2,000, including 600 intermediate range); some such as the DF-26 or the hypersonic DF-17 can be quickly nuclear-tipped.[28]

The PLA has also developed asymmetric warfare weapons to gain battlefield advantage: hypersonic missiles, anti-satellite or electromagnetic weapons. It knows that any war, especially with the United States, will begin in outer space and cyberspace. China's military doctrine since early this decade holds that to prevail on the battlefield, it must take command of space and dominate the networks.[29] In 2007 and again in 2010 and 2013, the PLA tested an anti-satellite weapon (destroying an old satellite for the first time with a surface-to-air missile), highlighting its new capabilities.[30] Meanwhile, China has set up a satellite navigation system (*Beidou* or Polar Star) which, since 2020 (30 *Beidou*-3 satellites) going by Pentagon analyses, allows it—as well as the PLA—to be free of dependence on American GPS. It also has a fleet of 120 reconnaissance and remote sensing satellites, half used by the PLA. Simultaneously, the PLA is developing directed-energy weapons to neutralize enemy satellites. Also, learning from the United States, especially its National Security Agency, the PLA is strengthening its cybernetic attack capabilities by regularly hacking foreign sites, mostly US ones, often to obtain scientific and technological secrets.[31]

In other areas, especially maritime, China seeks to impose a new power balance, based on the number of ships and submarines launched annually.[32]

Aircraft carrier projects are Chinese maritime ambitions' most spectacular part. Already possessing two operational aircraft carriers (*Liaoning* since 2012 and *Shandong* since 2019), the PLA will have three by 2024, once the *Fujian* enters service. Construction of a fourth one, probably nuclear-powered, started in 2018 and should be completed by 2025. While for budgetary and technical reasons, the nuclear-powered aircraft carriers project was temporarily halted in late 2019, it resumed in 2021 and will enable the PLA to eventually deploy six aircraft carriers. Should a conflict break out over Taiwan or the South China Sea, the PLA's aircraft carriers will not play a decisive role. The aircraft carrier is mainly a power attribute and signals ability to project power beyond national territories. Taiwan's civilian and military targets are now within range of Chinese aircraft and ground-based missiles. With four carrier groups soon, China's Navy can take on the US Seventh Fleet, even if regularly backed by the Third Fleet based in the Arabian-Persian Gulf, and impose on the United States an unfavorable balance of forces in the western Pacific.

Broadly, in terms of number of ships despite the imperfectness of this comparison, China's Navy has been world leader since 2019, ahead of the US's (355 vessels against 296 in 2021, 340 in 2022).[33] Most striking is the Chinese shipyards' pace of building new vessels and submarines: 119 vessels between 2005 and 2019 including 12 destroyers, 11 frigates, 42 corvettes, 35 patrol boats, and 17 amphibious vehicles.[34] Thus, despite the 2012 US announcement of placing 60 percent of its naval forces in Asia-Pacific (against 50% previously) and the Pentagon's plans, the United States is unlikely to regain preeminence. In 2022, the United States was estimated to possess 296 battle force ships, a more credible comparison basis, while China already had 340, rising to 400 by 2025 and 440 by 2030. The US Navy's 2016-set plan was acquiring 355 vessels by 2034.[35]

This modernization effort concerns not only the PLA Navy, but also the coast guard and maritime militia which since the early 2010s have played an increasing role in securing and controlling territorial waters, China-claimed "historic waters," and Exclusive Economic Zones (EEZs). They are deployed on the front lines, especially in the South China Sea and around the Diaoyu, to assert the activities' "domestic" character. China now has the largest coast guard fleet: 260 vessels, 140 of them large—some of the latter white-painted Jiangkai-class PLA frigates.[36] The coast guards oversee three areas (South China Sea, East China Sea, and North China Sea, i.e., Bohai Gulf, Yellow Sea). The number of boats of maritime militia vessels is unknown: often fishing vessels converted or temporarily mobilized and civilian-staffed.[37] Meanwhile, vessels are being specially built for the militia, for example, the 86 Hainan island ordered in 2016.[38] Maritime militia, like all militia, function under the People's Armed Police (PAP, 900,000 personnel), the PLA branch charged with internal security.

To better coordinate actions by various services enforcing Chinese sovereignty in its claimed maritime domain, the government has taken some major decisions. In March 2013 it merged four maritime surveillance agencies, including the coast guard, with the state oceanic administration. Five years later, in March 2018, it subsumed this administration directly under the Central Military Commission (CMC). In July that year, it placed the coast guard under the PAP's direction, itself under the CMC (previously it also reported to the Ministry of Public Security). These reforms have strengthened PLA control over the coast guard and maritime militia, as well as Xi's grip on them.

All aimed at strengthening the PLA's "anti-access/area denial or A2/AD" capabilities, in other words, deterring the United States from intervening in a conflict over Taiwan or other territorial issues, or at least delaying such intervention. It also aims to establish domination over the chain of islands from Okinawa to Singapore via Taiwan, the Philippines, and Borneo.

In sophistication and firepower terms, the US Navy is likely to stay a step ahead of China's. But its technological and qualitative lead is gradually eroding.[39] In the event of a war in the Western Pacific, will it be able to deploy enough ships and submarines to rule the seas?

The United States might take comfort in the belief that for the foreseeable future it can control the skies: who controls the sky, controls the sea. Such air superiority is still evident and decisive, in all scenarios, including in the South China Sea and around Taiwan.[40] Again, this superiority is declining.

In 2022, the PLA Air Force was already the region's largest, with more than 2,800 aircraft, including about 2,250 combat aircraft (1,800 fighters and

450 bombers), including 800 of the fourth and fifth generation, a proportion expected to rise in coming years (J-20, D-31). Moreover, the number and variety of its home-built drones is growing as also its anti-aircraft capabilities, modernized with Russian help.[41] Only the US Air Force is larger (3,400 combat aircrafts), and moreover technologically superior, possessing a large number of fifth-generation aircrafts (F-22, F-35).[42] However, this absolute numerical superiority is of little value, as in terms of combat aircraft numbers capable of being used in any conflict around China, the US superiority, even with Japanese support, is less and less assured. Also, this technological lead will weaken. Apart from fourth generation fighters (Sukhoi 25, 30, and 35), transport aircrafts (Ilyushin 76), tanker aircrafts (Il 78), anti-ship missiles (Sunburn SS-N-22), and defense systems (S-300 and S-400 surface-to-air missiles) bought from Russia, China has developed its own armaments, including a range of drones.[43]

Xi complemented this PLA strength acceleration with a thorough armed forces reorganization, to transform it into a more modern, flexible, reliable, and above all better-integrated tool. In 2013, he launched an unprecedented anti-corruption drive within the Party but also in the military, jailing many, including General Guo Boxiong, former CMC first Vice-Chairman, accused of selling promotions. In 2015, largely inspired by US methods and other modern armies, Xi centralized military command, placing all PLA wings under the direct control of the Party's CMC, which he chairs. He replaced the seven land-army-dominated military regions with five "combat zones" or "war theaters" (*zhanqu*) in which the main PLA branches must coordinate (Army, Air Force, and Navy for coastal areas). He formed new services, such as Rocket Force (*huojianjun*, strategic and conventional missiles, the former Second Artillery) and "Strategic Support Force" (*zhanluë zhiyuan budui*, in charge of cybernetic, electronic, and space warfare), to better respond to new threats. In 2016, Xi named himself commander-in-chief of the PLA's Joint Operations Command, signaling that he would directly lead the conduct of any war if necessary.[44]

Although more ambitious and active than his predecessors, Xi has been proceeding gradually. It was only in 2013 that he established the first Air Defense Identification Zone (ADIZ) in the East China Sea. First adopted by the United States during the Cold War to repel any surprise Soviet nuclear attack, it obliges civil and military planes crossing the zone to report to the authorities of the designating country. While the ADIZ does not mean national airspace extension, it enhances the state's surveillance of contiguous areas. The problem however comes from the fact that the 2013 Beijing-established ADIZ covers the Diaoyu and thus encroaches on Japan's ADIZ, and to a lesser extent South Korea's. Tokyo and Seoul protested but to no avail. Moreover, while the PLA Air Force is still unable to fully control this ADIZ, Japanese and US planes continuing to fly in the disputed areas, it raises the risks of incidents, even collisions. There has since been speculation over the establishment of another Chinese ADIZ covering almost the entire South China Sea. Facing criticism from ASEAN countries, especially those with territorial claims in the area (Vietnam, Malaysia, Philippines), the ADIZ decision has not been announced as of early 2023.

The unprecedented PLA modernization briefly presented above has one purpose: vanquishing the United States in a war aimed to protect what China deems its core interests, especially its territorial integrity and specifically conquer the naval perimeter claimed since 1949.

THE UNITED STATES

The United States has long accumulated enough weaponry to win any conventional war, and nuclear arms needed to destroy the planet many times over.

Briefly, a twofold question for the top world power: Could nationalist passions, or rather US elites' growing hostility to China, become a factor for war? How has the United States adapted to the PLA's rise to prevail in a possible conflict? While the political elites remain divided on how to confront China, they are in increasing agreement to resist, including militarily, its international ambitions, even contesting the regime's legitimacy. A new Cold War looms.

Rising Opposition to China

Few Americans view China positively now. Trade disputes and the COVID-19 pandemic have heightened this trend, which goes back to 2012, in other words, Xi's rise to power.

According to the Pew Research Center, between 2005 and 2011, Americans were more likely to have a positive view of China (52% against 29% who had a negative view in 2006 and 51% compared to 36% in 2011), excepting the global financial crisis year, 2008, and the Beijing Olympics (39% compared to 42%). Since 2012 (40% against 40%), US opinion has changed profoundly: negative views increasingly prevail: 55 percent against 34 percent in 2014 and 66 percent against 26 percent in 2020 after a relative and provisional respite in 2017 (47% vs. 44%) before Trump launched an anti-China trade war.[45]

Most Americans are nationalists: 91 percent believe that it is better for the world if the United States remains the leading power and 83 percent think that is still a reality, albeit less true in economic matters (59%). Republicans are marginally more "anti-Chinese" than Democrats (72% against 62%).

Same holds for university graduates (68% against 64% non-graduates) and older people (71% of those over 50 against 53% of those under 30). Most Americans have harbored a negative opinion of Xi (58% against 28% in 2014) but this has worsened markedly since 2019 (71% against 22% in 2020).

By 2020 more Americans believed Chinese power and influence posed a major threat: 62 percent compared to 41 percent four years earlier.[46] Their worries were mostly over China's negative impact on environmental protection (91% seriously or somewhat seriously concerned), cyberattacks (87%) and responsibility for US trade deficit (85%), ahead of job losses to its advantage (84%), rise of its military power (84%), human rights violations (82%), or growing technological prowess (78%).

The COVID-19 crisis and the Russian invasion of Ukraine have accentuated these trends: in summer 2020, 73 percent of Americans had an unfavorable view of China (compared to 22% with a positive perception) as well as the way it managed the crisis (64% against 31%), although Democrats were less critical than Republicans (38% against 73%).[47] In March 2022, more than 90 percent of Americans estimated that China–Russia partnership was a problem; then, unfavorable opinion of China reached 82 percent; and two thirds of Americans felt that China was a major threat.[48]

US businesses retain strong ties with China. Also, many liberals believe the Trump Administration had gone too far in confronting China or had not used the right methods to defend US interests. Yet anti-China consensus has overall strengthened in the United States. While the elites are deeply divided, divisions Trump helped deepen, they are united on the need to confront Xi's China.[49] Since Biden's January 2021 inauguration, this consensus has only been confirmed.

A Rising Anti-China Strategic Posture

Americans' realization of China's rise dates back to the twenty-first century's first decade, before the Beijing Olympics and the global financial crisis. The George W. Bush Administration began deploying more forces in Asia and strengthening ties with allies in the region. It also sought to strengthen bilateral free trade agreements with Asian countries with open economies and who were more respectful of international standards, especially in terms of the environment, intellectual property, and labor law, leading in February 2008 to twelve countries' talks for a Trans-Pacific Partnership (TPP).[50] The TPP was clearly aimed at countering China's growing commercial might. The latter's economic rise, especially its power assertion from summer 2008, persuaded the United States to go further. In November 2011, Obama launched the idea of a "pivot" toward Asia-Pacific (and to Europe's detriment), an expression quickly replaced by strategic "rebalancing" in favor of this region. Shortly thereafter, in June 2012, the Pentagon announced that 60 percent of US naval forces would be redeployed by 2020 to Asia-Pacific.[51] In April 2016, the Pentagon adopted the Southeast Asia Maritime Security Initiative to help ASEAN countries (including Indonesia, Malaysia, the Philippines, Thailand, and Vietnam) better counter Beijing's initiatives in the South China Sea. The same year, the Obama Administration signed the TPP agreement which, however, was not ratified. Then, the US government still believed it could influence China by adopting a policy combining cooperation and countering efforts.

After Trump took office, Washington adopted a more anti-Beijing strategic posture. Although he pulled out of the TPP soon thereafter, Trump boosted the priority his predecessors had accorded the Asia-Pacific, not hesitating to further neglect Europe and NATO. In November 2017 in Vietnam, he presented his vision of a free and open Indo-Pacific region based, among other things, on the rule of law, individual rights, freedom of navigation and free trade accords, promoting at the same time equity and reciprocity principles. It was then that Washington decided to include, more openly than earlier, New Delhi in its calculations and strategies vis-à-vis Beijing. Shortly thereafter, it unveiled new national security (December 2017) and defense strategies (2018) clearly prioritizing competition with China. In June 2019 elaborating on this strategy in terms of advanced acquisitions and deployment, the Department of Defense specifically targeted China, henceforth deemed a "revisionist power."[52] In November 2019, the State Department extended these initiatives by unveiling its vision of a free and open Indo-Pacific.[53]

In the following years, the Trump Administration grew more critical of Xi's China, denouncing his Belt and Road Initiative and the "debt trap" it rekindled. The United States boosted its economic and security relations with regional allies, notably Japan and South Korea. It relaunched the quadrilateral security dialogue (Quad) with Japan, Australia, and India, first held in 2007, raising it to ministerial level. Moreover, it kept boosting "freedom of navigation operations" (FONOPS) in the South China Sea to remind Beijing of the excessive nature of its territorial and maritime claims, granting more autonomy to Hawaii-based INDOPACOM (Indo-Pacific Command, ex-PACOM) officers to decide on such operations' opportuneness.

The "United States Strategic Approach to the People's Republic of China," a document the Trump Administration published in May 2020, largely reflects this change.[54] It criticized naive liberal approaches to China that expected its gradual political and economic opening. It argued that China's ruling party had abused the liberal order to protect its trade interests while seeking to reshape the international order to its advantage. It also warned of the Chinese government's intentions, seeking to push its ideology in multilateral organizations, especially the UN system, adding:

The CCP's expanding use of economic, political, and military power to compel acquiescence from nation states harms vital American interests and undermines the sovereignty and dignity of countries and individuals around the world.

Adopting "principled realism," the document noted the economic, ideological, and security challenges China presented. It gave unprecedented priority to combating Chinese espionage, especially technological and industrial. Finally, it set out two essential objectives:

> First, to improve the resiliency of our institutions, alliances, and partnerships to prevail against the challenges the PRC presents; and second, to compel Beijing to cease or reduce actions harmful to the United States' vital, national interests and those of our allies and partners.

This new US "strategic approach" is important, especially for Europeans, in three ways: First, facing reality but also pressed by advisers like Matt Pottinger, the then National Security Council's Asia Director, the Trump Administration recognized alliances' importance. The text welcomed changes in the European Union's China policy, especially the March 2019 document, "EU-China: A Strategic Outlook," which for the first time called China a "systemic rival." Although it sought to change the Chinese government's conduct internationally and internally, especially on human rights and Xinjiang, it did not openly seek to change China's "domestic governance model." Finally, while it prioritized economic, strategic, and ideological "competition" with China, it did not abandon cooperation and engagement, calling for a "result-oriented engagement."

The United States also intends to maintain its military lead over China. The US Navy plans to acquire a sufficient number of vessels to keep its status as the world's most powerful in the future. Its Air Force remains the largest and most sophisticated, although China's, now the third in aircraft numbers behind Russia, is gradually catching up. Since 2019, the Pentagon has been preparing to deploy medium-range missiles in the Western Pacific to counter China's threat. As for strategic weapons, Washington, like Moscow, can easily retain superiority in terms of launchers and nuclear warheads. Thus, US response to the new PLA-imposed strategy is based on strengthening conventional deterrence means.[55]

In his July 23, 2020, Nixon Library speech, then Secretary of State Mike Pompeo went further, stating that by opening up to China, the "free world" had created a new "Frankenstein." He openly attacked China's ruling party and, while not invoking regime change, called for a political system change.[56] He warned:

If the free world doesn't change communist China, communist China will surely change us. . . . Securing our freedoms from the Chinese Communist Party is the mission of our time.

[C]hanging the CCP's behavior cannot be the mission of the Chinese people alone. Free nations have to work to defend freedom.

Moreover, borrowing Ronald Reagan's famous 1980s dictum regarding the Soviet Union ("trust but verify"), Pompeo proposed adopting a modus operandi toward China based on mistrust and verification of all actions: "distrust and verify." Pompeo held that the era of "blind engagement" was over. However, "containment" of China was ruled out, given that its economy, unlike the former Soviet one, is globally integrated. Henceforth, facing conflict or "cold war," democracies must unite against China: not a normal regime but an aberration, a party-state that does not play by the same rules as the rest of the world. China depends more on the United States economically than vice versa. Thus: "We must induce China to change in more creative and assertive ways, because Beijing's actions threaten our people and our prosperity." But Pompeo also intended "engaging" Chinese people and "empowering" them, hoping to drive a wedge between them and the Party so the regime could evolve. This was the Trump Administration strategy's weakness: Chinese society is closely monitored and unable to participate in political life; moreover, it is blinded by a powerful CCP-stimulated nationalism; is the society ready to fight for freedom and democracy? Or, as I have written elsewhere, will it not continue, for the foreseeable future, to prefer greater prosperity and security over freedom and democracy?[57]

Had the United States under Trump the means to counter China's rise? Its Indo-Pacific strategy lacked funding. The US investment amounts announced in 2018 ($113 million) in digital economy, energy, and infrastructure and even the BUILD Act ($60 billion to back private investment in developing countries) struggled to compete with Xi's BRI.[58]

Can Biden remedy these weaknesses and acquire the means to maintain leadership in the Western Pacific? Firmer on human rights, the Democratic administration has tried strengthening its hand by improving ties with Asian and European allies. Albeit aware of the impossibility of complete economic decoupling and having reopened cooperation with China (at least on climate change), on the security level it intends maintaining the earlier course, especially on Taiwan (cf. chapter 3), in the South China Sea (chapter 4), or Japan ties (chapter 5). It plans to continue prevailing in strategic competition with China or any other nation.[59]

The first high-level meeting between Biden Administration and Chinese government officials in Anchorage, Alaska, in March 2021—Secretary of

State Antony Blinken and National Security Advisor Jack Sullivan on the US side, Politburo member Yang Jiechi and Foreign Minister Wang Yi on the Chinese side—underscored the continuity of America's China policy. Since then, the Biden Administration has kept in place most of the sanctions imposed by the previous administration against China. It has added some, often in coordination with European and Canadian allies, because of the deterioration of the human rights situation in Hong Kong and Xinjiang. It has expanded the "entity list" of Chinese companies banned from doing business in the United States. Besides, Congress' Democrats and Republicans introduced a new bill—the US Innovation and Competition Act of 2021—aimed at stopping China's global expansion on all fronts, including technological and financial ones, and everywhere in the world, especially in Africa and Latin America. Adopted by the Congress in June 2021 with a $250 billion budget, it has influenced the US's China policy. The G7 summit in June 2021 as well as the four virtual meetings that Biden held with Xi in 2021–2022 have confirmed Biden's plan to thwart China's rise, as well as his intention to involve more actively US allies in this strategy. One of the best illustrations of this new US strategy was the conclusion of the AUKUS pact with Australia and the United Kingdom in September 2021 (cf. thereafter).

As soon as Russia invaded Ukraine, Washington put pressure on Beijing not to sell military equipment to Moscow. In February 2022, the Biden Administration adopted a new Indo-Pacific strategy elevating US competition with China, although claimed to be managed "responsibly," to one of its three top priorities (with the pandemic and climate change).[60] In May 2022, Biden openly indicated the US's willingness to defend Taiwan militarily in case of an attack from China (to date he has publicly made this commitment four times since he came into office). And in August 2022, while mentioning the Pentagon's concern, he refrained from objecting to, let alone preventing, House of Representatives Speaker Nancy Pelosi's visit to Taiwan, triggering a fierce reaction from China (see chapter 4). While the Biden–Xi meeting in Bali in November 2022 has lowered the temperature between the two great powers, it has not narrowed their differences in any way whatsoever.

As the leading world power, the United States is used to setting international standards albeit with allies' help and imposing respect for them worldwide, particularly for economic and financial ones and the law of the sea. Finding its global leadership threatened, it seeks to better protect its technological advance. Huawei's exclusion from the US market illustrates this. The adoption of the CHIPS and Science Act in August 2022 and the Inflation Reduction Act in October 2022 as well as the Ministry of Commerce's decision taken around the same time to prevent China from acceding to the most sophisticated semi-conductors produced worldwide (particularly from the United States, Japan, South Korea, and Taiwan) have confirmed America's willingness to stay ahead in partially decoupling with the Chinese economy and boosting its own capacity in cutting-edge industries.

Keenly watching the PLA's rise, the United States has gradually realized the impossibility of sustaining in the Indo-Pacific and especially the Western Pacific the strategic domination it has enjoyed since World War II. How to prevent China from knocking it off from the region's top spot: this has been haunting the US establishment. The Chinese regime's authoritarian nature helps it in this respect but without bestowing a decisive advantage. Wouldn't it be better to challenge the PLA militarily before it becomes too powerful?

As shall be discussed, perhaps not. For Democrats as well as Republicans, China "poses the greatest threat to America today, and the greatest threat to democracy and freedom world-wide since World War II."[61] But as General Milley frankly said in late 2020: "We don't want great-power competition to turn into great-power war. That would be a disaster."[62]

Since 1783 the United States has deemed itself an Asia-Pacific power and intends to remain one regardless of changing power relations.[63] It wants to continue playing a security role, allowing it to maintain a balance among major powers in what it now calls the Indo-Pacific. Thus, its strategy in the foreseeable future is bound to remain mainly directed at China, raising the risks of armed incidents, even war.[64]

CHINA'S MAIN NEIGHBORS: JAPAN, INDIA, AUSTRALIA

China's neighbors such as Japan, India, and Australia lack the military means to challenge the PLA, although many of them are security-treaty-bound with the United States. The question is how to peacefully coexist with the Chinese giant and keep a favorable balance of power in the Indo-Pacific; how to prevent China from being tempted to undertake armed operation, such as to seize Taiwan, the Diaoyu (Senkaku) or the South China Sea islets controlled by Vietnam, the Philippines, or Malaysia.

Japan

Japan faces a dilemma: China is since 2003 its top trading partner, despite being its main security threat, eclipsing North Korean and Russian ones. After talks on the continental shelf delimitation in the East China Sea (Shirakaba–Chunxiao area) in 2008 failed, tension has risen around the Senkaku, with increasing incursions of Chinese naval vessels and coast guards in the territorial or contiguous waters around the disputed islands. After Japan's decision in 2012 to "nationalize" three of the Senkaku islands and, shortly thereafter, Xi's rise to power, relations have grown more tense (cf. chapter 5).

In 2021, more than 90 percent of the Japanese viewed China negatively.[65] This trend has grown after each crisis. In 2013, just 5 percent of the Japanese viewed China positively. This percentage rose a little to 17 percent in 2018 before falling to 14 percent the following year. In 2021, only 2.6 percent of Japanese thought that Japan-China relations were "good." Overall, a large majority of the Japanese are hostile to China and well disposed toward Taiwan, once Japan's colony (which paradoxically and unlike Korea, reciprocates the sentiment).[66] Tensions with China have helped boost Japanese nationalism. Postwar Japanese nationalism, mostly constitution-bound, including its albeit minority revisionist tendencies, now has difficulty competing with the Chinese, but it would be wrong to underestimate it.[67]

China and Japan reached a compromise in 2014 on the Senkaku which basically resolves nothing but has helped stabilize relations. In the following years, relations further improved: the then Japanese Prime Minister Shinzo Abe visited China in 2018 (the previous prime ministerial one was in 2011) followed by a Xi-Abe meeting on the Osaka G20 summit sidelines in July 2019. The COVID-19 crisis, rising Sino–US tensions, Sino–Indian border incidents, increased Chinese incursions around the Senkaku, and the National Security Law imposition on Hong Kong put paid to a proposed 2020 Xi visit to Japan, which had been in preparation for two years. These developments have contributed to fracturing the ruling Liberal Democratic Party (LDP)'s China policy. Japan's China-market-dependent businesses remain cautious. The Japanese establishment is trying to reduce this dependence and strengthen its security relationship with the United States and other Quad countries (India, Australia). It was Japan, through Abe while in Kenya in August 2016, that first put forward the "vision of an open and free Indo-Pacific," that is, two continents and oceans brought together around the principles of international law, freedom of navigation, and free trade, the only guarantors of regional stability and prosperity.[68]

Since early last decade, China has been the Japanese defense policy's main concern and target. In Tokyo's view, Beijing is now "a substantial threat" to its security. In its 2020 White Paper, Tokyo said the rising PLA might and activism—what it calls the "struggle" against the Senkaku, ADIZ establishment, "regular patrols" by the Chinese Navy and Air Force near the archipelago, especially in the East China Sea, the Sea of Japan, and the Pacific Ocean—"have become a matter of serious concern for the region, including Japan and the international community."[69] The 2022 White Paper sounds greater alarm, clearly criticizing China's plan to change the status quo around the Senkaku, in the South China Sea, and the Taiwan Strait.[70] Published after Russia's invasion of Ukraine, it underscores Beijing's close partnership with

Moscow and the growing risks of war in the Taiwan Strait. The PLA's opacity, its fait accompli policy in the Shirakaba (Chunxiao) area and around the Senkaku, the notable rise in its financial resources and projection capacities compared to Japanese defense which has been stagnating for many years below the 50 billion dollars level, are among Japan's main concerns.

The PLA's rising might has led Japan to modify its defense policy. After a gradual decrease, Japan's defense budget has steadily risen since 2013, from 4,645 billion yen in 2012 to 5,400 billion yen in 2021–2022 ($50 billion, from $45 billion at 2021 average rate). While it should increase to 6 trillion yen ($46 billion at the 2023 exchange rate) in 2022–2023, Japan's defense budget should double to reach 2 percent of GDP (against 1% today) by 2027, so the LDP intends. Similarly, the management of situations in "gray areas" has become the main priority, ahead of others—the defense of remote archipelagic islands (including the Senkaku) and strengthening cybernetic and electromagnetic defenses.

Other Japanese defense "pillars" remain the security treaty with the United States and international cooperation. But here too, the strengthening of coordination with the United States since new defense guidelines took effect in 2015 as well as international cooperation through the Quad are important adaptations to an environment that has become more dangerous. This scenario obviously includes Taiwan, whose location and greater vulnerability to China cannot leave Japan indifferent.

Since the 1990s, the US-Japan treaty's role has shifted from managing the Soviet threat to that of the Chinese one. On many occasions the guidelines for cooperation between Japan's Self-Defense Forces (SDF) and the advanced US system, especially on the archipelago, have been strengthened, most recently in April 2015.[71] The two military apparatuses have created an alliance coordination mechanism allowing them to exchange real time information both to better monitor the gray areas surrounding the archipelago and prepare for any military crisis. This greater coordination aims to more effectively counter Chinese incursions mobilizing coast guards rather than PLA boats (see chapter 5) as well as cyberattacks from China.[72] These new guidelines and especially this mechanism facilitates conducting joint operations, including outside Japan's territorial waters or airspace. They also facilitate cooperation with a third country, such as Australia and India.[73]

Unable for political reasons—opposition from Kômeitô, an LDP-allied Buddhist party—to revise article 9 of the Constitution (the famous renunciation to war article), the Abe government circumvented the hurdle by persuading the Diet to adopt in September 2015 a series of laws allowing Japan to take part in some situations in "collective defense," that is, in coordination with the Americans. These laws notably authorize the SDF to provide logistical support to other countries engaged in military operations even if these are not directly related to Japan's security: Taiwan obviously, but this law can also apply to the South China Sea where US and Japanese navies are already performing coordinated surveillance operations and exchanging intelligence. In principle, Japan's forces would not be called upon to fight, hence in the LDP's view the laws' compliance with the Constitution. But the development has major strategic consequences, particularly with regard to China. Prime Minister Fumio Kishida or his successors are unlikely to question it.

Simultaneously, Japan has gotten around to the intelligence sharing system with the closest US allies (the "Five Eyes" including Australia, Canada, New Zealand, and Britain), with whom it is already widely linked but would like to engage more.[74]

Besides, arms purchases, particularly from the United States, have risen. In July 2020, the latter agreed to sell Japan 105 F-35s ($23 billion), including 42 short take-offs ones. This will help Japan's Air SDF to strengthen archipelagic maritime security.[75] In 2019, Tokyo boosted its interceptor missile purchases. However, in July 2020, Japan abandoned acquiring the Aegis Ashore anti-missile defense system, deemed too expensive ($4.2 billion) and ineffective (especially in the event of a massive attack, i.e., saturation, of North Korean missiles). But this reversal has opened a debate on Japan's need to change its use-of-force doctrine, restrained by its constitution's Article 9 and deemed too defensive, in favor of adopting an offensive capability and deterrent, intended to preemptively neutralize missile launching bases of any potential enemy. Meanwhile, Japan is rethinking its strategy, so as to adopt an integrated anti-missile air defense system.[76]

Japan's defense policy confronts three problems: changing threats and especially the need to implement measures adapted for "hybrid warfare" and the use of "gray zones" by China (see chapter 5); the political but also human limits imposed on any financial defense effort; and the US alliance's uncertainties.

For example, given the steady decrease in Japan's population, the number of people eligible to join the SDF is becoming more problematic each year, the 18–32 age group expected to fall from nearly 19 million now to 14 million by 2050. The albeit strengthening of US–Japan links are far from having enabled Japan to become a full US ally in the event of a crisis or armed conflict. Thus, any common amphibious operation seems difficult to organize.[77] In doctrinal terms, there is a long way to go before the two sides' armed forces can cooperate in the use of forces and training.[78] Finally, despite the increasingly clear stands Washington and Tokyo have taken, Japanese public opinion has growing doubts about US commitment in the event of a Chinese attack on the Senkaku (see chapter 5).

India

India has long prided its independence. Long close to the former Soviet Union, despite a vaunted non-alignment, its foreign and security policies have deeply changed since the Cold War's end. Having become a declared nuclear power in 1998, it has also sought to improve its China ties. But it is mostly focused on its immediate neighborhood—Pakistan too having tested in 1998, the subcontinent and the Indian Ocean region.

China's rise has led India to get closer to the United States. The 2008 Indo–US civil nuclear accord sped up this rapprochement. The United States is now India's top trading partner ($119 billion in FY 2021–2022) against China ($115 b). Long allied to the Soviet Union, then Russia, for armaments, India has gradually diversified its sources, especially benefiting countries such as France (36 Rafale sales in 2016). Late in the first decade of this century, it began procuring US armaments (P-81 reconnaissance aircraft, C-130J and C-17 transport aircraft, CH-47 heavy helicopters, and AH-64-E Apache attack helicopters). After a slowdown between 2015 and 2019, such purchases have resumed (Sikorsky MH-60R naval helicopters). Meanwhile, India's Quad links to Japan and Australia and its ambition to be more active in East Asia have prompted it to strengthen ties with ASEAN countries, especially those having complicated relations with China, such as Vietnam and to a lesser extent Indonesia. Since early this century, New Delhi and Beijing have sought to strengthen relations and consolidate their partnership, bilaterally and through regional organizations as the BRICS and the Shanghai Cooperation Organization which India and Pakistan were admitted into in 2017. The 2018 Modi-Xi meeting in Wuhan seemed to crown this rapprochement. But Sino-Indian tensions have resumed, especially on their Himalayan border, an unresolved dispute. The 2017 military standoff on the Doklam Plateau and the 2020 deadly confrontation in the Galwan Valley in Ladakh-Aksai Chin highlighted this rapprochement's fragility as well as the depth of the two countries' power rivalry (see chapter 6).

India's defense policy has gradually adapted to the new PLA-imposed strategic environment. Its nuclear doctrine is mainly turned toward Pakistan and China. Its maritime strategy aims primarily to strengthen its security interests in the Indian Ocean, such that China's Navy would remain vulnerable there. Hence India has tried to counter China's Djibouti naval base by trying to establish its own base in the Seychelles (Assumption Island), unsuccessfully thus far, or in Mauritius's North Agaléga Island, with apparently more success. But Delhi has over the past decade also become more ambitious east of the Malacca Strait, showing growing interest and concern over Beijing's strategy in the South China Sea. Despite its relative caution over the 2016 arbitration award which broadly backed the Philippines' stand,[79] India now seems to favor setting up a coalition of democracies to more effectively counter China's ambitions.

Meanwhile, India has increased joint naval drills with the US, Japanese, Australian, and other Western powers, such as France in the Indo-Pacific. Organized bilaterally by the Indian and US sides since 1992, the Indian Navy's annual Malabar drills became trilateral in 2015 when Japan began participating. Japan's Navy had taken part in such drills in 2009, 2011, and 2014 when they were conducted off the archipelago, which provoked protests from China, but its participation was then ad hoc. In 2020, for the first time since 2007 Australia was invited to participate in the exercises, lending more substance to the Quad.

India's relations with Russia have remained ambiguous because of its persistent dependence upon Russian military equipment. In February 2022, New Delhi abstained in the United Nations after Putin had decided to invade Ukraine, refraining from condemning the aggression. Later, in September 2022, the Indian military participated in a Russia-organized multinational military exercise called "Vostok 2022" together with the Chinese PLA. Yet India–China relations have remained tense and, overall, India has clearly moved closer to the US and its allies, mainly concerned with China's rise.

Earlier, Indian public opinion was less hostile than Japanese toward China. But the country's image deteriorated in recent years. In 2019, only 23 percent of Indians viewed China favorably and 46 percent negatively against 35 percent and 41 percent respectively in 2013.[80] Since the 2020 border incidents, the trends have accentuated: 91 percent of Indians favor banning Chinese apps and 59 percent back embarking on a war against China (34% are opposed).[81] Meanwhile, Indian nationalism continues to assert itself, especially after the BJP's return to power and the rising tensions with China (and Pakistan).

Thus, the international environment and India's internal context make for a real strategic rapprochement with the United States and Japan but also with Australia and others such as France.[82]

Australia

Somewhat like Japan, *mutatis mutandis*, Australia confronts a paradox: China is its top trading partner. Australia is also linked since World War II's end to the United States by a treaty putting it fully in the Western camp. Its increasingly close security ties with Japan and India led to the Quad's formation, together with the United States.

While China is not openly deemed a threat by the Quad, especially Australia, PLA modernization has forced it to adjust security policy. A direct result of this adjustment was a very rapid rise in Australia's defense budget, which for the first time in twenty-five years reached 2 percent of GDP in

2020–2021. On July 1, 2020, Canberra unveiled a ten-year military spending plan up 40 percent compared to the previous 2016 one (270 billion against 195 billion Australian dollars). The plan is to improve armed forces' dissuasive capacities, especially the Navy's, and the Australian cybersecurity systems' while facing, in Canberra's view, "the most important strategic realignment since the second world war" in the Asia-Pacific.[83] Australia is trying to adapt to a new environment marked by rising Sino–US "strategic rivalry," the desire of the Trump and now Biden Administrations to rely more broadly on regional allies and thus the risk of some US disengagement. Australian Navy's participation in freedom of navigation operations in the South China Sea illustrates this new ambition. But Canberra cannot go too far in defying Beijing if it values economic ties.

In Autumn 2020, China sought to take advantage of this tension. It made many demands that were almost impossible for Australia to meet, such as lifting the exclusion of Huawei from its telecommunications market and ending criticism of its policies in Xinjiang and Hong Kong. Simultaneously, the Morrison government imposed some trade sanctions on China. While Australian public opinion remains divided, reservations or even hostile perceptions of China are growing. Clive Hamilton's 2019 book exposing Beijing's attempts to influence Canberra's foreign policy, especially its China policy, has divided the country.[84] But its impact was all the greater as it was followed by another work, written with Mareike Ohlberg, revealing a much more global Chinese strategy aimed not only at taking control of global narrative on China but also at forcing Western elites, aided by various pressure methods, to adopt pro-China diplomacy.[85] Thus, in Australia too, China ended up stoking nationalism and anti-China feelings.

The conclusion of the AUKUS pact in September 2021 confirmed and amplified Australia's concern over China. Concluded between Australia, the United Kingdom, and the United States and including the delivery for the first time ever of US-made nuclear-powered submarines to a non-nuclear power, it dramatically although only potentially (the first US-delivered submarine won't be operational before 2040) enhanced Australia's military capabilities. While this pact's conclusion provoked some collateral damage with some allies—France was upset to see its own diesel submarine deal being scrapped—and triggered a fierce reaction from China, it clearly signaled to the latter that Australia would probably not have any choice but to get involved if a war in the Taiwan Strait broke out.

The May 2022 political majority change has not fundamentally modified Australia's security policy and growing preoccupations with China. The AUKUS pact has not been questioned. And before becoming prime minister, Anthony Albanese had already pledged to spend more on defense, his predecessor having decided to increase defense spending by 7.4 percent in 2022–2023 (AUD48.6 billion or US$36 billion).

CONCLUSION

Passions and ammunition: rising tensions too between China on the one hand and the United States and its main Asia-Pacific allies and partners on the other—principally Japan but also India and Australia. Most ASEAN countries, being highly dependent on China, seek to maintain good relations with the two great powers dominating the region; including Indonesia, Malaysia, the Philippines, and Vietnam, which have however reasons to oppose China's South China Sea strategy (see chapter 4). Other US allies—South Korea and Thailand—too have their own reasons not to rattle China. A few states have more or less aligned themselves with China, which acts as a counterweight to regional powers they face: Pakistan because of India; Cambodia vis-à-vis Vietnam; and Laos neighboring Thailand. As for ally North Korea, it is rather a liability for Beijing than an asset in confronting Washington. Overall, a pre-conflict regrouping seems to be taking place: against China, the United States may seek to use the Quad and AUKUS. How will the Quad react should a Sino–US war break out in the Taiwan Strait, South China Sea, or around the Senkaku?

This remains hard to predict, obviously. However, fueled by an unquestionable rise of nationalisms, a rapid military modernization and also a deepening ideological rivalry between democracies and dictatorships, the current strategic configuration will play an essential part, should the Sino–US cold war turn hot.

Notes

1. "Full text of Xi Jinping's report at the 19th CPC Congress," *China Daily*, November 4, 2017
https://www.chinadaily.com.cn/china/19thcpcnationalcongress/2017-11/04/content_34115212.htm.
2. Emphases added.
3. *Xuexi shibao* (Study Times), May 15, 2020, http://www.xhby.net/zt/zyq/202006/t20200615_6688417.shtml; cited by Frédéric Lemaître, "En Chine, la 'pensée Xi Jinping' ne fait pas l'unanimité" ('Xi Jinping thought' does not enjoy unanimous backing), *Le Monde*, June 16, 2020, https://www.lemonde.fr/international/article/2020/06/16/en-chine-la-pensee-xi-jinping-ne-fait-pas-l-unanimite_6043030_3210.html.

4. See Xi Jingping's Speech at the Foreign Policy Conference held on November 28–29, 2014, http://www.fmprc.gov.cn/mfa_eng/zxxx_662805/t1215680.shtml.

5. "The Many Facets of Chinese Nationalism," *China Perspectives*, June 2005, https://www.researchgate.net/publication/30445836_The_Many_Facets_of_Chinese_Nationalism.

6. See chapter 5 of Bill Hayton's fascinating book, *The Invention of China*, New Haven: Yale University Press, 2020.

7. Gui Yong, Fu Yu and Yi Xin, "Shengwen haishi jiangwen? Toushe dangdai qingnian daxuesheng minzuzhuyi sichao" (Effervescence or cooling? Nationalism trends among students), *Sixiang yanjiu jiaoyu* (Research and ideological education), 2019, No. 1, pp. 107–11, https://www.ixueshu.com/document/b6a0a2e89f6b9322fa1ef62390bdd5c8318947a18e7f9386.html.

8. Alastair Iain Johnston, "Is Chinese Nationalism Rising? Evidence from Beijing," *International Security*, Vol. 41, No. 3, Winter 2016/17, pp. 7–43.

9. Peter Gries, Derek Steiger, and Tao Wang, "Popular Nationalism and China's Japan Policy: The Diaoyu Islands Protests, 2012–2013," *Journal of Contemporary China*, Vol. 25, No. 98, 2016, pp. 264–76.

10. Vietnam is a frequent victim of fake news. Zhao Yunxian, "Zai piliang shengchan de jia xinwen beihou, minzuzhuyi yinhun busan, 'hou zhenxiang' yili budao." (In the context of large-scale fake news production, nationalism prevails and "post-truth" prevails), *Jiemian xinwen* (World news), April 30, 2020, https://www.jiemian.com/article/4318301.html.

11. Wenna Zeng and Colin Sparks, "Popular Nationalism: Global Times and the US–China Trade War," *International Communication Gazette*, Vol. 82, No. 1, 2020, pp. 26–41.

12. Evan Osnos, "Born Red: How Xi Jinping, an unremarkable provincial administrator, became China's most authoritarian leader since Mao," *The New Yorker*, April 6, 2015, https://www.newyorker.com/magazine/2015/04/06/born-red.

13. Tang Yonghong, "Taiwan cong E-Wu jushi yanbian zhong neng xuedao shenme?" (What can Taiwan learn from the evolution of the situation in Russia and Ukraine?), *Aisixiang*, June 4, 2022, https://m.aisixiang.com/data/134418.html.

14. Ketian Zhang, "'Patriots' with Different Characteristics: Deconstructing the Chinese Anti-Japan Protests in 2012," Massachusetts Institute of Technology Political Science Department, *Research Paper*, No. 2015–18, September 3, 2015, https://papers.ssrn.com/sol3/papers.cfm?abstract_id=2655750.

15. Jessica Chen Weiss, *Powerful Patriots: Nationalist Protest in China's Foreign Relations*, Oxford, Oxford University Press, 2014.

16. Duan Xiaolin, "Unanswered Questions: Why We May Be Wrong About Chinese Nationalism and Its Foreign Policy Implications," *Journal of Contemporary China*, Vol. 26, No. 108, 2017, pp. 886–900; Kai Quek and Alastair Iain Johnston, "Can China Back Down? Crisis De-escalation in the Shadow of Popular Opposition," *International Security*, Vol. 42, No. 3, Winter 2017/18, pp. 7–36.

17. Nancy A. Youssef, "China Aims to Outpace U.S. Militarily, American Commander Says" (featuring comments by the US Chairman of the Joint Chiefs of Staff

Mark Milley), *Wall Street Journal*, December 8, 2020, https://www.wsj.com/articles/
china-aims-to-outpace-u-s-militarily-american-commander-says-11607459776.

18. "Full Text of 2019 Defense White Paper: 'China's National Defense in the New
Era' (English & Chinese Versions)" China's defense white paper, July 2019, Andrew
S. Erickson, *China analysis from original sources*, http://www.andrewerickson.com
/2019/07/full-text-of-defense-white-paper-chinas-national-defense-in-the-new-era
-english-chinese-versions/.

19. Diego Lopes da Silva, Nan Tian, Lucie Béraud-Sudreau, Alexandra Mark-
steiner, and Xiao Liang, Trends in World Military Expenditure 2021, *SIPRI Fact
Sheet*, April 2022. https://www.sipri.org/sites/default/files/2022-04/fs_2204_milex
_2021_0.pdf.

20. See my "China's Military Base in Djibouti: A Microcosm of China's Growing
Competition with the United States and New Bipolarity," *Journal of Contemporary
China*, Vol. 29, No. 125, September 2020, pp. 731–47.

21. The other doctrine being non-use against a non-nuclear power. Cf. Defence
white paper, 2019, op. cit.

22. Danny Gittings, "General Zhu Goes Ballistic," *Wall Street Journal*, July 18,
2005, https://www.wsj.com/articles/SB112165176626988025.

23. "Global Nuclear Arsenals Are Expected to Grow as States Continue to Mod-
ernize–New SIPRI Yearbook Out Now," *SIPRI Press Release*, June 13, 2022, https://
sipri.org/media/press-release/2022/global-nuclear-arsenals-are-expected-grow-states
-continue-modernize-new-sipri-yearbook-out-now. *Military and Security Developments Involving the People's Republic of China 2022.* Annual Report to Congress, Washington, DC: Office of the Secretary of Defense, November 29, 2022,
https://media.defense.gov/2022/Nov/29/2003122279/-1/-1/1/2022-MILITARY-AND
-SECURITY-DEVELOPMENTS-INVOLVING-THE-PEOPLES-REPUBLIC-OF
-CHINA.PDF, p. 94.

24. "Fact Sheet: China's Nuclear Inventory, Center for Arms Control and
Non-Proliferation," April 2, 2020, https://armscontrolcenter.org/fact-sheet-chinas
-nuclear-arsenal/.

25. Hu Xijin, "China Needs to Increase its Nuclear Warheads to 1,000," *Global
Times*, May 8, 2020, https://www.globaltimes.cn/content/1187766.shtml.

26. *Military and Security Developments involving the People's Republic of China
2021,* Annual Report to Congress, Washington, DC: Office of the Secretary of
Defense, November 3, 2021 https://media.defense.gov/2021/Nov/03/2002885874/-1/
-1/0/2021-CMPR-FINAL.PDF, p. 90. *Military and Security Developments Involving
the People's Republic of China 2022*, op. cit. p. 94.

27. Ulrich Kühn, Alexey Arbatov, David Santoro, and Tong Zhao, "Trilateral Arms
Control? Perspectives from Washington, Moscow and Beijing," Research Report, No.
002, Institute for Peace Research and Security Policy, March 2020, https://ifsh.de/file/
publication/Research_Report/002/20200224_IFSH_Research_Report_002_final.pdf;
David E. Sanger and William J. Broad, "A New Superpower Competition Between
Beijing and Washington: China's Nuclear Buildup," *The New York Times*, June 30,
2020, https://www.nytimes.com/2020/06/30/us/politics/trump-russia-china-nuclear
.html.

28. *Military and Security Developments Involving the People's Republic of China 2021*, op. cit., pp. 49, 61, 163. "Statement of Admiral Harry B. Harris Jr., U.S. Navy Commander, U.S. Pacific Command before The House Armed Services Committee on U.S. Pacific Command Posture," April 16, 2017, https://docs.house.gov/meetings /AS/AS00/20170426/105870/HHRG-115-AS00-Wstate-HarrisH-20170426.PDF. *Military and Security Developments Involving the People's Republic of China 2022*, op. cit. pp. 64–65.

29. Shou Xiaosong, ed., *Zhanlüexue* (Military strategy studies), Junshi kexue chubanshe (Military strategy publishing house), 2013, p. 96, cited by *2020 Report to Congress of the U.S.-China Economic and Security Review Commission*, Washington, DC: U.S. Government Publishing Office, December 2020, https://www.uscc.gov/sites /default/files/2020-12/2020_Annual_Report_to_Congress.pdf, p. 393.

30. Brian Weeden, "Anti-Satellite Tests in Space—The Case of China," Secure World Foundation, August 16, 2013. https://swfound.org/media/115643/china_asat _testing_fact_sheet_aug_2013.pdf.

31. *Military and Security Developments involving the People's Republic of China 2021*, op. cit., pp. 19, 64, 88–89. *Military and Security Developments Involving the People's Republic of China 2022*, op. cit., pp. 91–94. *The New York Times*, May 6, 2019, https://www.nytimes.com/2019/05/06/us/politics/china-hacking-cyber.html.

32. Ronald O'Rourke, *China Naval Modernization: Implications for U.S. Navy Capabilities—Background and Issues for Congress*, Washington, DC: Congressional Research Service, March 8, 2022, https://crsreports.congress.gov/product/pdf/RL/ RL33153.r

33. *Military and Security Developments Involving the People's Republic of China 2021*, op. cit., pp. ii, 48–49, 71. *Military and Security Developments Involving the People's Republic of China 2022*, op. cit., p. 50.

34. O'Rourke, *China Naval Modernization*, op. cit.

35. Ronald O'Rourke, *Navy Force Structure and Shipbuilding Plans: Background and Issues for Congress*, Washington, DC: Congressional Research Service, June 3, 2020, https://fas.org/sgp/crs/weapons/RL32665.pdf. *Military and Security Developments Involving the People's Republic of China 2022*, op. cit. p. 52.

36. *Military and Security Developments Involving the People's Republic of China 2021*, op. cit., pp. 75–76. A total of 260 ships and an additional 450 coastal patrol craft, according to *Military and Security Developments Involving the People's Republic of China 2022*, op. cit., p. 78. Other sources report a fleet of around 500,000 tons (1,300 vessels).

37. On maritime forces, see Derek Grossman and Logan Ma, "A Short History of China's Fishing Militia and What it May Tell US," *The Rand Blog*, April 6, 2020, https://www.rand.org/blog/2020/04/a-short-history-of-chinas-fishing-militia -and-what.html; Andrew S. Erickson, "The China Maritime Militia Bookshelf: Latest Data & Official Statements + My Fact Sheet & Recommendations," *China Analysis from Original Sources*, August 2, 2020, https://www.andrewerickson.com/2020/08 /the-china-maritime-militia-bookshelf-latest-data-official-statements-my-fact-sheet -recommendations-2/.

38. *Military and Security Developments involving the People's Republic of China 2020*, Annual Report to Congress, Washington DC: Office of the Secretary of Defense, September 1, 2020, https://media.defense.gov/2020/Sep/01/2002488689/-1/-1/1/2020-DOD-CHINA-MILITARY-POWER-REPORT-FINAL.PDF, p. 72.

39. Op. cit., pp. 48–49.

40. Eric Heginbotham, Michael Nixon, Forrest E. Morgan, Jacob L. Heim, Jeff Hagen, Sheng Tao Li, Jeffrey Engstrom, Martin C. Libicki, Paul DeLuca, David A. Shlapak, David R. Frelinger, Burgess Laird, Kyle Brady, Lyle J. Morris, et al., *The U.S.-China Military Scorecard, Forces, Geography, and the Evolving Balance of Power, 1996–2017*, Washington, DC: Rand Corporation, https://www.rand.org/pubs/research_reports/RR392.html; "An Interactive Look at the U.S.-China Military Scorecard," Rand Project Air Force, http://www.rand.org/paf/project/us-china-scorecard.html.

41. *Military and Security Developments Involving the People's Republic of China 2022*, op. cit., pp. 59–62.

42. Sebastien Roblin, "China's Air Force Is Completely Enormous (But Can it Beat America?): Although it Is Catching Up," *The National Interest*, December 27, 2019, https://nationalinterest.org/blog/buzz/chinas-air-force-completely-enormous-can-it-beat-america-109096.

43. Scott W. Harold, *Defeat, Not Merely Compete, China's View of its Military Aerospace Goals, and Requirements in Relation to the United States*, Washington, DC: Rand Corporation, 2018, https://www.rand.org/content/dam/rand/pubs/research_reports/RR2500/RR2588/RAND_RR2588.pdf; John A. Tirpak, "USAF Three Priorities: China, China, China. Air Force Leaders Warn: The U.S. Will Lose Air Superiority Without Rapid Change," https://www.airforcemag.com/article/usaf-three-priorities-china-china-china/.

44. Phillip C. Saunders, Arthur S. Ding, Andrew Scobell, Andrew N. D. Yang, and Joel Wuthnow, eds., *Chairman Xi Remakes the PLA. Assessing China's Military Reforms*, Washington, DC: National Defense University Press, 2019.

45. Kat Devlin, Laura Silver, and Christine Huang, "U.S. Views of China Increasingly Negative Amid Coronavirus Outbreak," Pew Research Center, April 21, 2020. https://www.pewresearch.org/global/2020/04/21/u-s-views-of-china-increasingly-negative-amid-coronavirus-outbreak/.

46. Jacob Poushter and Moira Fagan, "Americans See Spread of Disease as Top International Threat, Along With Terrorism, Nuclear Weapons, Cyberattacks," Pew Research Center, April 13, 2020. https://www.pewresearch.org/global/2020/04/13/americans-see-spread-of-disease-as-top-international-threat-along-with-terrorism-nuclear-weapons-cyberattacks/.

47. Laura Silver, Kat Devlin, and Christine Huang, "Americans Fault China for Its Role in the Spread of COVID-19," https://www.pewresearch.org/global/2020/07/30/americans-fault-china-for-its-role-in-the-spread-of-covid-19/.

48. *Reuters*, "Americans' Unfavorable Views of China Hit New High, Pew Survey Shows," April 28, 2022, https://www.reuters.com/world/china/americans-unfavorable-views-china-hit-new-high-pew-2022-04-28/.

49. Eleanor Morley, "The US Is Divided, But its Elites Are United against China," Red Flag, July 1, 2020, https://redflag.org.au/node/7248.

50. Nina Silove, "The Pivot Before the Pivot: U.S. Strategy to Preserve the Power Balance in Asia," *International Security*, Vol. 40, No. 4, Spring 2016, p. 46.

51. "Leon Panetta: US to Deploy 60% of Navy Fleet to Pacific," *BBC News*, 2 June 2012, https://www.bbc.com/news/world-us-canada-18305750.

52. "Indo-Pacific Strategy Report," Washington, DC, Department of Defense, 2019.

53. "A Free and Open Indo-Pacific: Advancing a Shared Vision," Washington, DC, Department of State, 2019.

54. https://www.whitehouse.gov/wp-content/uploads/2020/05/U.S.-Strategic -Approach-to-The-Peoples-Republic-of-China-Report-5.24v1.pdf.

55. David Ochmanek, "Sustaining U.S. Leadership in the Asia-Pacific Region, Perspectives, Rand Corporation," PE-142-OSD (2015), https://www.rand.org/pubs/ perspectives/PE142.html

56. United States Strategic Approach to the People's Republic of China, https://trumpwhitehouse.archives.gov/wp-content/uploads/2020/05/U.S.-Strategic -Approach-to-The-Peoples-Republic-of-China-Report-5.24v1.pdf.

57. *China Tomorrow: Democracy or Dictatorship?* Lanham, MD: Rowman & Littlefield, 2019.

58. Joel Wuthnow, "Just Another Paper Tiger? Chinese Perspectives on the U.S. Indo-Pacific Strategy," *Strategic Forum*, Institute for National Strategic Studies, National Defense University, June 2020.

59. Interim National Security Strategic Guidance, White House, March 3, 2021, https://www.whitehouse.gov/wp-content/uploads/2021/03/NSC-1v2.pdf.

60. "Indo-Pacific Strategy of the United States," The White House, February 2022, https://www.whitehouse.gov/wp-content/uploads/2022/02/U.S.-Indo-Pacific-Strategy .pdf.

61. John Ratcliffe (former [Trump era] Director of National Intelligence), "China Is National Security Threat No. 1," *Wall Street Journal*, December 3, 2020, https://www.wsj.com/articles/china-is-national-security-threat-no-1-11607019599?st =4q4aapv90wivrpv&reflink=article_copyURL_share.

62. Nancy A. Yousseff, "China Aims to Outpace U.S. Militarily, American Commander Says," *Wall Street Journal*, December 8, 2020, https://www.wsj.com/articles/ china-aims-to-outpace-u-s-militarily-american-commander-says-11607459776.

63. Michael J. Green, *By More than Providence: Grand Strategy and American Power in the Asia Pacific since 1783*, New York: Columbia University Press, 2017.

64. For a full presentation of the Trump Administration's China policy, see Mike Pillsbury, ed., *A Guide to the Trump Administration's China Policy Statements*, Washington, DC: Hudson Institute, 2020, https://s3.amazonaws.com/media.hudson.org /A%20Guide%20to%20the%20Trump%20Administration's%20China%20Policy %20Statements.pdf.

65. *The Dong-a Ilbo*, "90% of Japanese 'dislike China' and 66% of Chinese 'dislike Japan'" October 22, 2021, https://www.donga.com/en/article/all/20211022/2999473 /1.

66. Laura Silver, Kat Devlin, and Christine Huang, "Attitudes toward China," Pew Research Center, December 5, 2019, https://www.pewresearch.org/global/2019/12/05 /attitudes-toward-china-2019/; "How Are Global Views on China Trending?" China Power, https://chinapower.csis.org/global-views/; Laura Silver, "China's International Image Remains Broadly Negative as Views of the US Rebound," Pew Research Center, June 30, 2021, https://www.pewresearch.org/fact-tank/2021/06/30/chinas -international-image-remains-broadly-negative-as-views-of-the-u-s-rebound/.

67. Sven Saaler, "Nationalism and History in Contemporary China," *The Asia-Pacific Journal*, Vol. 14, No. 20, October 15, 2016, https://apjjf.org/-Sven -Saaler/4966/article.pdf.

68. Government of Japan, *Towards Free and Open Indo-Pacific*, November 2019, https://www.mofa.go.jp/files/000407643.pdf.

69. Ministry of Defense, *Defense of Japan 2020*, Part I, Chapter 2, Section 2, p. 58, https://www.mod.go.jp/en/publ/w_paper/wp2020/pdf/index.html.

70. Ministry of Defense, Defense of Japan 2022, https://www.mod.go.jp/en/publ /w_paper/wp2022/DOJ2022_Digest_EN.pdf.

71. "The Guidelines for U.S.-Japan Defense Cooperation," April 27, 2015, https://archive.defense.gov/pubs/20150427_--_GUIDELINES_FOR_US-JAPAN _DEFENSE_COOPERATION.pdf.

72. Scott W. Harold, Yoshiaki Nakagawa, Junichi Fukuda, John A. Davis, Keiko Kono, Dean Cheng, and Kazuto Suzuki, *The U.S.–Japan Alliance and Deterring Gray Zone Coercion in the Maritime, Cyber, and Space Domains*, Santa Monica, CA: Rand Corporation, CF-379-GOJ, 2017.

73. Tetsuo Kotani, "The Maritime Security Implications of the New U.S.-Japan Guidelines," April 30, 2015, https://amti.csis.org/the-maritime-security-implications -of-the-new-u-s-japan-guidelines/.

74. Daishi Abe and Rieko Miki, "Japan Sets its Sights on 'Six Eyes' Intelligence Status," *Financial Times*, August 25, 2020, https://www.ft.com/content/a73798d1 -1ac1-4a8b-964f-2bb28c34ae4e.

75. Valerie Insinna, "US Gives the Green Light to Japan's $23B F-35 Buy," *Defense News*, July 9, 2020, https://www.defensenews.com/smr/2020/07/09/us-gives -the-green-light-to-japans-massive-23b-f-35-buy/.

76. Rieko Miki, "The Price of Peace: Why Japan Scrapped a $4.2bn US Missile System," *Nikkei Asian Review*, August 5, 2020, https://asia.nikkei.com/Spotlight/The -Big-Story/The-price-of-peace-Why-Japan-scrapped-a-4.2bn-US-missile-system.

77. Scott W. Harold, Koichiro Bansho, Jeffrey W. Hornung, Koichi Isobe, and Richard L. Simcock II, *U.S.-Japan Alliance Conference. Meeting the Challenge of Amphibious Operations*, Washington, DC: Rand, National Defense Research Institute, 2018, p. 53.

78. Jeffrey W. Hornung, *Modeling a Stronger U.S.–Japan Alliance: Assessing U.S. Alliance Structures*, Washington, DC: Center for Strategic and International Studies, November 2015; Jeffrey W. Hornung and Mike M. Mochizuki, "Japan: Still an Exceptional Ally," *Washington Quarterly*, Vol. 39, No. 1, Spring 2016.

79. India merely "noted" this, decision, backing freedom of navigation and peaceful resolution of disputes, "Statement on Award of Arbitral Tribunal on South China

Sea Under Annexure VII of UNCLOS," July 12, 2016, https://www.mea.gov.in/press
-releases.htm?dtl/27019/Statement+on+Award+of+Arbitral+Tribunal+on+South+Ch
ina+Sea+Under+Annexure+VII+of+UNCLOS.

80. Laura Silver, Kat Devlin, and Christine Huang, "Attitudes toward China," Pew
Research Center, December 5, 2019, https://www.pewresearch.org/global/2019/12/05
/attitudes-toward-china-2019/; "Global Indicators Database," Pew Research Center,
March 2020, https://www.pewresearch.org/global/database/indicator/24/country/in/.

81. Sandeep Unnithan, "Enemy Number One," *India Today*, August 8, 2020, https:
//www.indiatoday.in/magazine/nation/story/20200817-enemy-number-one-1708698
-2020-08-08.

82. Rupakjyoti Borah, *The Strategic Relations between India, the United States and
Japan in the Indo-Pacific: When Three Is Not a Crowd*, Singapore: World Scientific
Publishing, 2020.

83. "2020 Defence Strategic Update," https://www.defence.gov.au/strategicupdate
-2020/; Australian Government, Department of Defence, July 1, 2020; *2020 Force
Structure Plan*, https://www.defence.gov.au/about/publications/2020-force-structure
-plan,

84. *Silent Invasion: China's Influence in Australia*, Sydney: Hardie Grant
Books, 2018.

85. Clive Hamilton and Marieke Ohlberg, *Hidden Hand: Exposing How the Chinese Communist Party Is Reshaping the World*, Sydney: Hardie Grant Books, 2020.

2

War Risks Debate in China

Starting after Tiananmen, this debate underwent significant development during Hu Jintao's presidency (2002–2012). It started with the initiation of China's "peaceful rise" idea, then adoption of a "peaceful development" strategy in order to defuse fears of war its growing rivalry with the United States had stoked. Obvious since the 1995–1996 Taiwan Strait crisis, or the so-called missile crisis, this rivalry more clearly showed itself after the accidental bombing of China's embassy in Belgrade in 1999 and during the April 2001 EP-3 incident—US surveillance aircraft intercepted by a Chinese fighter in international airspace south of Hainan Island.[1] Since then, both the government and Chinese experts have been trying to show that China has always been a peaceful power, unlike Western ones, especially the United States. Xi Jinping has largely adopted this essentialist approach to war and peace.

The campaign Hu launched in 2003 for the Party's adoption of the "peaceful rise" (*heping jueqi*) concept was aimed at dousing external concerns and refuting the "Chinese threat theory" (*Zhongguo weixielun*)—that armed conflict between China and the United States or its allies was inevitable. Under pressure from conservatives, the "peaceful rise" formula was quickly abandoned as in their view there could be no guarantee that China's rise would be peaceful.[2] But reprising the "peace and development" (*heping yu fazhan*) precept it had adopted at the reforms' start, the Party adopted "peaceful development" (*heping fazhan*) as its foreign policy plank.

As if by mirror effect, US perceptions and analyses of this rise directly affected Chinese debates. Well before Allison's analyses, John Mearsheimer's *The Tragedy of Great Power Politics*, presaging in 2003 the inevitability of a Sino–US armed conflict, lent arguments to Chinese realists. Among the most famous, Tsinghua University's Yan Xuetong campaigned for China acquiring a powerful military rivaling the US one and, positing the inevitability of conflict over Taiwan, went so far as to advise the government and the PLA to attack the "rebel island" in the near future. While Yan later admitted error in judgment, he long remained attached to hard realistic positions (see below).

Burgeoning tensions from 2010 over the Senkaku (Diaoyu) islets in the East China Sea administered by Tokyo and claimed by Beijing, then from 2012 in the South China Sea, where China began building multiple artificial islands, as well as the launch in 2011 by the Obama Administration of the strategic rebalancing (or pivot) in favor of the Asia-Pacific have clearly heightened discussions among China experts. While the government was propagating, not unsuccessfully, the idea that the United States could not accept China's rise to great power, experts began to express doubts about the current power transition's claimed peaceful nature.

Because it is in these terms that most Chinese international relations experts—albeit not all—now conceive the world order evolving: for them, on the one hand, China is rising, the United States, established power, declining; on the other, the latter is unlikely to accept being challenged by the rising power without resisting, and probably without fighting. So there are many justifications for boosting defense efforts and preparing for war.

It was in this context that in 2012, Xi, then still vice president, reacted to US concerns about Chinese ambitions by launching the concept of "new type of great power relations" (*xinxing daguo guanxi*). Just as ten years earlier the idea of peaceful rise, the "new type of great power relations" aimed at managing an increasingly conflicting relationship and to marginalize, even to mask as much as possible, the insoluble differences marking it.[3]

It was in this context that Allison's articles were published in 2012 and his book in 2017. His analyses, quickly disseminated in China, stoked myriad comments, pitting experts against one another, especially the realists against the constructivists, the "warmongers" against the pacifists.

While Xi has been promoting China's "peaceful development" and a "new type of great power relations" with the United States, he is readying a gradually more active PLA preparation for conflict. Since taking office, he has overseen creeping control of the South China Sea and the waters surrounding the Senkaku. And he is increasingly threatening Taiwan with "non-peaceful" reunification if the democratic island does not give in to Beijing's "one country, two systems" formula.

While Chinese experts are divided on whether to use force against Taiwan, the United States, Japan, or the South China Sea, most have taken a realistic approach to international relations. In military and especially propaganda circles, "warmongers" are on the rise and often seem to dominate the debates. So many theses in obvious tension with the idea widespread in China today that Chinese culture is more attached to peace than Western culture. However, no hasty conclusions need be drawn from the turn of discussions among Party-dependent Chinese specialists, the Party being an institution which, in all circumstances, has the last word. And it is far from certain that Russia's invasion of Ukraine has strengthen the warmongers' camp.

CHINA'S OFFICIAL POSITION: XI
INTENDS AVOIDING WAR

Adopted under Hu, the idea of a "peaceful development" path for China in an increasingly multipolar and globalized context has remained central since Xi rose to power. Presented by Xi as "laws of history," that is, objective forces triggered by the evolution of productive ones, and reflecting Marxist theses' accuracy, these tendencies are proffered with the aim of helping China take advantage of it by proposing "win-win" solutions, but also to avoid war.[4] This obsession shows in all of Xi's foreign policy speeches and of top foreign policymakers like Yang Jiechi and Wang Yi. Any war, even local, can slow down China's economic development and rise to power. The "new type of great power relations" concept stems from this fear of armed conflict.

This is also why Chinese leaders reacted quickly to Allison's theses, seeking to demonstrate by word and deed that the Thucydides Trap could perfectly be avoided. Thus, the adoption by Xi and his diplomats of the aforementioned "new type of relations between great powers" was retrospectively presented as the "intellectual framework" favoring precisely this trap's neutralization. The supposed acceptance—albeit quickly denied—by Obama of the "new type of great power relations" concept at the Sunnylands summit (June 2013) then filled many Chinese analysts with optimism.[5]

Xi's launch of "One Belt One Road" (*yidai yilu*, known since 2015 as the Belt and Road Initiative, BRI) in 2013 was later understood by many including He Yafei, a former Chinese vice foreign minister, as contributing to thwarting the Thucydides Trap: favoring, in Beijing's view, Sino–US cooperation in a region fraught with as many risks as opportunities, the BRI should enable the first and second world power to better assess their respective intentions. It would "cushion" their strategic competition.[6] Although the BRI's strategic and hegemonic dimension are glaringly obvious, Chinese analysts have often embraced this idea to proclaim China's peaceful and integrating ambitions.[7]

But somehow upping the ante, China thinks the United States has to do the heavy lifting to avoid the Thucydides Trap. Not only is the United States required to apply more seriously the principle which it has already endorsed of "mutual respect," that is, respect for China's "fundamental interests" (*hexin liyi*): including Taiwan, Tibet, Xinjiang, the South China Sea, and the regime's nature. But Washington must also accept to change the post-1945 world order to make it more "inclusive," to better "take into account the interests of all." In order to provide this "common roof," the Americans are called upon to stop ostracizing "China for having a different political system" and to modify security agreements to cover its security interests.[8] This 2016 statement by then Vice Foreign Minister Fu Ying, albeit harsh and somewhat unrealistic, highlights the risk of two countries' inability to avoid this trap, a risk that has since greatly increased.

Contrasting with this pessimism, despite deteriorating Sino–US relations caused especially by the Trump Administration's trade war, in 2018 Cui Tiankai, the then Chinese ambassador in Washington, made more confident remarks. Holding that Beijing and Washington continue to be in "the same boat," he said Allison's ideas, which he avowedly held in esteem, had been distorted: his goal was to do everything to thwart the Thucydides Trap. However, in his view too, the factors for war were not in China, but with the Americans who stirred up trade disputes, the Taiwan question, or other issues undermining China's territorial integrity.[9]

Other arguments abound: so far, China has benefited greatly from globalization, having embraced it, and above all having accepted it in its way with all the restrictions that a ruling Party-State believes it must impose through its control of and large subsidies to the economy's commanding heights, flagrantly violating WTO rules. China's economy now matters vis-à-vis most of its partners, helping Beijing impose a power balance favorable to itself, with the notable exception of the United States, and thus achieve its ends without starting a war. This is why China has done everything to promote interdependent relations, with its neighbors and developing countries as also with the whole world, commercially and industrially as well as in scientific and technological realms.

In January 2013, in one of his first foreign policy speeches as Party General Secretary, Xi declared:

> "The tide of history is mighty. Those who follow it will prosper, while those who resist it will perish." Looking back on history, we can see that those who launch aggression or sought expansion by force all ended in failure. This is a law of history. A prosperous and stable world provides China with opportunities, and China's development also offers an opportunity for the world as a whole. Whether we will succeed in our pursuit of peaceful development to a large extent hinges on whether we can turn opportunities in the rest of the world into China's opportunities and China's opportunities into those for the rest of the world so that China and other countries can engage in sound interactions and make mutually benefit progress.[10]

We will not seek to discuss the Marxist character or otherwise of this law of history. Nor will we debate here the irony of Xi's prediction in the context of the ongoing Russian invasion of Ukraine. But this quote clearly shows that Chinese authorities continue to prioritize economic development and a peaceful and gradual rise in the country's international influence. Indeed, the BRI launched in 2013, Beijing's unprecedented activism in the UN system, its global approach to national security, its ambitious technological modernization projects (Made in China 2025), its united front strategy to win over elites in an ever-increasing number of countries, and the instrumentalization of its economic and commercial power, all these decisions pointing to a strategy of boosting above all peaceful power and thus intended to avoid at all costs armed conflict, whether with neighbors or the United States.

China can achieve its ends in many areas without resorting to war. As Xi himself noted: "As China has increased its dependence on the world and its involvement in world affairs, so has the world deepened its dependence on China and had greater impact on China."[11]

Such greater dependence of many states on China has directly led it to play a greater role in world affairs. Xi's report to the 19th CCP Congress (2017) showed this clearly (see chapter 1). It is on this basis that the Party leadership developed its "Xi Jinping Thought on Foreign Affairs." As Yang Jiechi, Xi's top diplomatic adviser and Party Politburo member until 2022, noted, according to this "thought" (*sixiang*, a term recalling "Mao Zedong Thought"), peace, development, and win-win solutions remain priorities now. China must draw on its rise to power to improve "global governance," using Xi's own words at the 19th Congress, build "a new type of international relations" as well as "a community with a shared future for mankind" (*renlei mingyun gongtongti*).[12]

It is not only great power relations, especially with the United States, that China intends to change, but also the whole international order by using its influence in world arenas, such as the UN, and its ascendancy over all countries economically or financially indebted to it. We have witnessed how tenaciously Chinese diplomats try, albeit with uneven success, to have international organizations and China's partners adopt the "common destiny" concept.

Meanwhile, a more combative or "wolf-warrior diplomacy" (*zhanlang waijiao*) has been on the rise, referencing *Wolf Warrior 2 (Zhanlang er)*, a film starring a Chinese Rambo capable of protecting the nation's interests and nationals in a civil-war-torn African country. Officially launched following the Trump Administration's 2018 trade and ideological war, this diplomacy in fact precedes the rise in Sino–US tensions. It stokes domestic nationalism and bares China's belligerent ambitions (cf. chapter 7).

Fueling an unprecedented deterioration in relations with many partners (Australia, France, India, Japan, etc.) and magnified by the COVID-19 crisis, this aggressive diplomacy was temporarily attenuated mid-2020 so as to avoid a downward slide in US–China relations at a time when President Trump, unsure of reelection, sought to take advantage of these tensions. After the US boosted sanctions against China—excluding Huawei from the US market, closing China's Houston consulate, requiring Confucius Institutes to register as "foreign missions," threats to exclude TikTok and Wechat applications, retaliatory measures against Hong Kong after the National Security Law took effect on July 1, 2020—the unprecedented strengthening of ties between the Trump Administration and Taiwan and the launch of virulent attacks against China's political system, Beijing had the choice between heightening or lowering the tension. Wisely, it chose the latter, hoping that if Joe Biden won, he would have more leeway to reintroduce a less unfavorable China policy.

It was a tactical retreat and only vis-à-vis Washington. On August 4, 2020, Chinese Ambassador Cui Tiankai asked the United States if it were "ready to live in peace" with China—as if that depended on Washington only.[13] Three days later, in a long article, expressing support for stabilization of Sino–US relations and return to cooperation and non-confrontation, Yang Jiechi made no proposal likely to interest the Trump Administration, simply asking it, as if addressing lost sheep, to "correct mistakes" and get back on the right track.[14] Shortly thereafter, many senior Chinese voiced readiness to discuss with Washington any subject whatsoever, but did not offer any concrete concessions on one of the many disputes between the two capitals, even as trade talks continued. In the aftermath, the PLA said it had instructed its sailors and airmen to "not fire the first shot" in the event of a confrontation with Americans in the South China Sea.[15] Welcoming the Houston consulate staff, Foreign Minister Wang Yi declared on August 17 that, "dialogue and non-confrontation is still the mainstream opinion among the public in both countries, expressing his confidence that China–U.S. relations will be reborn after the current difficulties."[16]

On the same day, a reassuring cum inflexible commentary from the official Xinhua News Agency was crystal clear:

> China has no intention to replace the United States, nor will it be intimidated by the hostile words and acts of some U.S. politicians. The Chinese people will only rally more closely around the CPC and work together with other countries for a community with a shared future for mankind.[17]

A reassuring statement, as China's government thought it necessary to remind everyone that it would not to fall into the Thucydides Trap: its project's aim was not destabilization, nor achieving power transition but establishing a new, fairer multilateralism. As Xi said in 2017 regarding Sino–US ties: "As long as we maintain communication and treat each other with sincerity, the 'Thucydides's trap' can be avoided."[18] But inflexible too, as Beijing remains self-assured both in terms of the nature of its regime and the strategy of encircling Washington and its Western allies from the periphery, that is to say the south and all countries of the north ready to cooperate with it and endorse its "fundamental interests."

Biden's rise to power has in no way changed this guideline. While seeking to take advantage of a new American administration to attempt, with little hope, a "reset" of bilateral ties, China has remained both ambitious in its real objectives and rigid on issues it obsesses about, such as Taiwan. The March 2021 Anchorage meeting, Xi's participation in the Biden-organized virtual summit on climate change in April 2021, and the successive virtual or face-to-face conversations between both presidents have shown this quite well. They have also revealed how much, behind the rhetoric for internal use, Beijing has been eager to engage with the new US administration with a strong desire for dialogue and stabilization of relations.

But Sino–US differences have remained intact. For example, Chinese propaganda virulently denounced the US Innovation and Competition Act of 2021 even before its adoption, calling it a "risk creator" pushing the two countries toward "confrontation."[19] In the following months, many Biden Administration initiatives triggered fierce reactions from Beijing, including increasing arms sales to Taiwan, its silent endorsement of House of Representative Speaker Nancy Pelosi's Taipei visit in August 2022 and the adoption a few days later of the CHIPS and Science Act aimed at preventing China from catching up with the United States in semi-conductor technologies.[20]

As shall be discussed, such differences remain a belligerence-inducing spark, not only in Americans' views but also in many Chinese experts.'

DEBATES AMONG CHINESE EXPERTS

In China, it is particularly difficult distinguishing experts from privy councilors, independent academics from specialists spreading Party-State propaganda, more so under Xi. Nevertheless, debates among them, including on the serious issue of war, remain lively and pluralistic.

These debates fluctuate, depending on the evolution of Sino–US relations and, to a lesser extent, Sino–Japanese or Sino–Taiwanese ones, but also Chinese perceptions of their country's might. Thus, throughout the Obama presidency (2009–2016), dominated by an engagement policy toward China despite the strategic rebalancing announced in 2011, the realists, favoring power relations, remained most influential, to the detriment of the constructivists, who believe in the stabilizing virtue of interdependence and economic and human integration. After Trump entered the White House, especially since the December 2017 publication of new US national security policy and outbreak of the trade war with China the following spring, the latter gained influence.

As shall be seen, from 2019 onward, the rise in Sino–US frictions again strengthened the camp of realists and supporters not only of aggressive diplomacy but also of war, if need be, especially to settle "the Taiwan issue." With Biden, this camp could only get stronger and more vocal. Nevertheless, most of these flatterers have had to adjust their position when their master, Xi, asks them to. For example, in mid-2020 Xi began to take fright and moderated his hostility towards the Trump Administration, leading many Chinese experts to moderate their view. In the same vein, after Russia's invasion of Ukraine and even Nancy Pelosi's Taiwan visit, he has been keen to keep a strong communication channel with his American counterpart, compelling analysts again to nuance their anti-US invectives.

It is as if, like their diplomats, Chinese experts take advantage of US softness to push their country's advantage and adopt more moderate positions as soon as the latter hardens its position and applies punitive measures.

The aforementioned Yan Xuetong best illustrates this evolution. In 2012, he argued that a Sino–Japanese military confrontation around the Senkaku (Diaoyu) was probable, adding that he believed the United States would not intervene.[21] More generally, he then claimed that the more ambitious and offensive foreign policy advocated by Xi increased war risks, if not with the United States, at least with China's neighbors.[22] Hence the need for China to abandon promoting non-alignment and consider forging its own alliances, for example with Pakistan.[23]

However, after Trump's election, Yan turned more cautious and optimistic. In a world that had become bipolar, the greatest danger of war continued to come from a declaration of independence by Taiwan. He believed the risks of any Sino–US conflict's nuclearization would remain the best bulwark against war.[24] He did not think that the United States could start a real "cold war" against China because, like the latter, it now refused to take on too many international responsibilities; moreover, unlike Moscow, Beijing was doing its best to avoid getting involved in indirect armed conflicts with Washington.[25] Yan went further: he believed the Sino–US trade war would encourage China, not to close, but to open up even more economically, as its continued rise in power depended on it. Thus, having turned realist-constructivist, Yan thought like Xi that globalization protected China against the vulnerabilities of interdependence.[26]

In his 2019 book, *Leadership and the Rise of Great Powers*,[27] Yan adopted a "moral-realistic" position, again tending to minimize the risks of war and even a new cold war: drawing inspiration from the Warring States period (475–221 BC) and its thinkers such as Confucius and Sun Zi, he believed the *humane authority* of political power—a Confucian-inspired notion much different from Joseph Nye's *soft power*—was the only attribute that could enable China to replace the United States as world hegemon by promoting moral values within society and on the international scene capable of winning the majority's consent. Carefully avoiding dwelling on the nature of China's regime, Yan acknowledged that this process would take time but remained optimistic. In essence, this was not much different from the new international order and the "community with a shared future for mankind" dear to Xi.

More recently, Yan has stuck to this guarded optimism, assessing US–China relations more as an "uneasy peace" rather than a new "cold war" and believing that regular virtual or face-to-face talks between Xi and Biden can help prevent any military incident in the Taiwan Strait turning into a war.[28] Yan's main worry comes from the danger of being overwhelmed by great power competition.[29] Interestingly, Yan has been very critical of Russia's invasion of Ukraine and sees in this war only a "predicament" for China.[30]

Clearly, Chinese experts remain divided on war risks and, since 2019, on the emergence of a new cold war with the United States and the West. China's unprecedented rise, especially the reduction in the gap, not only in GDP value terms but "global power" with the United States, have led some, including the economist Hu Angang, to trumpet right from 2011 the country's coming accession to world number one rank.[31] Fueling Western and especially American fears this unlimited confidence in China's capacities and triumphalism have drawn much criticism since Beijing's trade war with Washington began. A group of alumni of Tsinghua University, where Hu teaches, even called for his expulsion for using misleading data exaggerating China's economic and technological prowess.[32]

Moreover, many analysts continue to challenge this overconfidence in China's might. Thus, Wu Jianmin, former ambassador to France and then president of the Central Foreign Affairs University, launched in 2016, shortly before his accidental death, into a public controversy with Hu Xijin, head of *Global Times* (*Huanqiu shibao*), the official newspaper known for its nationalist positions and occasional warmongering, asking him to be more cautious and reasonable over the South China Sea where the latter advised the use of force, if not against the United States at least with regard to the Philippines' claims.[33]

Another dividing line separates traditional realist analysts à la Morgenthau or Kenneth Waltz who believe Sino–US confrontation is structural, stemming from changes in their force equations, from those inspired by the neoclassical realism of a Randall Schweller, taking into account internal and thus ideological dimensions of the regimes involved. For some, the Thucydides Trap is manageable if the two governments adopt a defensive strategy.[34] Others hold that the two economies' growing interdependence raises the cost of any armed conflict but cannot in itself prevent it.

A final dividing line pits realists against constructivists. Among the latter may be mentioned the theorist Tang Shiping, who is concerned over the intellectual domination of the former. Indeed, holding like Robert Jervis that in international relations perceptions and especially misperceptions are fundamental, he thinks the neoclassical realists' "competition bias" is both misleading and dangerous, and a source of additional dangers and war risks.[35]

More broadly, many experts, especially the most official among them, echoing their government's view, note that China does not wish to replace the United States as the sole superpower, nor to fundamentally challenge the post–World War II international order, but simply to reform and improve it. For example, Cui Liru, former director of the Chinese Institute of Contemporary International Relations, has concluded that the Thucydides Trap does not apply to Sino–US relations, which are much more dominated by cooperation and mutual respect than confrontation.[36]

More recently, in the wake of the Sino–US trade war, other writers have taken up Cui's and Yan's arguments: current difficulties should not be an excuse to abandon reforms and shut China off; it does not aim to dethrone the United States; it must consolidate its gains, moderate its ambitions, and avoid, unlike the defunct Soviet Union, embarking on an arms race with the United States; if China, on the other hand, deepens its opening, its rise is inevitable, so let confidence prevail.[37] Obviously behind this dispute there is a domestic political dimension which is beyond this book's scope: it may simply be noted that in general the constructivists are more favorable to reforms and to cooperation with the West while the realists are more attached to protecting the one-party system from outside interference and thus suspicious of the United States and other democracies.

These reflections question the reality of the US–China power transition which many Chinese experts still believe in. Most of them agree on an economic transition, albeit slower than initially expected; but what about the transition in military power and even diplomatic influence or *soft power*? Besides, isn't the world becoming more multipolar?

So many questions relativize, even in Chinese analysts' minds, the reality of the Thucydides Trap. As Qin Yaqing, of China Foreign Affairs University, points out, in a perhaps now outdated controversy with Yan Xuetong, this overly famous trap cannot mechanically apply to China. However, Qin remains cautious: he believes the best way to avoid it is to forge with the United States the "new type of relationship between great powers" that Xi has been promoting since 2012.[38] These are the conclusions also of younger researchers who highlight the profound differences between the time of Thucydides and the present period and also propose concrete solutions, such as better preparation to manage crises and avoid any Sino–US war. They also believe, rather naively, that today's Chinese and Americans are less likely than Sparta and Athens to go to war to resolve differences.[39] The rise of Chinese nationalism and militarism as well as anti-PRC sentiments in the United States contradict their optimism.

Since 2019, influenced by the Trump Administration's policy stiffening, which Biden has continued, the debate terms have evolved, focusing on the outbreak of a new cold war but also rekindling fears of a hot one with the United States.

Sticking by their government's stance, many Chinese experts refuse to believe a new cold war could ensue, as China would find no advantage in it, and this despite rising Sino–US tensions. Thus some analysts, such as the very official "Guo Jiping" (a pseudonym) of the *People's Daily*, link the Thucydides Trap to the reappearance of what he calls, like the CCP, "Cold War mentality" (*lengzhan xintai*), presented as what the United States needs, believing only in zero-sum games and forging an enemy.[40] But others worry more: while they believe the chances of a new cold war remain minimal, they fear a more serious Sino–US conflict, even armed clashes.[41] Others still, rather more independent, such as Shi Yinhong, a noted commentator and Renmin University professor, do not hesitate to speak of a new cold war, marked not only by an ideological and strategic confrontation but also a partial decoupling of the two economies.[42] The growing preparation of the US and its allies such as Japan and even South Korea for a war with China over Taiwan makes Shi believe that both great powers are dangerously moving closer to the Thucydides Trap. While Beijing still wishes to avoid a direct armed confrontation with Washington, the latter needs to understand, in Shi's view, that it cannot abandon the military option vis-à-vis Taipei, otherwise the island would move toward formal independence.[43]

Equally independent and highly critical of the excessive power assertion Xi has promoted, Peking University's Wang Jisi, known for his guarded views, said in June 2020 that Sino–US relations were in worse and more dangerous state than US–Soviet ones were during the Cold War as the former are passing from a period of intense engagement and interdependence to disengagement, risk of decoupling, in short a *free fall*, forcing China to impose itself three essential limits: (1) peacefully resolving all disputes; (2) promoting economic cooperation; and (3) maintaining human relations between the two societies.[44] While his recommendations have had some perhaps temporary impact on his government, Wang is much more pessimistic today than in 2018 when he deemed improbable not only a "hot war" but also a new Sino–US "cold war."[45] After Biden took office, Wang has continued to try and reduce the gulf between the two countries but with no great success.[46] He still believes that both great powers are in a "hot peace" rather than a "cold war" situation.[47]

Nonetheless, he feels compelled to alert China's US experts about the slow and only relative decline of the United States, a superpower that will remain ahead of China despite its multiple domestic challenges: again a word of caution against some Chinese hubris.[48]

Wang is not alone in worrying about the impact of even a partial decoupling of Chinese and American economies on raising war risks.[49] Like him, however, some continue to believe the United States will never have the means, nor the intention, to "contain" China, believing rather—given the changing power balance in the Western Pacific—in the continuation of "competitive coexistence" (*jingzhengxing gongchu*) between the two great powers.[50]

Meanwhile, several analysts see in the PLA's gesticulations in the Taiwan Strait preparations of a military operation against the island, and thus the realization of one of Xi's flagship projects: reunification at all costs and as soon as possible with the rebellious island, reunification without which the "Chinese nation's renaissance" (*Zhonghua minzu da fuxing*) can never be complete. Some zealous academics close to the regime have proliferated variations on this theme. Thus Jin Canrong, associate dean of the School of International Relations at Renmin University, said in February 2019 that China had already accumulated enough arms (especially, according to him, 3,000 conventional short- or medium-range missiles) to impose on the United States a power balance it had never faced in the Western Pacific.[51] In August that year, he even declared that in the event of a conflict in the Taiwan Strait, the PLA had the means to destroy all US bases and aircraft carriers in Asia.[52] Raising the stakes, the *Global Times*'s Hu Xijin recommended in May 2020 tripling nuclear warheads' stock (to 1,000 from about 300 now) to boost China's deterrent capacity against the United States (see chapter 1).[53]

But in August 2020, the Party line changed and some analysts had to lower their arrogance and their enthusiasm somewhat. It was as if, approaching the precipice and thus prospects of a real war, the Party, the PLA, and Chinese elites prudently decided to retreat. As noted earlier, avoiding falling into what was seen in China as a Trumpian trap and preparing for the future, regardless of which president would be elected in November 2020, had become the priority. The analyses thus followed in the diplomats' footsteps, competing in moderation, and in a way, joining the wise Wang Jisi in his views.[54] Jin Canrong and Hu Xijin changed their tone completely, one calling to avoid any provocation and the other deciding to censor any overly nationalistic or warmongering statement.[55] Some defense experts, such as Xu Guangyu, adviser to the China Arms Control and Disarmament Association, downplayed the threatening nature of US activity in Chinese-claimed maritime domain (more than 1,000 overflights in the two previous years), stressing instead the opportunity the surveillance flights offered the PLA to "simulate" enemy operations.[56] Shi Yinhong warned against expecting the Democratic

US administration to adopt a less hostile policy and tried to emphasize that if Beijing did not consider concessions, relations could only deteriorate.[57]

In mid-2020, most experts rallied around a more cautious policy which, not overlooking structural confrontation with the United States, tried to reduce cold war risks and hot ones too. Meanwhile, for many Chinese experts, such greater moderation was only a tactical retreat, imposed by Trump and circumstances. Even if they harbor strong doubts over the current strategy succeeding, most of them continue to believe that China, following Sun Zi's dictum, could win without fighting and replace the United States, at least in Asia, without going to war.[58] In short, they hold that to reverse the power balance in China's favor, modernization of the military, particularly focused on Taiwan, Japan, and the South China Sea remains essential.

After the Biden Administration took office, Chinese experts were optimistic for a while: many believed or wanted to believe in the reset of Sino–US ties on a sounder basis. However, nothing happened. Most of them quickly resumed denouncing "hostile" US attitude, especially after the latter declared that China posed "the greatest long-term security threat of the 21st century," while continuing to remind anyone who would listen that China did not wish to supplant the latter, which remained invited to play a "constructive role" in the Asia-Pacific. While some analysts believe the Thucydides Trap can still be avoided, the Chinese military holds that the best way to avoid it is to boost the budget and strengthen PLA capabilities.[59]

The growing US–China tensions in 2022 have not really moved the fault lines among Chinese experts. Warmongers have been increasingly vocal, particularly before and after Nancy Pelosi's Taiwan visit. In a sense, the provocative exercise conducted by the PLA in the vicinity of the island as the visit was taking place was aimed at satisfying this segment of the Chinese public opinion (cf. chapter 3). In a tweet, Hu Xijin, former editor-in-chief of *Global Times*, even asked the PLA to shoot her plane before it lands in Taipei.[60] Nonetheless, it is interesting to note that this type of message was later taken down from the web and censored. Earlier, in December 2021, the same Hu had stepped down from his position at the *Global Times*. In early 2022, academics such as Jin Canrong already estimated that the PLA could conquer Taiwan in seven days and predicted that it would take control of the island at the latest in 2027, on the occasion of the one hundredth anniversary of the PLA.[61] And Chinese media and experts have remained highly critical of the United States and the West. Nonetheless, they have also followed the trend.

The Russian invasion of Ukraine and, more importantly, US and European reaction to it have also led experts to be more cautious. For example, echoing Yan Xuetong and Shi Yinhong's concerns, Wang Jisi has directly warned the promotors of the US–China strategic competition that they were actually playing into America's hands, insisting that China has never supported an "armed reunification" (*wutong*) with Taiwan.[62] Zheng Yongnian, now professor at Chinese University of Hong Kong's Shenzhen campus and a strong supporter of Xi Jinping, has joined this group, qualifies US–China relations as neither black nor white, assessing the "confrontation" as "controllable" (*kekong de duikang*) and calling both Chinese and US experts to contribute more actively to an improvement of the bilateral relationship.[63] And Jia Qingguo, professor at Peking University's School of International Affairs, has called on both China and the United States to stabilize their relationship, starting by working together to put an end to the war in Ukraine.[64]

Finally, what do Chinese experts think of Thucydides's Trap? Transposing their own relationship to the government to the United States context, many of them see in Allison's writings a coordinated action of a Harvard intellectual serving the US administration and might. Popularized after Obama launched the "Asia pivot," the Thucydides Trap has been perceived in China as intended both to preserve the United States' supreme status and reduce as much as possible the risks of an armed conflict with the main ascending power.[65]

However, two obvious uncertainties, that could potentially provoke an armed conflict, remain. On the one hand, beyond Allison, the influence of American neo-realists like Mearsheimer or Aaron Friedberg is destined to remain strong among Chinese experts, leading them more toward confrontation than toward building an unobtainable confidence with the United States.[66] On the other, current Sino–US tensions, persisting and even intensifying under Biden, can only persuade the PLA to continue earnestly preparing for a possible local or world war.[67]

REALPOLITIK AND TRADITIONAL CHINESE CULTURE

These Chinese criticisms of Allison and war risks are far from fully consistent with the idea propagated now by the Party and its propaganda organs as well as many experts that Chinese culture is less inclined to war, and therefore to any hegemonic project, than Western culture.[68]

This idea is not completely new even though for a long time China's pacifism was rather based on the vicissitudes the country had undergone since the Opium War (1840). But it has flourished since the mid-2000s, following the peaceful rise debate in 2002–2003 and the publication of a white paper titled "China's Peaceful Development" in 2005.[69] It has become a major propaganda theme since the rise to power of Xi who now constantly seeks to show that "there is no gene for invasion in Chinese people's blood" but only that of peace, and that a powerful country, if it "thinks well," is not necessarily a hegemon (*ba*).[70]

The authorities mobilized much talent to demonstrate the truth of this thesis. To this end, the Party has given greater prominence to Confucian ideology—now rehabilitated after being reviled by Mao—and to the concepts of peace, harmony, cooperation, and even selflessness; and this to the detriment of the Legalist School of thought (*fajia*) which, based on the principles of military force, control, and punishment, has always been of great help both to build the Empire and face threats. Reminiscent of the famous dialogue between Li Si, minister of Qin Shihuang, the first Emperor, and the Confucian Xun Zi: "For four generations now, [Qin (of the warring kingdom that united the Empire in 221 BC)] has scored victories. His armies are the strongest in the world and his rule has subjugated other feudal lords. It is not through benevolence or moral rectitude that we have achieved this. But by taking advantage of opportunities (*bian*)."[71]

This *realpolitik* lesson has failed to disarm Party propaganda and some Chinese analysts. For example, the latter claim that from the Han dynasty to the Qing, China never invaded any foreign country, ignoring among other things the extension of the Tang Empire to Talas (today's Kyrgyzstan) in the eighth century, Tibet's annexation by the Yuan in the thirteenth century, and Xinjiang's by the Manchus in the eighteenth century.[72] Similarly, the travels of Zheng He, the famous Muslim eunuch from the early Ming Dynasty, who traveled the seas to African coasts at the beginning of the fifteenth century, have been widely exploited to demonstrate China's non-belligerent intentions, at the risk of hiding part of the historical truth.[73] In reality, Zheng He was armed, fought with many chieftains on his way and even got involved in local conflicts far from China's coast.[74]

Similarly, many authors have sought to highlight the link between traditional Chinese culture's pacifism and that of the socialist era, omitting all reference to the eminently Soviet foundations of the Party's discourse on peace, including the "five principles of peaceful coexistence" introduced in 1954, being only an extension.[75] They also sought to show that PLA modernization had only a defensive aim.[76]

Some analysts go further, holding for example that Confucian culture is leading China to pursue not its personal interests but all of humanity's.[77] This is also how the notion of "community of shared destiny for mankind" needs be understood. In other words, Xi's regime embodies the moral rectitude of yesterday's *junzi* ("superior men" or *literati*) and is able to contribute more than Western powers to the international community.

This essentialist approach to Chinese strategic culture has been repeatedly invalidated by analyses of imperial history. One of the most relevant is Alistair Johnston's *Cultural Realism: Strategic Culture and Grand Strategy in Chinese History.*[78] It clearly shows how much the strategic culture of governments in late Ming dynasty was based on considerations of realpolitik, such as actual balance of forces with the adversary, rather than on a specific strategic culture and Confucian moral principles persuading them to spare the enemy and avoid war. Moreover, as noted earlier, many Chinese international relations experts are seduced more by realist theses than by the constructivist school. Of course, most of these realists continue referring to Sun Zi and his famous advice that the greatest military victories are those won without fighting. But clearly, they openly ignore the Confucian ideals being propagated by Chinese authorities and are more ready than earlier to send the PLA to battle.

Obviously, such a war would be presented as defensive, and thus morally justified, including by Confucians. Party propaganda has already acquired all needed tools to legitimize such armed engagement should the Americans exert too much pressure in the South China Sea or if Taiwan shows too much desire to move toward formal independence or simply closes the door to any unification within a reasonable time. Since 2005, the anti-secession law authorizes China's government to act in this direction (cf. chapter 3).

In other words, the discourse on the fundamentally peaceful character of the Chinese is a smokescreen to contain the "China threat" narrative and delegitimize ex ante any military action by the adversary. It exaggerates the otherness of China's cultural heritage in order to take advantage of it. In fact, it is just as ideological as the "peace" (*mir*) discourse the Soviet Union served up ad nauseam in the Cold War era. Above all, it has failed to defuse the strategic dilemma that China's ambitions and the military assets it has accumulated have created over the past three decades.

CONCLUSION

China, peaceful power? This is what the Chinese government and experts close to it sell to the world. Reality is different. Recent developments in war risk discourse and debates show useful ideas. China is eagerly preparing for war, not just in one form but several types of armed conflict. While it mainly envisages a local war, it does not exclude an escalation to the extreme, especially with the United States. In that sense, the Chinese leadership and military are closer to Clausewitz than to Sun Zi. As a rising great power capable of challenging the established one, it has clearly entered into a duel with the latter, in order to complete national reunification and ultimately exclude it from the Western Pacific.

Meanwhile China seems worried and hesitant to take high risks. So long as Washington believed in engagement, Beijing and its experts could push.

But under the Trump presidency, the situation became more perilous although for a while China pursued its sharp diplomacy. Since Biden's election, the danger hasn't dissipated but rather intensified. Hence the need to deescalate somewhat, especially regarding Taiwan, and to revive discourse on China's basically peaceful nature. However, both China and the United States know perfectly well that the risks of war cannot be completely eliminated; on the one hand because the concentration of Chinese and US ships and planes in the disputed areas surrounding China could at any time cause an armed incident which would then have to be managed and resolved at all costs; on the other hand, because Beijing's intentions have not changed an iota: Taiwan, the South China Sea, the Diaoyu (Senkaku), the first chain of islands, so many territories and areas it has to control if it wants to complete and succeed in the avowed renaissance of the Chinese nation.

Notes

1. The Chinese plane crashed at sea, its pilot died, and the EP-3 had to crash-land in Hainan. The US crew were released after long and tough negotiations and the plane was returned much later.

2. On "peaceful rise," see Bonnie Glaser and Evan S. Medeiros, "The Changing Ecology of Foreign Policy-Making in China: The Ascension and Demise of the Theory of 'Peaceful Rise,'" *The China Quarterly*, No. 190, July 2007, pp. 291–310.

3. Foreign Minister Wang Yi explicitly said this new model of relations would help the United States and China to avoid falling into the Thucydides Trap, "Transcript of Interview with Wang Yi," *Financial Times*, January 29, 2014, http://www.ft.com/cms /s/0/c0b29fd8-88e2-11e3-bb5f-00144feab7de.html#ixzz2romBvrDS.

4. Tanner Greer, "The Theory of History That Guides Xi Jinping," *Palladium*, July 8, 2020, https://palladiummag.com/2020/07/08/the-theory-of-history-that-guides-xi -jinping/.

5. Susan Rice, Barack Obama's national security adviser, openly endorsed this formula, drawing much criticism. Wang Dong, "The Xi-Obama Moment: A Post-Summit Assessment," *Commentary*, The National Bureau of Asian Research, October 21, 2013, p. 2.

6. Liu Yafei, "Why China's Belt and Road Plan Is the Best Way to Lift the Global Economy," *Huffington Post*, October 21, 2015, https://www.huffingtonpost.com/he -yafei/china-road-belt-global-economy_b_8338916.html.

7. Wenshan Jia, "Cooperation Based on Belt and Road Can Overcome Risk of War Between China, US," *Global Times*, July 3, 2017, http://www.globaltimes.cn/content /1054699.shtml?from=groupmessage.

8. Fu Ying, "How Can the U.S. and China Avoid Sliding into Conflict?" *Bloomberg News*, September 1, 2016, https://gcaptain.com/can-u-s-china-avoid-sliding-conflict/.

9. "Remarks by Ambassador Cui Tiankai at the 8th US-China Civil Dialogue," July 26, 2018, https://www.fmprc.gov.cn/mfa_eng/wjb_663304/zwjg_665342/zwbd_665378/t1580426.shtml

10. Xi Jinping, "Strengthen the Foundation for Pursuing Peaceful Development," January 28, 2013, *The Governance of China*, Beijing: Foreign Languages Press, 2014, Volume 1, p. 272.

11. Xi Jinping, "China's Diplomacy Must Befit its Major-Country Status," November 28, 2014, *The Governance of China*, Beijing: Foreign Languages Press, 2017, Volume 2, p. 481.

12. Yang Jiechi, "Yi Xi Jinping waijiao sixiang wei zhidao shenru tuijin xin shidai duiwai gongzuo" (Guided by Xi Jinping Thought in diplomatic matters, promoting overseas work more deeply in the new era), *Qiushi* (Seeking Truth), 2018/15, http://www.qstheory.cn/dukan/qs/2018-08/01/c_1123209510.htm.

13. Holly Chik, "US-China Decoupling: Does Clash of Ideologies Raise Too Many Non-negotiables?" *South China Morning Post* (*SCMP*), August 16, 2020, https://www.scmp.com/news/china/diplomacy/article/3097546/us-china-decoupling-does-clash-ideologies-raise-too-many-non.

14. "Full Text of Yang Jiechi's Signed Article on China-US Relations," *Global Times*, August 7, 2020, https://www.globaltimes.cn/content/1197044.shtml

15. Wendy Wu and Minnie Chan, "South China Sea: Chinese Military Told Not to Fire First Shot in Stand-off with US Forces," *SCMP*, August 11, 2020, https://www.scmp.com/news/china/diplomacy/article/3096978/south-china-sea-chinese-military-told-not-fire-first-shot.

16. "Chinese FM Greets Diplomats Returning from Closed Houston Consulate," *CGTN*, August 17, 2020, https://news.cgtn.com/news/2020-08-17/Chinese-diplomats-of-closed-Houston-consulate-leave-U-S--T1Fevcferm/index.html.

17. "Commentary: Reviving McCarthyism Is anachronistic," *Xinhua*, August 17, 2020, http://www.xinhuanet.com/english/2020-08/17/c_139296662.htm (CPC stands for Communist Party of China).

18. Xi Jinping, "Work Together to Build a Community of Shared Future for Mankind," Speech, Geneva, 18 January 2017, https://america.cgtn.com/2017/01/18/full-text-of-xi-jinping-keynote-speech-at-the-united-nations-office-in-geneva.

19. "Proposed US Act Outrageous Risk Creator: China Daily Editorial," *China Daily*, April 25, 2021, https://www.chinadaily.com.cn/a/202104/25/ WS60854f71a31024ad-0baba389.html; Li Qingqing, "Strategic Competition Act Further Pushes China-US ties toward Confrontation," *Global Times*, April 22, 2021, https://www.globaltimes.cn/page/202104/1221842.shtml.

20. GT Staff Reporters, "US CHIPS Act 'Economic Coercion' against China; But Won't Succeed in Changing Global Semiconductor Industrial Distribution: Expert," *Global Times*, August 10, 2022, https://www.globaltimes.cn/page/202208/1272694.shtml. Chris Miller, *Chip War: The Fight for the World's Most Critical Technology*, New York, Scribner, 2022.

21. Malcolm Moore, "Military Conflict Looms between China and Japan," *The Telegraph*, September 27, 2012, https://www.telegraph.co.uk/news/worldnews/asia/china/9571032/Military-conflict-looms-between-China-and-Japan.html.

22. Xuetong Yan, "From Keeping a Low Profile to Striving for Achievement," *The Chinese Journal of International Politics*, Vol. 7, No. 2, June 1, 2014, pp. 153–84, https://doi.org/10.1093/cjip/pou027. Xuetong Yan, Professor and Dean of Institute of Modern International Relations, Tsinghua University.* *Corresponding author: Email: yanxt@tsinghua.edu.cn. Search for other works by this author on: Oxford Academic Google Scholar.

23. Idea that was censored, and removed from the *Global Times* site where it appeared in March 2016. Cf. also "Q. and A.: Yan Xuetong Urges China to Adopt a More Assertive Foreign Policy," *The New York Times*, February 9, 2016, https://www.nytimes.com/2016/02/10/world/asia/china-foreign-policy-yan-xuetong.html.

24. "Yan Xuetong on the Bipolar State of Our World," *China Media Project*, June 26, 2018, http://chinamediaproject.org/2018/06/26/yan-xuetong-on-the-bipolar-state-of-our-world/.

25. Yan Xuetong, "Trump Can't Start a Cold War with China, Even if He Wants to," *Washington Post*, February 6, 2018, https://www.washingtonpost.com/news/theworldpost/wp/2018/02/06/china-trump/?utm_term=.51e8f7e1c1d8.

26. Yan Xuetong, "To Rejuvenate, China Must Continue Opening Up," *Washington Post*, August 23, 2018, https://www.washingtonpost.com/news/theworldpost/wp/2018/08/23/trade-war-2/?noredirect=on&utm_term=.f30da14ef2a0.

27. Princeton University Press, especially pp. 200 onward.

28. Yan Xuetong, "Avoiding War but Always Worried," *China US Focus*, December 28, 2021, https://www.chinausfocus.com/foreign-policy/avoiding-war-but-always-worried.

29. Yan Xuetong, "Daguo jingzheng de yiqi manfu de wei" (The danger of an overwhelmed great power competition) *Guoji Zhengzhi Kexue* (International Political Science), 2022, No. 2, pp. III–V, https://t.cnki.net/kcms/detail?v=3uoqIhG8C46NmWw7YpEsKMypi3qVj28Lnd4ijJJLBTppkzmUJwl_dSOZz2Q_yfxvvmjYTKHIWe62mo_p5vJKRlZvYA6eaK7Q&uniplatform=NZKPT.

30. Teddy Ng, "China Has Gained Nothing from Ukraine War and It Will Only Prompt Further Breaches of International Rules, Says Leading Scholar," *SCMP*, May 12, 2022, https://www.scmp.com/news/china/diplomacy/article/3177503/china-has-gained-nothing-ukraine-war-and-it-will-only-prompt; Yan Xuetong, "China's Ukraine Conundrum," *Foreign Affairs*, May 2, 2022, https://www.foreignaffairs.com/articles/china/2022-05-02/chinas-ukraine-conundrum.

31. Hu Angang, *China in 2020: A New Type of Superpower*, Washington, DC: Brookings Institution Press, 2011.

32. Cary Huang, "China's Social Media Users Call for Sacking of 'Triumphalist' Academic, as Anti-hype Movement Grows," *SCMP*, August 3, 2018, https://www.scmp.com/news/china/policies-politics/article/2158054/chinas-social-media-users-call-sacking-triumphalist.

33. For a discussion of this polemic, cf. Jean-Pierre Cabestan, "Editorial," Dossier, "What Kind of International Order Does China Want," *China Perspectives*, 2016/2, pp. 3–6.

34. Mo Shengkai and Chen Yue, "The U.S.-China 'Thucydides Trap': A View from Beijing," The *National Interest*, July 10, 2016, https://nationalinterest.org/feature/the -us-china-thucydides-trap-view-beijing-16903?page=0%2C1.

35. Tang Shiping, "Taking Stock of Neoclassical Realism," *International Studies Review*, Vol. 11, No. 4, 2009, pp. 799–803.

36. Cui Liru, "Managing Strategic Competition Between China and the U.S.," *China US Focus*, August 10, 2016, https://www.chinausfocus.com/foreign-policy/ managing-strategic-competition-between-china-and-the-u-s.

37. Sun Jinsong, Liu Yuebin, Wang Zhaoqin, Peng Gongpu, and Zuo Fengrong, "Stepping Back and Looking at the Long Term: Observing External Challenges We Face Based on the Laws of the Rise and Fall of Great Powers," *Renmin Ribao* (People's Daily), September 11, 2018, http://paper.people.com.cn/rmrb/html /2018-09/11/nw.D110000renmrb_20180911_1-02.htm?mc_cid=fb1f4ddb04&mc_eid =2d8b6cc43c.

38. Yaqing Qin, "Continuity through Change: Background Knowledge and China's International Strategy," *The Chinese Journal of International Politics*, Vol. 7, No. 3, September 1, 2014, pp. 285–314, Yaqing Qin** Professor of International Studies at China Foreign Affairs University.** Corresponding author. Email: yqqin@cfau.edu. cn. Search for other works by this author on: Oxford Academic Google Scholar, https: //doi.org/10.1093/cjip/pou034.

39. Li Shengli and Lü Huili, "Why Are China and the U.S. Not Destined to Fall into the 'Thucydides' Trap,'" *China Quarterly of International Strategic Studies*, Vol. 4, No. 4, 2018, pp. 495–514.

40. Guo Jiping's "Commentary on International Affairs," "Shishang benwu 'Xiuxidide xianjin'" (There is no Thucydides Trap in the world), *Renminwang*, June 18, 2019, http://paper.people.com.cn/rmrb/html/2019-06/18/nw.D110000renmrb _20190618_5-01.htm.

41. Fan Jishe, "ZhongMei guanxi zheng chuyu shenmeyang de zhuangtai?" (What is the state of Sino-US relations?), *Pengpai* (The Paper), February 24, 2020, https:// www.thepaper.cn/newsDetail_forward_6131263.

42. Finbarr Bermingham and Cissy Zhou, "Coronavirus: China and US in 'New Cold War' as Relations Hit Lowest Point in 'More than 40 Years,' Spurred on by Pandemic," *SCMP*, May 5, 2020, https://www.scmp.com/economy/china-economy/ article/3082968/coronavirus-china-us-new-cold-war-relations-hit-lowest-point.

43. Shi Yinhong, "Meiguo tongmeng yu lianmeng tixi de duiHua junshi taishi xianzhuang" (The current military posture of US alliances and coalition systems towards China), *Yatai Anquan yu Haiyang Yanjiu* (Asia-Pacific Security and Maritime Affairs), 2022, No. 2, pp. 1–13, https://t.cnki.net/kcms/detail?v=3uoqIhG8C46Nm Ww7YpEsKMypi3qVj28Lnd4ijJJLBTppkzmUJwl_dT-0v7d3ZPhUrrBMQ_H7vnSz _xEYe7459syx0IjqvABV&uniplatform=NZKPT.

44. Wang Jisi, "Light at the End of a Bumpy Tunnel?," *China US Focus*, June 18, 2018, https://www.chinausfocus.com/foreign-policy/light-at-the-end-of-a-bumpy -tunnel.

45. "America and China: Destined for Conflict or Cooperation? We Asked 14 of the World's Most Renowned Experts," *The National Interest*, July 30, 2018, https:

//nationalinterest.org/feature/america-and-china-destined-conflict-or-cooperation-we-asked-14-worlds-most-renowned-experts?page=0%2C4.

46. Wang Jisi, "The Understanding Gap," *China-US Focus*, March 11, 2021, https://www.chinausfocus.com/foreign-policy/the-understanding-gap.

47. Wang Jisi, "The Hot Peace Paradigm," *China US Focus*, January 2, 2022, https://www.chinausfocus.com/foreign-policy/the-hot-peace-paradigm.

48. "Meiguo neizheng waijiao yanbian de biaoxian yu dongyin: Wang Jisi jiao-shou zhuanfang" (The Performance and Motivation of the Evolution of the United States' Domestic Politics and Foreign Policy: Special Interview of Professor Wang Jisi), *Dangdai Meiguo Pinglun* (Contemporary American Review), 2022, Vol. 6, No. 1, pp. 1–16, https://t.cnki.net/kcms/detail?v=3uoqIhG8C46NmWw7YpEsKMypi 3qVj28Lnd4ijJJLBTppkzmUJwl_dWYnToYuyQ93VTYgT4Hix1oIRCtXBWNvtR3 _U1YdxDAE&uniplatform=NZKPT.

49. Li Yan, "ZhongMei zai Yatai diqu de anquan maodun: yanbian yu luoji" (Sino-US security contradictions in the Asia-Pacific: evolution and logic), *Guoji anquan yanjiu* (International security studies), No. 2, April 7, 2020, http://www.cicir .ac.cn/NEW/opinion.html?id=69d1fb83-ca29-446a-bda2-5e5389124da6.

50. Yang Wenjing, "ZhongMei Yatai 'jingzhengxing gongchu' moshi tanxi" (Analysis of Sino-US 'competitive coexistence' model in the Asia-Pacific), *Xiandai guoji guanxi* (Relations internationales contemporaines), No. 3, October 30, 2019, http://www.cicir.ac.cn/NEW/opinion.html?id=73035d47-525d-4467-a690-40ab58eeeca9.

51. William Zheng, "China's Military Build-up Just Starting—a Lot More to Come, Expert Warns," *SCMP*, February 24, 2019, https://www.scmp.com/news/china /diplomacy/article/2187487/chinas-military-build-you-aint-seen-nothing-yet-expert -says.

52. Anthony Kuhn's tweet, August 5, 2019, https://twitter.com/akuhnnprnews/ status/1158351554300112896?lang=en.

53. Hu Xijin, "China Needs to Increase Its Nuclear Warheads to 1,000," *Global Times*, May 8, 2020, https://www.globaltimes.cn/content/1187766.shtml.

54. Javier C. Hernández, "As Relations With U.S. Sink, China Tones Down 'Hot-headed' Nationalism," *The New York Times*, August 15, 2020, ttps://www.nytimes .com/2020/08/15/world/asia/china-us-nationalism.html.

55. "Restraint in the Taiwan Straits Is the Solution: Global Times Editorial," *Global Times*, August 17, 2020.

56. Yang Sheng, "'Simulated Enemy' Helps PLA Drill for Real Combat Capability," *Global Times*, August 17, 2020, https://www.globaltimes.cn/content/1198023 .shtml.

57. Hernández, "As Relations With U.S. Sink," op. cit.

58. Sun Zi's famous dictum is "To win one hundred victories in one hundred battles is not the acme of skill. To subdue the enemy without fighting is the acme of skill" (*Baizhan baisheng fei shanzhi shan zhe ye, bu zhan er qu ren zhi bing, shanzhi shan zhe ye*).

59. "Can China and US Escape 'Thucydides Trap'? A Dialogue Between Graham Allison and Wang Huiyao," China-US Focus, April 20, 2021, https://www.chinausfo -cus.com/foreign-policy/can-china-and-us-escape-thucydides-trap-; *SCMP*, March

8, 2021, https://www.scmp.com/news/china/politics/article/3124591/chinas-military-must-spend-more-meet-us-war-threat.

60. Steven Nelson, "Propagandist Warns China Could Down Nancy Pelosi's Plane During Taiwan Trip," *New York Post*, July 29, 20222, https://nypost.com/2022/07/29/china-could-shoot-nancy-pelosi-plane-during-taiwan-trip/.

61. Tsukasa Hadano, "China Eyes 'Armed Unification' with Taiwan by 2027: Key Academic," *Nikkei Asia*, January 31, 2022, https://asia.nikkei.com/Politics/International-relations/China-eyes-armed-unification-with-Taiwan-by-2027-key-academic.

62. Wang Jisi: "Youren zongxiang ba ZhongMei laru zhanhuo, ZhongMei fasheng zhanzheng yanlun bu neng zai kuada le" (Some people always want to draw China and the US into a war, The 'China-US war' discourse cannot be expanded any more), *Center for International Security and Strategy*, Tsinghua University, July 8, 2022, https://ciss.tsinghua.edu.cn/info/zmgx/5059.

63. Zheng Yongnian, Fazhan 2022 ZhongMei guanxi (The development of China-US Relations in 2022), *Center for China and Globalisation*, January 12, 2022, http://www.ccg.org.cn/archives/67699.

64. Jia Qingguo, "China-US Cooperation Is the Key to Peace," *East Asia Forum*, March 14, 2022, https://www.eastasiaforum.org/2022/03/14/china-us-cooperation-is-the-key-to-peace/

65. Jia, "Cooperation Based on Belt and Road . . . ," op. cit.

66. Aaron L. Friedberg, *A Contest for Supremacy: China, America, and the Struggle for Mastery in Asia*, New York: Norton, 2011, pp. 156–81.

67. Yang, "Simulated enemy," op. cit.

68. Sun Jisheng, "Chuantong wenhua yu shibada yilai Zhongguo waijiao huayu tixi goujian" (Traditional culture and the construction of Chinese diplomatic discourse since the 18th CCP Congress), *Guangming Wang* (Guangming.net), August 16, 2019, https://www.gmw.cn/xueshu/2019-08/16/content_33083529.htm. Wang Xinjun, "On China's Traditional Culture and Peaceful Development Strategy," Asia Paper, Institute for Security and Development Policy, Stockholm, August 2012, https://www.isdp.eu/content/uploads/publications/2012_wang_on-chinas-traditional-culture.pdf; Wang was then a researcher at the National Defence Policy Research Centre of the Academy of Military Sciences and a PLA senior colonel.

69. English edition: *China's Peaceful Development Road*, December 2005, http://www.china.org.cn/english/2005/Dec/152669.htm. Cf. also the second white paper on the issue of China's Peaceful Development, September 2011, http://english.www.gov.cn/archive/white_paper/2014/09/09/content_281474986284646.htm.

70. "Xi: There Is No Gene for Invasion in Our Blood," *China Daily*, May 16, 2014, https://usa.chinadaily.com.cn/china/2014-05/16/content_17511170.htm. "Xi Jinping's Speech in Commemoration of the 2,565th Anniversary of Confucius' Birth," September 24, 2014, *China US Focus*, http://library.chinausfocus.com/article-1534.html. Qiao Qingju, "Xishi waijiao de 'he' wenhua diyun: Zhongguoren xuemai meiyou qiongbing duwu de jiyin" (Xi's diplomacy and the cultural heritage of 'harmony': the Chinese lack the gene for military violence in their blood), *Renminwang* (People.com), July 15, 2015, http://cpc.people.cn/xuexi/n/2015/0715/c385474

-27309679.html. Qiao Qingfu was then philosophy professor at the Central Party School.

71. Cited by Arthur Waldron in his review of Alistair Johnston's book, *The China Quarterly*, Vol. 147, September 1996, p. 962.

72. Qiao, "Xishi waijiao de 'he' wenhua diyun," op. cit.

73. Wang, "On China's Traditional Culture," op. cit., p. 10.

74. Geoff Wade, "The Zheng He Voyages: A Reassessment," *Journal of the Malaysian Branch of the Royal Asiatic Society*, Vol. 78, No. 1 (288), 2005, pp. 37–58. Edward L. Dreyer, *Zheng He: China and the Oceans in the Early Ming, 1405–1433*, New York: Pearson Longman, 2007. Chia Lin Sien and Sally K. Church, eds., *Zheng He and the Afro-Asian World*, Melaka: Perbadanan Muzium, 2012.

75. He Xingliang, "Zhongguo chuantong 'heping' linian dui goujian renlei mingyun gongtongti de dangdai jiazhi" (The contemporary version of the traditional Chinese concept of "Peace" in building a community for humanity), *Qiushi* (Seeking Truth), March 2018, http://www.qstheory.cn/zhuanqu/qsft/2018-03/16/c_1122547235.htm.

76. Wang, "On China's Traditional Culture," op. cit., pp. 30–32.

77. Wang, "On China's Traditional Culture," op. cit., pp. 20–21, 25.

78. Princeton University Press, 1995.

3

Is a Sino–US War over Taiwan Likely?

Is a Sino–US war over Taiwan conceivable? The answer to this question, also the title of a book I published in 2004, is necessarily more complex than at the time.[1] Briefly presented in chapter 1, China's rise in general and the PLA's in particular have changed things. Despite all its efforts, Taiwan no longer has the means to resist a Chinese armed offensive on its own. Only a massive US military commitment might save the island if war breaks out, and allow the survival of the Republic of China (ROC), Taiwan's official name. However, the power balance between the PLA and US deployment in the Western Pacific is changing rapidly; in some ways the former already has the advantage. Yet for Beijing, the risks remain enormous, and perhaps insurmountable: first the operation failing, and then the conflict's possible nuclearization and finally the tough estimation of such an offensive's international consequences or challenges that would stem from a takeover of the island, its institutions, economy, and population.

The fundamental question is whether China will take such risks or prefer other options that are doubtless less radical and effective as also less dangerous and of which it has already demonstrated a foreshadowing: a limited military engagement, for example a temporary blockade of the island or takeover of Taiwan's outer islands such as Quemoy (Kinmen/Jinmen), located near the Fujian coast, or Pratas (Dongsha), an atoll more than 400 km southwest of Kaohsiung; a more systematic use of gray zones between war and peace (violations of air and maritime space around Taiwan, cyberattacks, disinformation, etc.); or an increase in PLA intimidation and posturing around the island. The military exercise conducted around Taiwan in August 2022 after US House of Representatives Speaker Nancy Pelosi's Taipei visit indicated greater intimidations. All these options would have only one objective: compel Taipei not only to accept the "one China" principle but also to negotiate an immediate or gradual reunification agreement with Beijing under the "one country, two systems" formula. But here again, what would be the reaction of Washington, Taipei's sole, albeit unofficial, protector, one which for several years has been sending increasingly clear signals to Beijing but faces a less favorable power balance than before?

In this chapter, I first briefly review the evolution of China's reunification strategy since 1979 and US commitments. Next, I present new specific measures the PLA has implemented to achieve a successful military operation against Taiwan. Then I analyze the evolution of debates on the merits and risks of a military operation against Taiwan, in China as in the United States. Then, I focus on Taiwan, the discussions going on there on the island's long-term security efforts to adapt its armed forces. Finally, I assess the risks attached to other options mentioned above. My guess is that the multiple dangers of a massive PLA offensive will continue to render one unlikely in the foreseeable future (ten years). As shall be discussed, Russia's Ukraine invasion on February 24, 2022, has influenced all the actors involved, compelling them to more carefully envisage direct and indirect consequences of an armed conflict in the Taiwan Strait. Beijing will undoubtedly continue, beyond Xi's reign, to advance its advantage in two ways: by getting the best out of most gray zones, the usefulness of which it has already tested both in the South China Sea and the East China Sea (cf. chapters 4 and 5); and by continuing its so-called united front operations to win over increasingly large segments of society and in particular Taiwanese elites. I conclude that it is not certain that this dual strategy suffices to persuade Taiwan to relinquish sovereignty and submit, which in a way brings us back to "square one": an armed attack. But at what cost?

EVOLUTION IN CHINESE REUNIFICATION STRATEGY AND US COMMITMENTS

No need to go into details here.[2] Taiwan has always been part of China's "core interests" (*hexin liyi*). Nevertheless, since Xi took power in 2012 it has become clear that reunification with Taiwan cannot be "passed down from generation to generation" and left unresolved. Since the 19th Party Congress in 2017, reunification has become one of the conditions for "the rejuvenation of the Chinese nation," to be complete by 2049, the PRC's centenary. Xi therefore wants to press the movement, and Tsai Ing-wen's 2016 election as Taiwan's president and her reelection in 2020 forced him to up the pressure on Taiwan, and thus on the United States. Tsai's Democratic Progressive Party (DPP), now in a majority, knows it cannot formally declare independence, to avoid provoking a casus belli with Beijing and spare Washington, Taipei's only protector. But it is fiercely opposed to any unification and does not recognize the so-called 92 consensus (*jiu'er gongshi*), a formula coined in 2000 by Su Chi, a Kuomintang (KMT) official, and immediately taken up by Beijing to describe the ambiguous compromise found in November 1992 in Hong Kong by mainland China and Taiwan negotiators by which there is only one China, the mainland side preferring not to seek to define it and the Taiwanese side (of the KMT era), letting each side of the strait retain its own interpretation (one China, two interpretations—*yi ge Zhongguo, geze biaoshu*). For Beijing, China is the PRC and Taiwan is a sacred and inalienable part of it (cf. Preamble to the 1982 Constitution); for Taipei, China is the ROC, which only exercises jurisdiction over Taiwan and other islands it administers (Pescadores Kinmen, Matsu in particular). Not the PRC but the "Chinese communists" exert jurisdiction on China's "mainland." As a mere fourteen states recognize the ROC in 2013, the asymmetry in this compromise is glaring.

The vast majority of Taiwanese have always opposed the "one country, two systems" formula Deng Xiaoping proposed from the early 1980s but this opposition has since consolidated, rising to 89 percent in 2020, a percentage that has remained rather stable since then (86% in late 2021, 79.3% in late 2022).[3] In 2022, some 76 percent of the Taiwanese supported their government's "rejection"? of this formula.[4] Its application in Hong Kong since 1997 and Macao since 1999 have for a long time exposed its limits. Ever narrower in Macao, these limits became even more evident in Hong Kong since the failure of the 2014 "Umbrella Movement" demanding that Beijing keep its promises and grant the special administrative region completely democratic institutions, and above all the terrible failure of the 2019 movement against extradition of suspects to the mainland. The terrible failure, because while the bill was withdrawn, political reforms not only remained at a standstill contrary to the movement's demand, but also were later reversed with the introduction in June 2020 of a new national security law in Hong Kong, the subsequent detention of more than 200 democrats and activists, the gradual destruction of civil society and complete overhaul in April 2021 of the Legislative Council's election system: in the December 2021 election, only twenty out of ninety deputies were directly elected and the pan-democrats who were not in jail had few incentives to run. Hong Kong's transformation into a quasi-authoritarian political system has helped further deepen the gap between China's one-party regime and Taiwan's democracy.

While the KMT continues to promote a rapprochement with the mainland and some form of agreement or modus vivendi around the "one China, two governments" idea, the DPP counts on US support to continue opposing the "One China" concept and the "92 consensus." What brings the "pan-Blue" coalition (KMT and allies) and "pan-Green" one (DPP and pro-independence parties) together is the principle that the ROC is a sovereign and independent state and growing doubts in the ranks of the KMT toward the "92 consensus" now qualified by its Chairman Eric Chu Li-luan, as a "non-consensus consensus";[5] what separates them are the ROC's geographical limits—one including the mainland, the other excluding it, although the ROC Constitution, not having been fundamentally revised, continues to formally include it. A delight for public international law experts.

But what matters most to Taiwan are US position and posture. They have always been ambiguous. The US government has never officially recognized Taiwan as part of China. Diplomatic documents dating back to the early 1950s, during the Korean War era, a conflict that froze the border between the two Chinas in the Taiwan Strait, show Taiwan's "undetermined status" in the US administration's view.

The 1972 Shanghai Communiqué signed at the end of Richard Nixon's China visit does not completely remove this ambiguity:

> The United States acknowledges that all Chinese on either side of the Taiwan Strait maintain there is but one China and that Taiwan is a part of China. The United States Government does not challenge that position. It reaffirms its interest in a peaceful settlement of the Taiwan question by the Chinese themselves.[6]

After the Sino–US diplomatic normalization in December 1978, the joint communiqué sounded no different: "The Government of the United States of America acknowledges the Chinese position that there is but one China and Taiwan is part of China."[7]

Although the Chinese side immediately translated *acknowledges* as *chengren* which in English means "recognize,"[8] the US government stuck to its position. All the more so since, in Washington's view, one of the conditions for recognizing China was precisely the Chinese promise to resolve the Taiwan issue peacefully. As President Carter said at the time:

> We were favorably impressed with Teng [Deng Xiaoping] and the rapidity with which he moved and agreed to accept our one-year treaty with Taiwan, our statement that the Taiwan issue should be settled peacefully would not be contradicted by China, and that we would sell defensive weapons to Taiwan after the treaty expires.[9]

Of course, Beijing also stated that the Taiwan issue was China's internal affair, that it alone could decide the settlement and that it could not commit itself to not using force: peaceful resolution was only a hope and not a condition of Sino–US normalization.[10] But on January 1, 1979, Deng launched a new peaceful unification (*heping tongyi*) policy targeting Taiwan. In April the same year, affirming its strong interest in status quo in the strait and the Taiwanese people's "well-being," the US Congress passed the Taiwan Relations Act (TRA), which reaffirmed that the United States views normalization with China as resting "upon the expectation that the future of Taiwan will be determined by peaceful means" and required any administration to maintain close security relations with the island.

The TRA stated:

> Any effort to determine the future of Taiwan by other than peaceful means, including by boycotts or embargoes is considered a threat to the peace and security of the Western Pacific area and of grave concern to the United States. States that the United States shall provide Taiwan with arms of a defensive character and shall maintain the capacity of the United States to resist any resort to force or other forms of coercion that would jeopardize the security, or social or economic system, of the people of Taiwan. . . .

> the United States shall provide Taiwan with arms of a defensive character and shall maintain the capacity of the United States to resist any resort to force or other forms of coercion that would jeopardize the security, or social or economic system, of the people of Taiwan.[11]

In August 1982, Deng persuaded President Reagan to commit to gradually reducing the amount of arms sold to Taiwan (Third Communiqué) but no deadline was set. And the "Six Assurances" secretly given to Taiwan the previous month contradicted this commitment and reaffirmed the TRA's supremacy. Among other things, Taiwan was assured it would continue receiving in the long-term armaments according to the threat level it faced and that its international status would remain undetermined for the United States.[12] Moreover, the Taiwan Strait's remilitarization starting in the early 1990s made the "Third Communiqué" obsolete, Washington having more or less explicitly linked its application to Beijing's adherence to peaceful reunification policy and above all a reduction in tensions in the strait.

Since then, successive US administrations have maintained a "strategic ambiguity" position in the event of a Chinese attack on Taiwan. They repeat that US reaction, its military commitment, its extent, and form will depend on the circumstances. In recent years, in view of mounting Chinese intimidation, pressure on the administration has increased from several think tanks, pundits, members of Congress, and even former military officials to evolve and introduce greater "strategic clarity."[13] In their view, this would help prevent the risk of war more effectively by strengthening US deterrence capacity.

The Trump Administration, after some "transactional" muddle,[14] adopted in May 2020 a new "strategic approach" to the PRC that has substantially reduced this ambiguity.[15] This document states in particular:

The United States maintains that any resolution of cross-Strait differences must be peaceful and according to the will of the people on both sides, without resorting to threat or coercion. Beijing's failure to honor its commitments under the communiqués, as demonstrated by its massive military buildup, compels the United States to continue to assist the Taiwan military in maintaining a credible self-defense, which deters aggression and helps to ensure peace and stability in the region.

Not long after, in August 2020, the US government not only declassified the "Six Assurances" but also added them to its "one China Policy," notably modifying its content and its spirit.[16] It is worth mentioning them again here:

First, the US has not agreed to set a date for ending arms sales to Taiwan; second, it has not agreed to consult with the PRC on arms sales to Taiwan; third, it will not play any mediation role between Taipei and Beijing; fourth, it has not agreed to revise the TRA; fifth, it has not altered its position regarding sovereignty over Taiwan; and sixth, it will not exert pressure on Taiwan to enter into negotiations with the PRC.[17]

The Trump Administration has also indirectly reduced the US "strategic ambiguity" by increasing arms sales (over $13 billion between 2017 and 2020), by strengthening unofficial ties with Taipei, sending members of its cabinet there (such as Health Secretary Alex Azar in August 2020) and promoting the adoption of several laws, such as the Taiwan Travel Act which facilitates exchanges, the TAIPEI Act and the Taiwan Assurance Act, that seek to boost Taiwan's international status.[18]

Concerned over rising PLA intimidation around Taiwan since 2016 and the evolution in Hong Kong since 2020, Washington wanted to "rebalance" the diplomatic-strategic situation in the strait to Taipei's benefit and Beijing's disadvantage. "Taiwan is critical to American interests in Asia," a former Pentagon official said in August 2020. This importance is not only strategic, but also technological.[19] Demonstrating this desire to "decouple," the Trump Administration encouraged a reduction in Taiwan's economic dependence on China in key sectors, for example inviting in 2020 in Arizona a $12 billion investment by the electronic chip firm TSMC (Taiwan Semiconductor Manufacturing Company). In other words, the more Xi pushes for reunification, the more the United States feels compelled to strengthen support for Taiwan's security.

President Biden has not modified but deepened this policy. One of his China advisers, Randall G. Schriver, already held in late 2020 that the Taiwan Strait constitutes the most serious threat to US security, not hesitating to compare it to the "Fulda gap" between West and East Germany.[20] In March 2021, the Biden Administration affirmed unwavering "rock-solid" support for Taiwan, "a leading democracy and a critical economic and security partner, in line with longstanding American commitments."[21] And it has continued to publicly refer to the "Six Assurances," in addition to the "Three Communiqués" and the TRA. Since then, reacting to the PLA's more frequent and more aggressive intimidations around Taiwan, President Biden himself has clearly indicated at least four times (August 2021, October 2021, May 2022, and September 2022) that if the island were attacked, the US military would intervene and defend it.[22] Each time, the State Department has tried to reassure Beijing, underscoring the fact that US policy had not changed. The Biden Administration has also several times reminded the Chinese government that "it does not support Taiwan independence" or at least, to quote the president's own words "does not encourage" it.[23] Nonetheless, Biden's statements were made on purpose, and everyone got the message. In other words, in coming years, US support for Taiwan will thus strengthen rather than weaken. The US National Security Strategy issued in October 2022 has clearly confirmed it, upholding the commitment under the TRA "to maintain [the US] capacity to resist any resort to force or coercion against Taiwan."[24] The US military is actively preparing for a possible confrontation with China later in the decade.

However, it is unlikely any US government would completely abandon "strategic ambiguity" which on the one hand offers more flexibility and thus more freedom and on the other hand puts Chinese authorities in an uncertain situation. Kurt Campbell, the Biden team's Indo-Pacific coordinator, noted this in May 2021, pointing out "significant drawbacks" in any "strategic clarity."[25] It is more certain that Washington maintains its "one China policy," based on the "Three Communiqués," the TRA and now the "Six Assurances" as well as a silent or explicit commitment to the "Three No's" (no to Taiwan independence, to two Chinas or one China and one Taiwan and Taiwan's participation in international organizations reserved for States) with probably greater flexibility regarding the third "no."[26]

The other major post-1979 development is that Taiwan has democratized and is now able to envisage a future other than that of reunification with an authoritarian state which would not only deprive it of de facto sovereignty and independence but would deny it equal status and control it with an ever-shorter leash, as in Hong Kong and Macao.

Beijing has therefore gradually changed its reunification policy, officially professing a peaceful strategy but increasingly accompanied by threats of the use of force, and consequently, an unprecedented accumulation of means toward this eventuality. Contrary to what some in Taiwan have speculated, especially in the "Blue" camp, the CCP has never abandoned extending the "one country, two systems" formula to Taiwan (it was actually Taiwan that Deng had in mind when he first mentioned it in 1983). Xi has repeatedly indicated this as the only way to "reunify" with Taiwan, despite the obvious differences between Taiwan's de facto independence and sovereignty and Hong Kong or Macao.[27] Beijing's White Paper on Taiwan issued in August 2022 has not only confirmed this objective, but also offered the island much stricter conditions: no more commitment is made on Taiwan's right to keep its armed forces; and in a direct threat to the DPP, it clearly indicates that only the "Taiwanese compatriots that support reunification" will be allowed to take part in the island's political life after reunification.[28] In his report to the 20th Party Congress, Xi Jinping has seemed more open to "consult . . . with people from all political parties" in Taiwan, but he has also confirmed his "firm support to patriots in Taiwan who desire unification, and join hands to keep pace with the trend of history."[29]

Simultaneously, not only has China increasingly directly threatened Taiwan (1995–1996 missile crisis, 1999 crisis, 2005 anti-secession law) but also has made reunification a major objective. This objective was linked, right from 2010, the Hu Jintao era, to China's "rejuvenation."[30] Similarly, while continuing to limit Beijing's elbow room, the TRA did not prevent Xi from adopting right from 2016 and the DPP's return power a much more aggressive reunification strategy. Without openly setting a deadline, he instructed the PLA to consider an offensive against Taiwan as a priority. China's defense white paper of July 2019 declared the CCP intentions in clearer and harsher terms than previous ones:

> China must be and will be reunited. China has the firm resolve and the ability to safeguard national sovereignty and territorial integrity, and will never allow the secession of any part of its territory by anyone, any organization or any political party by any means at any time. We make no promise to renounce the use of force, and reserve the option of taking all necessary measures. This is by no means targeted at our compatriots in Taiwan, but at the interference of external forces and the very small number of "Taiwan independence" separatists and their activities. The PLA will resolutely defeat anyone attempting to separate Taiwan from China and safeguard national unity at all costs.[31]

This statement warrants dissection. It is certainly an extension of everything Beijing has said post-1979: any renunciation of the use of force would be counterproductive as it would contribute to discouraging peaceful reunification. This is exactly what Deng said in the United States in February 1979.[32] The threat of the use of force is above all dissuasive and in line with Sun Zi's principles. The problem is both the Taiwan and the Defense White Papers hide the reality: the vast majority of Taiwanese not only oppose the "one country, two systems" formula's introduction but also any form of reunification. Only a minority now supports the so-called 92 consensus. Around two thirds of them (64%) identify as only Taiwanese (compared to 30% Taiwanese and Chinese and 3.5% Chinese).[33] As for "external interferences," that is to say the TRA and US role, they constitute the keystone of Taiwan's security and survival.

Consequently, more and more people in China openly believe that any peaceful reunification has become impossible and therefore only the use of force can resolve "the Taiwan question" and bring about China's rejuvenation. As shall be seen later, it is particularly difficult to distinguish experts' suggestions from the options Xi, the CCP, and the PLA are considering. Bear in mind for now that Chinese authorities have every interest in remaining ambiguous about their true intentions. Clearly, the PLA is preparing more actively each day for an armed conflict over Taiwan, which inevitably would engage in one way or another the United States, and perhaps its allies.

THE PLA'S SPECIFIC PREPARATIONS
FOR WAR AGAINST TAIWAN

The PLA is considering multiple options to force Taiwan to agree to reunification. Those most often mentioned include a massive missile strike, especially to decapitate Taiwan's political leadership and military command, a blockade of the island, occupation of a peripheral island (Kinmen, Matsu, or Pratas), and an invasion in the form of a landing. To these traditional options, others have been added recently, such as a generalized cyberattack. But as shall be seen, Chinese official sources rarely mention these scenarios, leaving the official press free to build hypotheses based on PLA exercises made public. It is still US sources which remain the most reliable.[34]

More than earlier, given changes in the power balance with Taiwan, the aim is no longer merely to neutralize Taiwanese forces but also to prevent any rapid US intervention. The objective is thus to present the United States, its allies, and the international community a fait accompli as quickly as possible, through some kind of *Blitzkrieg*, while preventing or substantially reducing, through massive use of long-range offensive weapons, any US military response capability.

To this end, the PLA has set two priorities: strengthening its anti-access (A2/AD) capabilities within the first island chain and establishing integrated command and control systems allowing it to mobilize large forces against any US intervention. On these two fronts, the PLA has learned from the United States.[35] More specifically, it seeks to acquire the full panoply of weapons and systems already with US forces: decapitation weapons for enemy command systems, high-precision and longer-range missiles and drones, landing, control of logistics flows over long distances, better information, surveillance and reconnaissance (ISR) systems, integrated air defense systems, more effective underwater detection systems, greater jamming capabilities, anti-satellites and cyberattacks, and so forth. As noted (cf. chapter 1), the PLA has also modified its organization in order to better serve these objectives: it has developed joint land-air-sea operations, recruited qualified technical personnel, rapidly expanded marine troops, multiplied night exercises, and so on.[36]

For this purpose, the PLA keeps publicizing its new offensive means against Taiwan. On the one hand, it is gradually developing new armaments that reinforce capacities. On the other, it is boosting maneuvers that simulate attacks on Taiwan, especially blockades or landings. Among new armaments, missiles and drones take priority. In December 2019, China announced having acquired a new long-range missile (probably a DF-17 variant) on board its most recent 10,000 to 12,000 ton type 055 destroyers (the first, the *Nanchang*, was commissioned in January 2020, the fourth and fifth 055 in April 2022, its eighth in January 2023) and capable of firing with higher precision from a greater distance (1,800 to 2,500 km), thus threatening both Guam and US aircraft-carriers.[37]

In August 2020, China announced the development of a new weapon specifically for use in an attack on Taiwan: The *Tianlei 500* (Sky Thunder), a 500 kg and 60 km range winged missile that can carry 6 kinds of ammunition and 240 submunitions capable of covering a 6,000 m2 radius and hitting various targets. It is of the cluster bombs category and China has not signed the convention banning them.[38]

Among military exercises made public in recent years, most point to a full-fledged invasion of the island but more recently, particularly in the aftermath of Nancy Pelosi's visit to Taiwan, to a blockade. In April 2019, the Nanjing-based eastern command—which would oversee any operation against Taiwan—organized a naval air exercise of strikes and joint maritime assault by the Navy and Air Force, engaging multiple electronic warfare boats, fighters, bombers, and AWACS.[39] In August 2020, PLA attack helicopters carried out drills simulating a cross-strait attack, with vertical landing said to play a "vital" role in the event of a military operation.[40]

China's Air Force is projecting its bombers (e.g., its H-6Ks) more often covering longer distances over the Western Pacific, and thus beyond Taiwan and the first island chain, for training purposes. The objective is also dissuasive: raise the potential threat to the United States in the event of a conflict over Taiwan.[41]

Some reports in the Chinese press are clearly intended to send diplomatic and psychological messages: reminding everyone about China's irredentism, intimidating Taiwan, and demonstrating growing superiority over US forces likely to be deployed in the area. In August 2020, two days after a destroyer (USS *Mustin*) of the VIIth fleet transited the Taiwan Strait, Beijing released an eight-minute video showing a new submarine (type 093B, a modified version of 093) simulate launching a torpedo against an enemy vessel. This submarine is equipped with YJ-18 anti-ship cruise missiles, a variant of the CJ-30 with a range of 540 km; its capabilities would equal the US Los Angeles Flight I and Flight III class submarines.[42]

Nationalist organs such as *Global Times* project optimism, believing the PLA can quickly seize control of Taiwan even before the United States has had time to react, and that at least a week would be needed to mobilize US military resources. US bases in the Western Pacific (Japan, Guam) are now vulnerable, within range of the PLA's DF17 (new hypersonic missile with 2,500 km range) and DF26 (4,000 km range) missiles. By deploying its two aircraft carriers, *Liaoning* and *Shandong*, to the east of Taiwan, China's Navy can block US relief. China's air defense can intercept any B1 bombers deployed near its coast to neutralize PLA vessels and missile bases.[43]

From August 4–7, 2022, as a protest against Pelosi's Taipei visit, the PLA conducted a larger type of exercise in the Taiwan Strait and around the island in seven zones located much closer to it than earlier, especially during the 1995–1996 missile crisis.[44] This unprecedented exercise—the fourth Taiwan Strait crisis in the eyes of many—was aimed at demonstrating the PLA's capability of strangling Taiwan by imposing a full blockage on it. While the difference between these maneuvers and a full-fledged blockade remains obvious, named on purpose "island closure military exercise," they have led to the cancellations of many civilian flights and diversion of many ships. Focusing on training, the PLA went for "joint blockade, sea target assault, strike on ground targets, and airspace control operation, and the joint combat capabilities of troops," the exercise including live-fire rockets and precise missile strikes (9 to 11), some of the missiles flying over the island before splashing in Japan's claimed EEZ (five in total). It involved the PLA's Air Force, Navy, and Rocket Force, operating jointly. More importantly, this exercise has tried to impose upon Taiwan and the United States a "new normal" that ignores the existence of a median line in the strait (usually respected prior to 2020), pretends to turn the whole strait into PRC domestic waters, demonstrates the PLA's capability to challenge Taiwan's airspace and territorial waters as well as putting additional pressure on the Taiwanese armed forces.

There was again a strong psychological war dimension in this exercise, exaggerating the PLA's capabilities and publishing pictures giving the wrong impression that PLA aircraft and ships taking part in it were very close to the island while, actually, none of them penetrated Taiwan's air space or territorial waters. Yet PLA fighters and bombers repeatedly penetrated Taiwan's ADIZ, for example on forty-nine occasions on August 5. Some drones were flown above Kinmen and Matsu. Moreover, the exercise was extended for two days until August 9, and challenged both Japan and the Philippines' EEZ, sending a signal to the whole region and beyond about Beijing's willingness and capability to solve by any means the so-called Taiwan issue.

Meanwhile the increasing Chinese military maneuvers and activities in the Taiwan Strait in recent years have provoked enhanced return of US sea and air transit. In August 2020, a B1 bomber flew over Taiwan with the aim both of demonstrating US resolve to ensure the island's defense and of gleaning more information on the PLA's new projection means. Condemned by Beijing, this show of force led some, including Wei Dongxu, a military affairs expert often quoted by *Global Times*, to call for caution and above all for continuation of the modernization effort. In his view, the PLA must stick to "active defense" strategy and strengthen air defense capabilities around its main military installations, especially missile bases, the only weapons currently capable of forcing Washington to "think twice" before rushing to Taiwan's aid.[45]

Although in 2022 voices of caution were less frequent or audible, the PLA made sure to keep its August exercise under the war threshold and avoid missteps. Contrary to some netizens' demand, Pelosi's plane or military escort was not intercepted, let alone shot. And no incident occurred. More generally, some social media commentators were disappointed by the weakness of their government's response to Pelosi's visit.

Taiwanese and US reactions to this exercise has been cautious in order to avoid any further escalation. However, showing no sign of panic, Taiwanese public opinion has not been really affected by it or by the Taiwan white paper published a few days later, which remains a non-starter for both DPP and KMT voters.[46] And the United States has resumed its naval passages in the Taiwan Strait, sending two cruisers through it in late August, demonstrating its willingness to preserve the status quo. In other words, the PLA is steadily improving its capabilities to project force across the Taiwan Strait in a more coordinated manner. Nonetheless, it may still have doubts about its readiness for a war against Taiwan and its August 2022 exercise has fed anti-PRC feelings in the United States, Europe, and Japan.

Finally, while US sources do not rule out China's recourse to nuclear weapons in the event of the conflict prolonging and getting bogged down, Chinese media remain discreet on this matter.[47]

EVOLUTION OF DEBATES IN CHINA
OVER AN ANTI-TAIWAN WAR

Being highly attentive to changes in the military power balance in the Taiwan Strait and more broadly in the Western Pacific, Chinese experts have been increasingly inclined since 2012 and more so since 2017 to contemplate a war against Taiwan. This has been spurred by Xi's plan to "reunite" with Taiwan before 2049 and by the increasingly unlikely prospect of peaceful reunification. In late 2016 Wang Zaixi, former deputy director of the State Council Taiwan Affairs Office, said the prospect of such reunification was receding. The same article quoted General Wang Hongguang, former deputy commander of the Nanjing Military Region, as saying a conflict with Taiwan "very likely" before 2020.[48] Similarly, believing he was relaying popular feeling, Zhou Zhihuai, a former director of the Institute of Taiwan Studies, Chinese Academy of Social Sciences, declared in 2017: "Mainland Chinese public opinion has been impatient with Taiwan for a long time."[49] On January 1, 2018, an editorial in the *Global Times* added: "Mainland Chinese will be very happy to see the PLA act and punish this pro-independence Taiwan."[50]

After Trump took office in January 2017, Chinese media began more often to question US willingness to continue defending Taiwan. "America First" meant for many Chinese analysts the possibility of abandoning Taiwan (*qi Tai*), a sentiment then getting stronger among some KMT officials on the basis of Trump's ambiguous remarks (see supra).[51] They were to become quickly disillusioned and change tack, focusing from 2018 on US analyses highlighting the Pentagon's unpreparedness for a generalized war in the strait (cf. *infra*).

However, these positions remain concentrated in mainstream media. Articles by major international research institutes, even those with military affiliation, avoid or sidestep the topic, focusing for instance on the capabilities of new PLA weaponry. Thus, the subject remains taboo or treated internally (*neibu*). Hence these debates are unrepresentative and generally display unfailing optimism, amplified online.[52] Quite likely a good part of the discussions made public have no other purpose than to stoke fears and uncertainties in Taiwanese society.

Tsai Ing-wen's January 2020 reelection as Taiwan's president reignited Chinese warmongering. Representing a no doubt widespread opinion within the PLA, General Wang Hongguang deemed it time to apply article 8 of the anti-secession law, that is, use force to achieve a goal unlikely ever to be approved by Taiwan's majority.[53] According to article 8, the state may resort to "non-peaceful means" (*fei heping fangshi*) to "reunite" Taiwan if peaceful reunification possibilities have been exhausted. Meanwhile the Chinese media make abundant use of pro-mainland Taiwanese. Luo Qingsheng, executive director of the Taiwan Institute for International Strategy, said in August 2020 that the United States would stay out of any cross-strait conflict and let Taiwan fight in a kind of "proxy war" (*daili zhanzheng*).[54]

Among experts who do not deem a war imminent is the aforementioned Yan Xuetong: he declared in May 2020 that even if a military incident occurred, the three parties, namely the United States, China, and Taiwan, would quickly manage it and avoid any escalation.[55] Similar to recent statements by General Qiao Liang, known for his book *Unrestricted Warfare* (see chapter 1), that a conflict around Taiwan would be too costly and Chinese society, especially in COVID-19 pandemic times, should focus on its well-being. By thus decoupling China's rejuvenation from national unification, he was directly criticizing Xi and his international ambitions.[56] Two months later, another (former) "hawk," National Defense University professor General Dai Xu, reportedly called for not underestimating the United States: not viewing it as a "paper tiger" and avoid giving the impression that China might surpass it.[57] Although these remarks need to be treated with caution, interestingly they have had some impact on Beijing's foreign policy discourse (cf. chapter 2).

But in popular media, this is a minority view. The DPP's hold on power boosts nationalists' and the PLA's arguments to take action.[58] Moreover, Chinese optimism is nurtured by growing doubts among US experts about American ability to secure Taiwan and defeat the PLA in the event of an all-out conflict. Presented hereunder are worst-case scenarios giving China the advantage over the United States as greedily proffered by Chinese media.[59] However, are these doubts sufficiently shared and strong enough to convince Xi to act? Nothing is less certain.

The Russian invasion of Ukraine and Biden's repeated commitments to defend Taiwan have had conflicting influences on the Chinese debate. The invasion has boosted the optimism of the warmongers at least until Putin started to run into difficulties. But the US reaction has contributed to splitting analysts and media influencers between the ones who are ready to take up the US military challenge and those who call for caution, particularly in the context of Pelosi's Taipei visit.

In that respect, Jin Canrong's changing views are worth noting. On the one hand, Jin estimates that China can learn a lot from the Ukraine war to get better prepared for a showdown in the Taiwan Strait, militarily but also in terms of mitigating the potential impact of economic sanctions against China. On the other hand, he is worried about the risks of nuclearization if the United States intervenes. He even thinks that it is in the Biden and the Tsai Administrations' interest to provoke a military crisis in the strait before the PLA is ready to confront the United States.[60] Following the PLA's unprecedented early August 2022 exercise around Taiwan and the publication of a new White Paper on Taiwan reunification not long after, some Chinese analysts, such as Zhang Weiwei of Fudan University and Jin Canrong, have become very vocal about their military's achievement and the prospects for an early unification. They have also underscored that after unification, the PLA would send troops to Taiwan and the central government would exclude all pro-independence Taiwanese from public affairs on the island and reeducate them.[61] Nonetheless, they are also aware that the PLA still needs time to get ready for an armed conflict in the strait, especially a confrontation implicating the United States.[62] And as noted earlier (cf. chapter 2), most experts are actually concerned about the risks of both China and the United States falling into the Thucydides Trap. This group includes Jia Qingguo, Shi Yinhong, Wang Jisi, Yan Xuetong, and Zheng Yongnian, to mention but a few.

Quoting their own experts, Chinese media have remained much more forceful about society's support for "preparing to war" against Taiwan and the island's early reunification.[63] Nationalist *Global Times* has presented the August 2022 PLA exercise conducted after Pelosi's visit to the island as a "unification operation's rehearsal."[64] Yet they cannot ignore the Biden Administration's and Taiwanese society's growing opposition to Xi's unification strategy. As a result, while still promoting "peaceful reunification," they try to convince their audience that the PLA has imposed a "new normal" around the island, putting the blame for the more dangerous situation on the United States and their "DPP pawns."[65] But one thing is clear: the promoters of the idea that the United States would abandon Taiwan have been sidelined and today, learning from the consequences of the war in Ukraine, the multiple risks (military, economic, and international) attached to an "armed reunification" (*wutong*) are clearly emphasized.[66]

EVOLUTION OF US DEBATES OVER AN ANTI-TAIWAN WAR

American Weaknesses

In recent years, observing the rapid PLA modernization, a growing number of American studies have revealed rising concern over US forces' ability to prevail in the event of an all-out conflict with China over Taiwan. In 2020, it became known that Pentagon analysts showed the United States losing on all counts, not when these simulations were carried out but in 2030, when the PLA would have acquired a greater number of missiles, aircraft-carriers, submarines, and destroyers.[67] This highlights the extent to which US diplomatic and military posture is no longer tenable in the medium term and that an adjustment is necessary, either by abandoning Taiwan, which remains unlikely, or by imposing on US forces, far-reaching reforms, something many analysts envisage.

These Pentagon analyses are partly based on previous work already exposing US weaknesses and moreover, new Chinese capabilities in the event of a conflict over Taiwan. A simulation carried out in 2019 by David Ochmanek and Robert Work, analysts from Rand, a think tank close to the US Air Force, came to the same conclusion: in the event of a high-end war with China (or

Russia in the Baltic states), "US Forces suffer heavy losses."[68] One of the reasons for this potential defeat in the event of a conflict is the greater vulnerability of US forward posture in the Western Pacific: it is vulnerable to attacks by new Chinese short-range missiles (DF -11A, DF-15B) and medium range (DF-21A to E) or intermediate range (DF-26) ones. US aircraft carriers will have to stay more than 1,000 nautical miles (nearly 2,000 km) from Chinese shores to be safe from most PLA missiles. Also, if they approach, onboard F-35s could be destroyed before they leave their base. The same applies to Japan- or Guam-based F35s. Poorly defended US tank brigades are also vulnerable to missiles and drones as well as helicopter attacks. In addition, US satellites, command systems, and communications networks could be destroyed or seriously damaged. In other words, if the PLA launched a "systems destruction war" against US forward deployment, the latter could quickly find itself paralyzed as it has accumulated too many weaknesses.

How to overcome these weaknesses? In Ochmanek and Work's view, by changing the way US armed forces wage war and shifting equipment priorities: first acquire many more missiles, especially long-range ones (the Army's MLRS), the Air Force's JACM-ER, and the Navy's LARSM "anti-ship" ones; many more defensive missiles such as Mobile Short-Range Air Defense (MSHORAD) batteries and Army Stinger missiles; and in the longer term, lasers, railguns, and high-energy microwave weapons to destroy enemy missiles; then, reinforce the command and control systems with better protected links, larger electronic warfare means, and more decoys; finally, wider use of artificial intelligence: no "killer robots" but "loyal wingmen" drones to assist pilots and mass data managers.

How to finance these projects? According to Ochmanek, $24 billion a year over five years should suffice if, simultaneously, the Pentagon reduces the number of aircraft carriers, amphibious boats, and combat brigades—whose unsuitability to new forms of conflict has long been debated—increases missile defense systems and strengthens capabilities to attack Chinese vessels using long-range missiles, such as aboard bombers. The aim is to be able to sink 350 PLA ships in the first seventy-two hours of conflict.[69] In these experts' view, the main difficulty is not financial but politico-bureaucratic: that of the Defense Department modifying current priorities.

Lyle Goldstein, of the US Naval War College, projects a similar scenario based on the most recent PLA training: in the event of a Chinese attack, the Taiwanese would "fold" in a week or two. Obviously, the PLA will have to face multiple risks linked to any *Blitzkrieg* across a 150 km sea area, often battered by bad weather (except in April and October). But PLA strategy has evolved, no longer favoring an amphibious landing on the model of Overlord (June 6, 1944) but a "vertical envelopment" by establishing multiple bridgeheads using paratroopers, frogmen, and helicopters while numerous salvos of missiles would endeavor simultaneously to decapitate Taiwan's command centers and destroy the majority of its air and naval bases. The PLA's advantage is its numerical superiority, including over US forces, the number of warships and civilian vessels it can mobilize (not 300 but 10,000 according to Goldstein), its impressive missile strike-force including greater precision, and finally the proximity to Taiwan.[70] If China manages to quickly occupy Taiwan, the cost of any US counterattack will become prohibitive or very high.[71]

In August 2020, four-star Admiral James Winnefeld, previously vice chairman of the Joint Chiefs of Staff, and former CIA Deputy Director Michael Morell painted an even more disturbing scenario: China could seize Taiwan in three days and no later than January 18, 2021, two days before the new US president was to take office. After a series of cyberattacks destroying electrical installations and other vital equipment, the PLA would impose an air and sea blockade of Taiwan prior to a full invasion. On the second day, stock markets crash, many countries protest but do nothing more. Paralyzed by multiple internal problems and divisions, the United States is unable to react. PLA landing begins on the third day, featuring thousands of quickly converted combat and fishing vessels, and it is too late for Americans to intervene militarily without the cost being prohibitive and outcome uncertain. President Tsai and her government are forced to capitulate and cede to a team ready to work with the victors.[72]

Of course, while the end of the Trump presidency was marred by unforeseen developments such as the Capitol crisis, this prediction did not materialize. In fact, this catastrophic scenario was immediately subject to much criticism in the United States. Critics focused on supposed US inability to react quickly prior to a possible change of president and on President Tsai's rapid capitulation.

The most recent analysis was made public by the CSIS in January 2023. The result of a wargame run twenty-four times, it is less pessimistic in a sense that in most scenarios, the United States together with Taiwan and Japan manage to defeat a conventional Chinese amphibious invasion and maintain the island's de facto independence.[73] Nonetheless, the cost is very high for all the parties implicated in the conflict. And to achieve this outcome, important conditions need to be met. The Taiwanese must decide to fight and not rapidly surrender (see thereafter); there is no "Ukraine model" since Taiwan is an island: it needs to accumulate large stocks of weapons and ammunitions before any conflict starts and the US military must quickly intervene. The United States must be able to use its bases in Japan. And the United States must be able to destroy the PLA fleet from outside the Chinese defense zone with the help of long-range missiles. Finally, to avoid a Pyrrhic victory, it is recommended that the United States makes clear its war objectives, refrain from striking the Chinese mainland to avoid any nuclearization of the conflict, and accept heavy casualties. This report's conclusion is clear: both the United States and Taiwan need to strengthen their deterrence. More specifically, the United States needs to fortify its air bases in Japan to increase aircraft survivability on the ground, prioritize undersea platforms rather than surface ships, continue the development of hypersonic weapons, and prioritize bombers equipped with long-range anti-ship cruise missiles over fighters. This report recognizes that China may privilege other actions, particularly a blockade. Nonetheless, it estimates that many of its recommendations also apply to these scenarios.

Such analyses have the same objective: to alert US political and military leadership to the need to better prepare and therefore to change: a series of "wake-up calls" going far beyond Taiwan's security. American appreciation of the risks of war goes beyond Taiwan and stems from the overall evolution of Sino–US military balance of power. As Bonnie Glaser, then an expert at the Center for Strategic and International Studies (CSIS), Washington, noted in the spring of 2020:

> Every simulation that has been conducted looking at the threat from China by 2030, and there have been various ones carried out, for example in the event of China invading Taiwan, have all ended up with the defeat of the US . . . Taiwan is the most volatile issue because that could escalate to a war with the US, even to a nuclear war.[74]

These analyses may be somewhat overly pessimistic. But they perfectly reflect the questions Americans are asking in light of new threats the PLA poses and the answers they generate, and this even before the Russian invasion of Ukraine. Note that while the hypotheses of Ochmanek, Work, and others exclude the conflict's nuclearization, those of Glaser and the CSIS report do not. This shall be further discussed infra.

US forces suffer from multiple weaknesses or inadequacies. Many analysts deem the vulnerability of US command systems, ships, and aircraft to cyberattacks particularly worrying.[75] They are also struggling to block Chinese long-range hypersonic anti-ship missiles.

Chinese Weaknesses

However, China and the PLA are not without weaknesses should they decide to attack Taiwan. The aforementioned simulations tend to neglect Taiwanese forces' resistance capacities. Of course, some US experts close to Taipei, such as Ian Easton, express a none-too-convincing optimism over the island's resistance capacities, especially faced with precise missile attacks, blockade, or Chinese espionage activities.[76] But, although on the whole less assured than before, many analysts such as Michael Beckley and William Murray integrate more realistically all the strengths and weaknesses of the three parties to any armed conflict should one erupt.[77]

Based on PLA strategists' available work, these experts rightly believe that any war China launches would first aim to neutralize as quickly as possible using conventional surface-to-surface or air-to-surface missiles the largest number of Taiwanese aircraft, ships, and command centers.[78] The aim of such an operation is obvious: controlling the skies and the waters of the strait and around the island in order to begin either a landing or a blockade, the two decisive operations likely to subjugate Taiwan. The question is, can such a lightning offensive succeed? Doubts abound.

The PLA now possesses around a thousand short-range ballistic missiles (DF-11, DF-15, and DF-16) or short-range cruise missiles (DH-10–300 to 1,500 km). It also has 700 fighters (compared to 400 in Taiwan) and 250 bombers attached to the eastern and southern theaters, the two combat zones to be engaged in any cross-strait operation. China thus enjoys an obvious superiority. But Taiwan has the advantage any defending army does.[79]

First of all, no attack preparation will go unnoticed by either Taiwan's intelligence services or US detection means, especially space- and submarine-based ones. In other words, Taiwan and the United States will have between one and two months to prepare. Taiwan's forces will have time to disperse their planes and ships, plan alternative airports, and move command centers underground.

Taiwan not only possesses three Patriot P-3 anti-missile defense systems (recently modernized) capable of stopping some of the Chinese missiles, but also missiles capable of neutralizing some of the missile bases or PLA aircraft: 50 short-range missile ramps installed in underground silos and 524 long-range surface-to-air missile launchers mostly self-propelled, thus mobile.[80] According to some sources, Taiwan also has special forces pre-positioned on the mainland and capable of neutralizing some missile bases.[81]

Chinese missiles, albeit more accurate than twenty years ago, with around 500 kg payload, can only cause relatively limited destruction. Their impact will be both psychological and physical. Historical precedents show that rather than breaking the defender's morale, such attacks strengthen it.

But imagine that Beijing considers the ground sufficiently prepared to initiate an invasion. The difficulties any expeditionary force will then face remain colossal in the medium term. The PLA will first have to ensure control of the skies—a tall order. It would have to be able to reach Taiwan's coast within eight hours and establish one or more bridgeheads on the few beaches where such operations are possible. It has to press into the adventure enough troops to prevail over Taiwan's military (about 165,000 officers and soldiers), even if one harbors doubts, contrary to Ian Easton's estimates, over the level of preparation and commitment of the island's 2.3 million reservists or the additional 70,000 conscripts that the extension of conscription to one year will supply in 2024 onward (see below). Such an undertaking would face major obstacles in terms of coordination, transport capabilities, and chances of survival against Taiwan's defense, particularly at sea and on land, which will have been only partially destroyed.

In reality, PLA's modernization plans for the Army and the Navy hardly point toward the establishment of a significant landing force. The Navy has certainly increased its amphibious capabilities with the launch of already three Yushen class ships (type 075 landing helicopter docks) in addition to the eight modern Yuzhao class (type 071 amphibious transport docks) transport and other existing platforms. However, the number of landing craft, including its Yuyi-class hovercrafts, remains limited (probably around 20). These lend the PLA the means to seize an outlying Taiwanese island (Pratas, Itu Aba in the South China Sea or Kinmen). Albeit somewhat easily achievable, such a goal remains politically questionable: it would propel Taiwan even further toward formal independence.[82] Moreover, this limited capacity does not signal preparations in the short or medium term for a landing on the main island. The Chinese Navy and Army's amphibious program rather prioritizes intervention means far from its territory, for example in Africa or the Middle East (cf. chapter 7).[83]

Such diversification of PLA missions diverts it from Taiwan. The new challenge for China's military is to be able to face several crises simultaneously: in the strait, in the South China Sea, around the Senkaku, or on the border with India or in Africa. So many "distractions" the United States could use or stoke. Precisely what Joel Wuthnow of the National Defense University in Washington thinks, leading him to relatively optimistic conclusions about the risks (and chances of success) of a PLA attack on Taiwan.[84]

Yet another reason for the PLA to have weighed other operations, especially a Taiwan blockade.

Blockade: Most Likely Military Operation

Some US analysts have said the PLA could carry out "strategic bombing" to force Taiwan to capitulate. This is most unlikely for several obvious reasons: the CCP has no plans to destroy the economy and decimate the population of a province it wants to annex; again, historical precedents show such an operation has limited chances of succeeding; moreover, any strategic bombing risks provoking not only a greater US military engagement than other types of attacks, but also international condemnation, further isolating China.[85]

For these reasons, a blockade has long been mentioned as the most probable scenario.[86] It has the advantage of seeming to remain peaceful at first, in other words stay within the gray zone strategy's limits, before turning aggressive and destructive. It could also force the Taiwanese to "shoot first," and therefore to become responsible for the hostilities. Taiwan is known to be highly dependent on the outside world for 60 percent of its food and 98 percent of its oil. It is also the place where around 90 percent of the most sophisticated semi-conductors in the world are manufactured. Its main ports are located on its western coast, facing the mainland. Experience shows any blockade is difficult to sustain and to remain airtight. To be effective, it must be preceded by a more or less complete neutralization of the adversary's air force and navy, which, as seen above, is not a given.

The main questions are whether a blockade can quickly damage Taiwanese morale and whether the Americans will be able to dismantle China's action. Again, precedents show that most beleaguered societies tend to tense up and resist as long as possible. Seeking to survive as a de facto independent state, Taiwan will be inclined to guard its sovereignty. Here too, US military support will be decisive, both to help Taiwan hold on and to break or dodge the blockade. The PLA Navy has emerged as the world's largest: it will have the means to mass a greater number of ships and submarines than US forces, even if the latter were backed by allies, such as Japan, which is far from certain. The risks for the United States engaging in such an operation have thus become much higher than during the 1995–1996 missile crisis.

However, can it back down? Will it be able to abandon Taiwan? On a strategic level, US credibility in the Indo-Pacific zone is at stake. If it does not try to break the Taiwan blockade, its Asian and Pacific allies, such as Australia, will have to face the consequences and thus a profound adaptation to the new strategic and military environment China will have imposed. Even if it resists pressure from Congress and the pro-Taiwan lobby to pass a Taiwan Defense Act, given the mood among American society and elites today, any future administration will be forced to act.

The good news for any US government is that it will have a fairly wide range of options to achieve objectives ranging from a counter-blockade of the Strait of Malacca which would deprive China of more than half its hydrocarbon imports, from hunting down PLA submarines in the strait using drones to escorting merchant ships supplying Taiwan.[87] US forces still enjoy a technological lead over the PLA and much greater combat experience than the latter. US ships and aircraft need not even be near the island: anti-ship missiles (LRASM) can be fired from more than 1,000 km away; its underwater drones can torpedo many Chinese ships and landing craft. Although the United States has lagged behind China (and Russia) in deploying medium-range hypersonic missiles, by 2023 it should be ready with a missile much faster than the PLA's (17 times versus 5 times the speed of sound).[88] This new capability is intended to break through Chinese defenses (A2/AD) from a greater distance and limit the risks US forward deployment could face.[89] And it may be envisaged that in order to avoid a war in the strait, the United States would intensify information, cybernetic, and economic war with China. In other words, the US military priority today is to invest in new capabilities to "bolster deterrence" and better "counter coercion" together with its allies. In the words of Secretary of Defense Lloyd Austin III, "integrated deterrence" has become the cornerstone of the US new national defense strategy.[90] As many actions that have preceded but are vindicated by the recommendations of the 2023 CSIS wargame report.

The bad news is that even if the United States wins the blockade battle, it is not certain to win the war: Taiwan is closer to China than to the US mainland and Beijing is probably more determined than Washington to achieve its ends. This sentiment is growing in US security circles today, obviously fed by the simulations mentioned above. More decisively, in my view, the nationalist passion Beijing has invested in the idea of reunification is the main driver of a military operation which, albeit risky, is in its view worth attempting.

In most US experts' views, such an operation is unlikely in the short term. The national security law's imposition on Hong Kong in June 2020, the Sino–Indian border skirmishes in mid-2020, or the rise in Sino–US friction in the South China Sea and the Taiwan Strait do not portend an attack on Taiwan. The CCP will remain mainly focused on emerging from the COVID-19 crisis, restructuring its economy and safeguarding minimal growth.[91] In contrast, many US analysts share medium- or long-term pessimism. Even the aforementioned Ian Easton shares this concern: he predicts a crisis in the Taiwan Strait in the next five years; he judges the PLA's chances of winning today at 20 percent but in five years could rise to 50 percent; and in the coming decade, with the Chinese military's rise, the situation will become increasingly unstable.[92] This sentiment is now shared by the US military establishment. In March 2021, before leaving his position as commander of INDOPACOM, Admiral Davidson declared that China could well attack Taiwan in the next six years, that US means of conventional deterrence against such an attack were "eroding," and that it was necessary to strengthen them, especially in Guam.[93] The Pacific Deterrence Initiative created in 2020 has this very aim. A few days later, his successor Admiral Aquilino made similar remarks shortly before his appointment: as the main flash point and war factor in the South and East China Seas, Taiwan could be the target of a PLA invasion "much sooner than you think"; consequently, only a strengthening of US military posture and of its allies' can prevent such an occurrence.[94] Of course, it was also a way for INDOPACOM to ask for more resources. But the risks of war with the PLA are real and the US armed forces are preparing for it already. The memo sent by US general Michael A. Minihan, head of Air Mobility Command, to his troops and made public in

January 2023 according to which a war could break out in 2025, after the next Taiwan and US presidential elections in 2004 has no other goal but to speed up this preparation.[95] Such risks are fraught with incalculable consequences: in the event of US engagement in a battle, which is likely (cf. infra), the risks of nuclearization cannot be excluded.

Risks of the Conflict's Nuclearization

These risks are highly difficult to assess. US analysts have long underestimated them. This is no longer so because of the erosion of US military superiority over China and the improvement and increase in the Chinese nuclear arsenal, especially the probable doubling of its intercontinental warheads (from 200 today to 400 in 2027).[96] That said, cogitation on the risks of nuclearization of a war around Taiwan remains underdeveloped, including in the United States, and deserves more attention.[97]

Washington's threat of recourse to nuclear weapons can be a deterrent. But if that threat fails, any US Air Force use of tactical nuclear weapons to stop a PLA invasion would risk an escalation.[98] Conversely, US superiority in strategic nuclear weapons could dissuade China from taking the plunge. However, with a consolidated second-strike capability, Beijing could renew the threat General Zhu Chenghu made in 2005: "You care more about Los Angeles than Taiwan!" The PLA's mid-2020 submarine-launched missile tests sought to flaunt this capability.[99] Following the US example, Chinese authorities are likely to go for theater nuclear weapons, nuclearizing the warheads of some of its 2,000 conventional short- and medium-range missiles. (This was the reason the Trump Administration cited in 2018 for denouncing the 1987 US-Soviet Intermediate-Range Nuclear Forces Treaty.)

The PLA's massive investment in conventional missiles, air force, navy, marine troops, and electronic and space warfare shows a strong desire to avoid such nuclearization. But can US forces defeat the PLA without nuclearizing the conflict?

It is already far from certain today, and will be even less so in 2030.[100] As we have seen, only a massive investment in hypersonic, electromagnetic, and electronic warfare weapons can help US forces to quickly neutralize China's Navy and thus avoid nuclearization of the conflict.[101] Will future administrations agree to make this effort? Can they?

The Biden Administration has demonstrated its willingness to invest enough resources in the military to continue to be able to deter any Chinese military action against Taiwan. It has sped up the expansion of the US Navy, intensified US Marines' training in island fighting, and worked more closely with Japan to upgrade military facilities on the Nansei islands, the southern part of the Ryukyu, located next to Taiwan (Ishigaki, Yunaguni) and deploy more marines there. The debate is ongoing in the United States about the likelihood of such an eventuality. Pessimists such as Oriana Mastro assess that nationalist passion will lead Xi Jinping to attempt armed unification in the coming years while more optimist analyses continue to think that an invasion or even a blockade remain unlikely in the coming decade and that peaceful reunification will remain the priority.[102] While I am more convinced by the latter, we will see below the specific impact of the Russian invasion of Ukraine on the likelihood of war in the Taiwan Strait.

In any case, in the foreseeable future, it is quite likely that if Taiwan were attacked, Washington would intervene, trying to avoid any nuclearization of the conflict. Although the now democratic island is not a US "vital interest," abandoning it would destroy US credibility in the eyes of Asian (and non-Asian) allies. Moreover, given its strategic location, Taiwan constitutes a lock restricting the Chinese Navy's access to the Western Pacific and contributes to guaranteeing the Japanese archipelago's security. Thus, its importance to the United States, Japan as well as other US allies such as South Korea and Australia, should not be underestimated.[103] Expressing its concern over rising tensions in the Taiwan Strait, the joint US–Japanese statement of April 2021 confirmed this.[104] Finally, as shall be discussed, the outcome of any war in the strait will also depend on the evolution of debates in Taiwan and its ability and resolve to resist any PLA aggression.

EVOLUTION OF DEBATES AND DEFENSE POLICY IN TAIWAN

The Taiwanese are divided on defense issues. The Pan-Green camp remains confident overall and believes that by making greater defense efforts and cultivating close US ties, Taiwan can continue ensuring its security. The Pan-Blue camp suffers from divisions and harbors concerns. However, both sides are strongly influenced by intensifying Chinese threats and the evolution of US debates on the chances of success, even the raison d'être, of any military intervention should a cross-strait conflict erupt.

The Pan-Green camp had for long somewhat neglected the island's defense needs, with overreliance on US guarantees and Japan's interest in maintaining status quo. But since Tsai took office in 2016, the DPP has evolved and tried to catch up, boosting defense spending and, with Pentagon help, addressing the many weaknesses of Taiwan's forces. In case of a Chinese attack, the current Taiwanese government's aim is to hold out not for merely twenty-four hours as has been reported, but one to two weeks, in order to allow time for US military intervention.

With Tsai, unlike one of her predecessors Chen Shui-bian (also DPP), preserving status quo rather than embracing more formal independence has become a priority. Her oft-repeated argument, and that of many Taiwanese, is that Taiwan is already independent under the official name of Republic of China (ROC). This greater caution is obviously intended first, to reassure Americans: recall George W. Bush's criticism—a president otherwise quite pro-Taiwan—in December 2003 alongside the Chinese Premier Wen Jiabao, against Chen Shui-bian's alleged mishandling of the status quo by organizing a referendum on the island's security which could have suggested movement toward independence. And second, it also aims to avoid giving Beijing the slightest pretext to contemplate hostilities against the island. The question is obviously whether this caution will be enough to protect Taiwan against an armed conflict with China.

In the Pan-Blue camp, pessimism is mainly rooted in DPP politics and Tsai's refusal to recognize the "92 consensus," which deprives her of a direct and open communication channel with Beijing. The KMT continues to believe that a return to this consensus would be a source of cross-strait peace and stability, thereby minimizing the force of CCP irredentism.[105]

Some in the Pan-Blue camp do not hesitate in adopting pro-China stances. For example, citing recent US simulations, KMT Central Committee member and former deputy director of the Mainland Affairs Council Ho Yi-cheng said the United States would jettison Taiwan in the event of a PLA attack, adding, without citing his sources, that only 15 percent of Taiwanese would be in favor of fighting (cf. infra). Most interestingly, his article was reproduced on the *Taihaiwang* site (Taiwan Strait.net) hosted by Baidu, China's main search engine.[106] Similarly, retired army general Wang Wen-wei, eighty-eight, has agreed to be utilized by Beijing propaganda, lending it his support for peaceful reunification and his hostility toward the United States. In his view, the latter seeks to use Taiwan to contain China but would remain on the sidelines should conflict break out.[107] He is far from being the only retired Taiwanese officer to think so.

Former Taiwan president and ex-KMT chairman Ma Ying-jeou made similar comments in August 2020: any PLA attack will be too fast for US action; the only solution for Taiwan is to avoid or prevent war by pursuing accommodation. This stand, deemed defeatist, is far from being shared by all the "Blues" and is decried in society: polls show nearly 60 percent of Taiwanese denounced it.[108]

On his part, the aforementioned Su Chi is worried about President Tsai's overly offensive strategy. He believes she was instrumentalized by Trump Administration "hawks" to confront China; she interfered in Hong Kong affairs by supporting the 2019 protest movements and envisages so close a security relationship with the United States that it would lead to a return of

US military presence in Taiwan. So many developments likely lead to a *casus belli* with Beijing.[109] This too is a minority opinion within the KMT.

First led by native Taiwanese Johnny Chiang Chi-chen and then Eric Chu Li-luan, the KMT that emerged from the January 2020 electoral defeat is much more realistic, and even centrist on Taiwan's security and future, that is to say, for his party, the ROC's survival. While continuing to officially adhere to the "92 consensus," which allows it to maintain a direct communication channel with Beijing, the KMT is strongly committed to Taiwan's sovereignty and security. When visiting the United States in June 2022, Eric Chu has gone further, admitting that what was agreed in Hong Kong in 1992 was a "'no consensus' consensus."[110] Having directly controlled the armed forces during the long martial law era (1949–1987), the KMT retains many supporters, particularly among the officer corps. A majority of the latter remain ready to defend the ROC within its current borders, but are not necessarily ready to defend an independent Taiwan's sovereignty, without ties to the Chinese nation, since the independence quest has inevitably drawn the PLA's ire. In this sense, while remaining centrist and suspicious of the mainland, the KMT is in a position that objectively tends to better serve US long-term interests than the DPP.

Tsai and DPP realists are acutely aware of the many complexities and nuances, knowing too well that if they mishandle the status quo, that is, the current institutional envelope—"the ROC on Taiwan," the United States could abandon them or put strong pressure on them to change course. Consequently, despite the doubts some "Blue" personalities harbor, the DPP and the KMT are united both to defend Taiwan's sovereignty and to maintain close security links with the United States, the only country that has agreed to sell it weapons and render help if China attacks.

Beyond the "Green" and "Blue" rivalry, debates on Taiwan's security focus on three essential questions: Given the irremediable evolution of military balance between China and the island, what defense strategy should be adopted? What financial and human resources can be mobilized to render this strategy credible? If war breaks out, will the Taiwanese be ready to fight?

An Active Defense and Asymmetric Strategy

What defense strategy should be adopted to minimize war risk and, if such conventional deterrence strategy fails, how to resist as long as possible before the Americans arrive? Such are the essential questions preoccupying Taiwan's political and military elites.

Having been forced twice by the United States (in 1977 and in 1988) to abandon all military nuclear programs, Taiwan has been seeking since the early 2000s a form of conventional deterrence and asymmetric defense strategy clearly aimed at demonstrating their ability to inflict enough damage on the adversary to force it to think twice before launching an attack.

With only 165,000 officers and soldiers, a relatively small army (staff: 89,000 compared to the PLA's 416,000 in its eastern and southern theaters), even more modest Navy (40,000 personnel, 4 destroyers, 22 frigates, and 2 submarines), and Air Force (35,000 personnel and 300 fighter planes and 450 including trainers), Taiwan's armed forces have few other options.

The problem is this asymmetric strategy did not immediately gain unanimous support and many politicians and military personnel have long opposed it, believing they could both pursue an ambitious active defense strategy which included, notably under Chen Shui-bian, advanced defense of the strait—the "decisive battle" was to take place there (*jingwai juezhan*)—and turn to the United States in the event of an attack. Several elements of this new strategy have gradually been implemented, such as the "porcupine" tactic, proposed by the American William Murray back in 2008, and intended to better protect Taiwan's vital installations.[111] But it was President Tsai who, starting in 2018 and especially after her second term began in May 2020, officially prioritized large-scale acquisition of asymmetric capabilities.

An often overlooked asset, Taiwan has a defense industry which, under the pressure of circumstances—US "de-recognition" in 1979—had perforce to be developed with notable support from the National Chung Shan Institute of Science and Technology. While some of its accomplishments have been controversial, such as the Indigenous Defense Fighter aircraft which does contribute to the island's air defense, a growing number of them directly serve the asymmetric strategy gradually put in place in recent years: various types of missiles, including medium range, drones, mines, radars.

In 2018, Taiwan's armed forces adopted an "Overall Defense Concept" aimed at putting in place a close air and sea defense strategy for the island.[112] In terms of equipment, this means that rather than possessing armaments capable of projecting force in the strait, Taiwan needs a greater number of offensive and defensive short-range systems able to withstand an enemy's initial bombing and to be deployed quickly on the island. It also needs to develop greater capabilities in electronic warfare and cyber defense and attack, a task Tsai's government has attached high priority to. In June 2017, the ROC armed forces instituted a fourth arm (or command) in charge of information, communications, and electronics (*zidongdianjun zhihuibu*) and especially of cybersecurity.[113]

Taiwan continues to prepare for a blockade and relies on its Air Force to maintain control of the skies over the strait and on its Navy for dismantling operations. Nevertheless, described as "resolute defense and effective deterrence," the new strategy revolves around three axes: protection of forces, decisive battle in the littoral zone, and the enemy's destruction on landing beaches.[114]

The first axis is to camouflage and render impenetrable as many command centers and equipment as possible: the aim is to guard against a massive missile attack. Then, the strategy intends organizing defense operations in two phases. The first is the decisive battle on the coasts stretching up to 100 km from the main island. This will be based on networks of underwater mines and surface buildings that will not yet have been destroyed. Taiwan's military has great expectations of the *Kuang Hwa* attack craft as well as the new fast and stealthy *Tuojiang*-class catamarans, and the sea-to-sea missiles they are equipped with (*Hsiung Feng* 2 and 3, Harpoons). The defense forces will also be counting on the ramps of self-propelled surface-to-sea missiles that will have been scattered in the island's mountains. The second phase will consist of striving to annihilate the enemy in an area extending 40 km from the coast and especially near the landing beaches. This area will be quickly mined by the Taiwanese Navy's new fast mine-layers.[115] The resistance against the invading armada will also be ensured by the missiles aboard multiple fast attack ships and ground-based mobile ramps.

Is this strategy credible? In public, Taiwanese military experts have long said the PLA lacks as yet the material and logistical means to land on the island.[116] And they think the geography—insularity, bad weather, mountainous terrain—serves their strategy. Among the advice Taiwanese experts have given is better use of the island's mountainous terrain where the surface-to-air and surface-to-sea missile ramps could be installed with greater safety.[117] However, in 2021, Taiwan Minister of Defense Chiu Kuo-cheng admitted that the PLA would have the ability, probably at a high cost, to mount a full-scale invasion by 2025.[118]

This is why Taiwan's armed forces have already set themselves several new priorities. The first is to strengthen asymmetric warfare means. These are already numerous: various types of short and medium-range ground-to-ground, air-to-ground and sea-to-ground missiles capable of neutralizing military objectives not only in the strait but also on the mainland (*Hsiung Feng* IIE, cruise missile *Wan Chien*[119]), torpedo craft, cyberattacks, and so forth.[120] With US help, they are steadily improving: underwater mines, portable missiles, coastal defense cruise missiles, anti-tank missiles, mobile artillery rocket systems, and drone jammers.

The second axis is military reorganization to better serve its new missions. The thirty-sixth edition of the annual military maneuvers known as *Han Kuang* (light of the Han) in July 2020 illustrated this adaptation effort quite well.[121] The first innovation was the creation of a combined arms battalion, similar to the US Marines. Composed of infantry and armored companies, naval and air support section, this battalion would operate and react quickly and autonomously. The second was the establishment of an anti-decapitation operations force, intended to protect the government and the military command, composed of a Military Police special company as well as Coast Guard elements and National Police special forces.

Moreover, Taiwan has accelerated the construction in Kaohsiung of eight and perhaps ten diesel submarines, promised by George Bush in 2001 but long delayed. The factory, benefiting from US and other countries' assistance but preferring to remain discreet, was inaugurated in 2019. Meanwhile, the United States began to deliver Mk 48 torpedoes (18 in 2020) and UGM-84L Harpoons Block II submarine missiles. In order to demonstrate the program's importance, a German-made torpedo was live-tested during the thirty-sixth *Han Kuang* maneuvers.

The Taiwanese military's third objective is to strengthen the mobilization capacity and thus the credibility of the vast reservist corps (2.3 million). The 2020 *Han Kuang* maneuvers for the first time included mobilizing reserve artillery units handling Howitzers. This is still a timid and above all symbolic evolution as this corps is yet a reality on paper only: only 300,000 reservists could immediately joint front-line battles (cf. infra).[122] But it is intended to make people aware of the greatest dangers facing Taiwan today.

Han Kuang 37 (2021) and 38 (2022) have intensified exercises simulating a PLA invasion and attacks on several parts of the island as well as in Taiwan's offshore Kinmen with the aim of addressing the armed forces' major weaknesses.[123]

To achieve these new objectives, President Tsai substantially boosted the defense budget in 2020. It had long stagnated around $10 billion and 2 percent of GDP, while the PLA's now exceeds 230 billion. Again, parity is impossible, but an additional financial effort was long overdue. Successive presidents, including Chen Shui-bian and Ma Ying-jeou, preferred to prioritize social programs; Tsai too at least until 2020. Now that has changed. In August 2020, she announced a 4.4 percent rise in the defense budget for 2021, rising to 11.1 percent if the special budget for purchasing 66 F-16 aircraft is included (nearly $1 billion for a total contract of $62 billion).[124] In August 2022, she went further, proposing a double-digit increase (13.9%) to US$19.41 billion, including US$3.6 billion for fighter jets and other equipment acquisitions as well as "special funds" for the Ministry of Defense.[125]

This responded to a long-standing US demand. With the heightened external threat and thanks to the Trump presidency (and Tsai's), the already close security ties between the two countries grew a little closer. As of 2019, 3,500 to 4,000 Pentagon officials visited Taiwan each year.[126] And this number has since increased. Interoperability between Taiwanese forces and the forward deployment of INDOPACOM has been significantly enhanced. In June 2020, US and Taiwanese special forces held joint training on the island. Meanwhile a larger number of Taiwanese forces have participated in maneuvers on US soil. But Taiwanese forces' responsibilities have become heavier: the US military expects them not to be limited to protecting "gray areas" against incursions by PLA vessels and aircraft.

Taiwan does not always receive the US armaments it desires (like the F-35). Nevertheless, in recent years, the two sides' coordination has improved greatly. In 2020, Taiwan purchased 66 F-16Vs, particularly suited to its needs. In August that year, Lockheed Martin set up its first Asian F-16 maintenance plant in Taiwan. After the Biden Administration came into office, arms sales have increased: in August 2021, the United States accepted to sell 155mm M109A6 Paladin Medium Self-Propelled Howitzer System and related equipment for an estimated cost of $750 million.[127] And in 2022, Taiwan's acquisitions (US$1.1 billion) included logistics support for Taiwan's Surveillance Radar Program, 60 Harpoon anti-ship missiles and 100 Sidewinder tactical air missiles.[128]

That said, Taiwan's military continues to face multiple challenges.[129] The new concept of defense is far from having fully entered the armies' daily reality. The military institution's rigidity and the various arms' compartmentalization remains a problem. While the Air Force and Navy have adapted better to new threats, the Army is lagging behind and struggling to take the measure of them. Many Taiwanese decision makers, Green and Blue, pay too much attention to the military equipment the Americans agree to supply and not enough to their integration into the armed forces and their real usefulness if war broke out. Thus, arms contracts often take the place of strategy and guaranteeing US support is viewed like sacred talismans capable of protecting the island from any external threat. It is not certain, for instance, that acquiring more of large ships such as the Kidd class destroyers integrated into Taiwan's Navy in 2005–2006 or the M1AT Abrams heavy tanks, too wide for most of the island's roads, yield much benefit. However, 108 of these tanks were again purchased in 2019 for two billion dollars. Similarly, in 2020 Taiwan acquired 36 additional amphibious assault vehicles (AAV-7) whose usefulness in the event of a PLA attack remains marginal.

The program to build 2,000-tonne diesel submarines—expensive ($5–$20 billion) and late—is far from enjoying unanimous backing, especially among KMT ranks. Reckoning that their size will render them dependent on ports that risk being mined if China blockaded, some submariners would have preferred smaller vessels (500 to 1,000 tons), which are more flexible and easily concealed.[130] Crucially, despite their projected usefulness in thwarting PLA plans to control the strait, these submarines will not be operational until 2025 or possibly 2028, even if the prototype is ready ahead of schedule in September 2023 and the first submarine is delivered to the ROC Navy in 2024.[131]

But the main weaknesses of Taiwan's forces are human. Since the early 2000s, the military has suffered from a critical shortage of qualified officers and personnel. Before 2000, compulsory military service (for men) lasted two years, as in South Korea. Gradually reduced to one year in 2008 and four months in 2013, it has become increasingly symbolic and useless. Taiwan is also finding it difficult recruiting and holding on to technicians capable of serving the new defense systems and competent computer specialists to strengthen cybersecurity, both defensive and offensive. Salaries, albeit revised, remain insufficient to attract talent. Pensions, costing the state dearly, have for their part shrunk. Career prospects are also far from attractive. Tarnished by several repeated incidents, some involving conscripts, the armed forces' image in Taiwanese society remains poor. In order to make up for lack of personnel, the government introduced voluntary military service in 2013. But it did not appeal to many young Taiwanese. The escalating Chinese threat has reignited debate over reinstating a longer conscription, leading the Tsai Administration, in December 2022, to extend military service back to one year from 2024 for men born after 2005 despite the unpopularity of this measure among young people (see infra).[132] This measure should add an extra 60,000 to 70,000 manpower annually to the professional force. However, the low birth rate (less than 1 percent) will directly reduce the impact of such a move. This worrying situation has dented society's confidence. A 2018 poll showed that 40 percent of Taiwanese believed their armed forces were utterly incapable of defending the island.[133]

Another oft-cited weakness is Taiwan's vulnerability to Chinese espionage. In fact, in recent years curbs have been tightened, especially on Chinese businessmen visiting the island or senior Taiwanese officials retiring on the mainland. But Beijing's main intelligence targets remain Taiwanese military personnel in service. Their clear aim is to demonstrate, especially to Washington, Taipei's inability to protect its defense secrets, in order to reduce as much as possible the delivery of the most sophisticated US equipment to the island.[134]

The reserve forces are far from operational. In principle highly numerous (2.3 million), they have little or no training and are badly equipped. Until 2021, most only received an annual five-day training session. Late that year, the Tsai Administration extended the training period to two weeks and increased combat training.[135] Since January 2023, women can volunteer for reserve force training, the military allowing 220 discharge female soldiers, to start with, to enroll in the training.[136] Women make up to 15 percent of Taiwan's military, mostly serving in non-combat roles. But the impact of this reform is doubtful, as well as the impact of some wealthy Taiwanese people's initiative, such as that of Robert Tsao Hsing-cheng, to contribute money (US$100 million in this case) for Taiwan's defense.[137] At least this reform and this initiative highlight a growing awareness, in the context of the war in Ukraine and more aggressive PLA operations around the island, that Taiwan is in danger.

Some are calling on Taiwan to study Israel, but that is unrealistic given the different nature of threats the two countries face. Believing the reservists are the "last resort defense of our homeland," President Tsai is aware of the problem but struggling to find solutions. Instead of creating a second army made up of operational reservists, some suggest more realistically the ensuring of, if conflict erupted, the defense of urban and rural communities.

Finally, in official documents, Taiwan's military continues to display an autonomous defense capability, without US military intervention. However, this position is increasingly untenable and hampers the forging of stronger Taipei–Washington coordination prior to any conflict.[138] Some in the United States believe that after a week or two of resistance, Taiwanese forces would have to leave the direction of the war and therefore the field of operation to advanced US deployment. But many questions remain unanswered and ultimately depend on Taiwanese people's fighting spirit.

Taiwanese People's Fighting Spirit

Many observers have expressed doubts about Taiwanese people's real will to fight. With Tanguy Le Pesant, I had, a few years ago (2009), tried to assess their defensive spirit. We concluded then that US commitment to the island's defense would play a decisive role. Without it, Taiwanese morale would drop very quickly and possibly lead them to capitulate.[139]

Today, most Taiwanese people's reaction remains more or less the same. Despite contradictions between polls—surveys with a "Green" tendency are naturally more optimistic than those by "Blue" researchers—the results are quite convergent. According to the former (Taiwan Foundation for Democracy), 57 percent of Taiwanese said in 2019 they were ready to defend the island if it were attacked (compared to 55% the previous year) while 31 percent thought the opposite (36% in 2018). In addition, some 82 percent of twenty- to twenty-nine-year-olds would take up arms if Beijing sought to impose unification by force.[140]

Meanwhile, according to ETToday, a Blue media, in July 2020, in the event of war, only 41 percent of Taiwanese would agree to fight while 49 percent of them would refuse to. Interestingly however, just two years earlier, the former accounted for only 24 percent and the latter 73 percent. The same poll revealed a clear consensus (more than 75%) favoring restoring conscription. It also showed a rise in supporters of eventual independence (33% against 23% in 2018) compared to the majority who favor status quo (51% against 55%) and the minority who ultimately prefer unification (12% versus 21%).[141]

A third survey in August 2020 by the Chinese Association for the Study of Public Opinion (*Zhonghua minyi yanjiu xiehui*), a Blue but quite reliable Taiwanese institution, confirmed, although with a lesser amplitude, the trends of the first survey: 48 percent of Taiwanese were ready to fight against 42 percent opposed to the idea. This result was closely linked to the belief shared by 59 percent of Taiwanese that US troops would be sent to Taiwan if conflict erupted (against 29%). Similarly, a majority of islanders (53%) support a rise in defense spending (against 34%). Nonetheless, for a large number of Taiwanese, these are hypothetical questions: in fact, as the third survey showed, 80 percent of them continued then to consider any Chinese attack unlikely (against 12% who think the opposite).[142]

More recent polls confirm these conflicting results, despite the war in Ukraine and the growing PLA intimidations, especially after Pelosi's Taiwan visit. According to a poll organized in March 2022 and published in May in the journal of the Institute of National Defense and Security Research in Taipei, more than half of Taiwanese (54% against 58% in September 2021) were confident in the nation's self-defense capabilities, and about 73 percent (against 75%) were willing to fight in the event of war. But, probably because of the US's non-direct involvement in the war in Ukraine, only 40 percent of the Taiwanese (against 57% in September) thought that the United States would send troops to the island. If the United States intervenes, 95 percent of them would fight, if not, only 65 percent of them would.[143]

In contrast, after the August 2022 PLA exercise, a Blue survey, probably based on a biased sample, indicated that most Taiwanese were not only worried about a war (64%) but also less willing to go to battle or let a member of their family to do so (65%), although half of them believed that the United States would intervene if a war broke out.[144] A month later, another Blue polling institute, the Taiwanese Public Opinion Foundation, indicated that 51.2 percent of the Taiwanese believed that if China invaded Taiwan, it would win the war against 29.6 percent who thought the opposite. However, according to this foundation, the results showed that a higher-than-expected number of Taiwanese were confident that the country's military could hold out and defeat the PLA.[145]

We need to take all these surveys with much caution because in case of war, many Taiwanese would not need to fight and, at the same time, options for all Taiwanese would dramatically narrow, especially if the island were isolated or faced a blockade.[146]

Yet the gradual change in thinking deserves attention: restoration of one-year conscription and increase in the defense effort now enjoy majority Taiwanese support. In December 2022, 73.2 percent of them supported the former, with the noticeable exception of the twenty- to twenty-four-year-old cohort: 35.6 percent agreed with the reform while 37.2 percent of them opposed it.[147] And the strengthening of US military support has also helped reassure the island's society and to boost its fighting spirit, even if it remains far below Israel's.

In sum, any armed conflict would prove disastrous for Taiwan. It could be so for China too and albeit to a lesser extent, for the United States.[148] It would also have devastating consequences for the world order and the world economy, not only because of the crucial role played by Taiwan in the semiconductor industry.[149] As Ni Lexiong, a Shanghai-based military expert, put it in September 2020: "If we fight a war with the US, we will make sure that we have absolute superiority and up to now we have not done so. Isn't it obvious?"[150] The real question is when will the PLA enjoy "absolute superiority" over US forces? By 2035? By 2050, more likely (cf. chapter 1).

Finally, one last matter is often overlooked, in the event of a successful Chinese invasion: the risks associated with the PLA and the CCP controlling the island and its population. Given the Taiwanese people's state of mind, their identity, and even their nationalism, one cannot exclude fierce and costly resistance. The island's topography could help them. The possible outbreak of a long and perilous period of guerrilla warfare is likely, if not to dissuade, at least to compel some Chinese officials to seriously weigh the pros and cons before embarking on any adventure.[151]

A war would highlight the strengths and weaknesses of the three militaries involved. It could well end with a paralysis halfway through the respective objectives pursued by each, for logistical reasons, due to combat inexperience, specific difficulties of the maritime environment and the objective at stake as well as nuclearization risks. It is therefore conceivable that the PLA will continue to think twice before embarking on a generalized conflict against Taiwan for a long time to come, because the state of war is a threshold which, once crossed, becomes very difficult to retreat from before a "rise to extremes," in Clausewitz's famous words.

GRAY ZONES: NON-MILITARY WAYS
OF SUBJUGATING TAIWAN

US awareness of the risks incurred and Taiwan's improved preparedness could for a long time dissuade China from embarking on a frontal conflict, and even a blockade of the island which inevitably would propel the three parties beyond the threshold of war.

Hence it seems to me that Beijing will continue preferring other methods to achieve its ends. Some, such as the use of gray zone coercion, carry risks but are most likely to affect Taiwanese morale. Others, such as cyberattacks or disinformation, are less dangerous but are already subject to countermeasures.

Finally, united front strategy, despite its modest successes for now, is likely to be pursued in parallel. All of these methods are similar to what is called "political warfare."[152]

More Frequent Use of Gray Zone Coercion

Unable to take physical control of the territories it claims, China began in the early 2010s to challenge the sovereignty exercised by occupiers over the territories in various ways. Since the start of that decade, as shall be seen (cf. chapter 5), PLA vessels and aircraft have regularly entered the territorial waters or airspace of Japanese-administered Senkaku (Diaoyu). In the South China Sea, Chinese entities are trying to establish jurisdiction over all sea and air space within the famous nine-dash line by creating artificial islands in the Spratlys and multiplying intimidation of other occupants (cf. chapter 4). In short, China has decided to make systematic use of the gray zones between war and peace.

Incursions into Taiwan's sea and air zones are both old and recent. The first date back to the 1958 crisis when the PLA unsuccessfully attacked Kinmen, the outlying island near the Fujian coast, and more recently to 1996 when a PLA missile (unarmed) overflew the main island. In 1999, after President Lee Teng-hui floated the idea that Taipei–Beijing relations were of quasi-state nature, the PLA Air Force violated the median line in the Taiwan strait. But it is since the DPP returned to power in 2016 and especially 2019 that PLA incursions near Taiwanese sea and air space have multiplied. These breaches were preceded by air and sea circumnavigations around the island, via the Bashi Channel, as the PLA sought to demonstrate its new projection capabilities. Since March 2019, and more so Tsai's reelection in January 2020, Beijing's pressure has increased substantially.[153]

From September 2020, Taiwan's defense ministry began to publicize the incursions of planes and PLA vessels in its ADIZ, highlighting an intensification of these incursions: 1,700 planes and more than 1,000 ships entered the area between 1990 and September 2020. In response, 3,000 interceptions were carried out, costing of one billion dollars annually, or approximately 9 percent of the defense budget. Between mid-September 2020 and end of March 2021, 135 additional incursions, engaging 329 PLA aircraft, took place. Since then, incursions have intensified, especially after Pelosi's Taiwan visit in early August 2022, reaching 446 in that single month.[154] In the year 2022, a total of 1,700 incursions in Taiwan's ADIZ have been registered. And in December 2022–January 2023, reaching 306 in less than two months, and 47 on a single day, December 25.[155] These are not only increasingly frequent but also involve a larger and more varied number of aircraft (bombers, fighters, anti-submarine warfare aircraft, electronic warfare aircraft, etc.), each time putting Taiwanese pilots a little more to the test and weighing more heavily on the island's finances.

There are two reasons for this: on the one hand, the increasingly uncertain prospect of peaceful reunification; on the other, the strengthening Taipei–Washington military-strategic cooperation, marked by an increase in arms sales and enhancement of quasi-official ties between the two sides.

In mid-2020, the PLA organized air and naval maneuvers, in the southwest of Taiwan and halfway to the ROC-controlled Pratas. These were held in international sea and air space but for the first time in twenty years (excepting in 2019) beyond the median line in the strait and within Taiwan's ADIZ. During US Health Secretary Alex Azar's Taiwan visit in August followed by Undersecretary of State for Economic Growth Keith Krach a month later, there were multiple violations of Taiwan's ADIZ by the PLA's Su-30 fighters and Y-8 transport aircrafts, forcing the island's air defense to intercept these intruders. They were the most serious incursions since 1996. Taiwan considered them a "serious provocation" and a threat to regional security and stability.[156]

The large-scale PLA exercise organized around Taiwan as a reaction to Pelosi's visit went further in terms of gray zone coercion. It was clearly presented as simulating a potential blockade of the island. Nonetheless, it needs to be reiterated that none of the PLA vessels or aircraft entered Taiwan's territorial waters or air space. Yet, for the first time on July 24, 2022, a Chinese unmanned aerial vehicle (UAV) penetrated the airspace of Lieyu, an island which is part of Kinmen. Unprepared and unable to identify whether it was a civilian or a military one, Taiwanese soldiers threw rocks at the drone. A few days later, a PLA drone was spotted over Matsu and in early August two other Chinese military drones flew over Kinmen, compelling the Taiwanese military to fly flares at them. On September 1, the latter finally shot down a Chinese civilian drone which had penetrated the Kinmen airspace.[157] These incursions have clearly and intentionally pushed to a higher and more dangerous level China's gray zone tactics, increasing the risks of military crisis. But they have also shown Taiwanese military's resolve and strict application of their standard operating procedures.

These gestures have many aims: punish Taiwan for any move toward independence or attempt to improve its international status; increase Taiwanese people's feeling of insecurity; create a new status quo or "new normal" around the island by reducing Taiwanese Air Force's and Navy's operational space; gather more information on the island's electronic signal intelligence; test the United States' resolve to defend Taiwan; please the PRC nationalists; and finally improve PLA airmen's capabilities, such as by organizing night flights near Taiwan for the first time in March 2020, with the aim of being able, when the time comes, to open a second front on Taiwan's eastern flank where important military bases are concentrated.[158]

Beijing presents these actions as so many affirmations of the People's Republic sovereignty over "the rebel island." The affirmation remains deliberately vague: intended to prevent any formal independence, it also aims to combat the "separatist" forces currently in power in Taiwan. Through these intimidations, the CCP has been seeking to weaken the DPP by holding it responsible for the present tensions and to persuade Taiwan's electorate by coercion to support the Pan-Blue camp, especially the KMT, which is more accommodating of Beijing. As Chinese Taiwan Affairs Office spokesperson Ma Xiaoguang said in September 2020: "using force to refuse unification is a dead end" (*yiwu jutong, silu yitiao*).[159]

Can Beijing push its advantage further? Unlikely. It would only help increase the risk of incidents and therefore of a flare-up in the strait situation.

First, such intimidations put the KMT in a delicate position. As a Taiwanese party, it can obviously criticize the DPP's policy, but cannot make a pact with the potential enemy. They also prompt the United States to react, boosting the passage of its vessels and planes through the strait, mostly on the Taiwanese side of the median line which divides the strait, and even through Taiwan's sea and air space.

The main consequence of these PLA incursions, unprecedented in scale, is an increase in the risk of incidents (collision, warning shots, live fire, etc.). In February 2020, according to Taiwanese sources, China's Air Force changed its rules of engagement: during an exercise simulating an attack against Taiwan, the United States, and Japan, a PLA J-11 entered the island's ADIZ and locked its radar on a Taiwanese F-16 which came to intercept it.[160] In September 2020 after some 40 PLA planes crossed the median line, Taiwan's Air Force modified its own rules of engagement, giving itself the right to open fire in the event of an alleged attack, although all authorization will still have to come from the top political leadership.[161] The first shooting of a Chinese UAV in September 2022 has demonstrated that Taiwan was serious about its rules of engagement. But it has also augmented the probability of a military crisis in the strait.

Besides these intimidations, other actions aimed at challenging both the median line and even Taiwan's jurisdiction over its territorial waters and exclusive economic zone. Since October 2019, Chinese vessels have been venturing into waters around the Pescadores (Penghu) archipelago to illegally extract sea sand. Several vessels and their crew have since been arrested by Taiwan's coast guard, notably in July 2020. In September 2020, these extraction attempts extended to the small archipelago of Matsu (Mazu) located near Fuzhou.[162] Similar actions have continued since then, for example in June 2021 and in April 2022.[163] Meanwhile a Chinese Foreign Ministry spokesman said, "Taiwan is an inalienable part of Chinese territory and there is no so-called middle line." He thereby confirmed Beijing's new, more offensive strategy.

In the longer term, through what could be called a new "nerve-wracking war," Beijing's objective is to affect Taiwanese morale, to "psychologically cripple" them and hold them responsible for the rise in tensions and any incidents.[164] But will these intimidations and challenges to the ROC borders succeed in persuading Taiwan's military to give up the fight and the Americans to abandon Taiwan? For the moment, while the risk of incidents has risen, they have had the opposite result.[165]

Cyberattacks and Disinformation

Another type of threat comes from two important tools, one new, one old, China seeks to use to weaken Taiwan: cyberattacks and disinformation.

I have already mentioned the possibility of attacks or even cyber warfare in the context of a conflict pitting China against Taiwan and the United States. Here, I consider these attacks taking place in a peaceful, near-normal environment. With Taiwan, cyber war has intensified since the DPP returned to power in 2016. Coming probably—for lack of formal proof or clear attribution—from specially trained PLA elements, these attacks target public, civilian, or military and private sites on the island, especially the electronics industry, more advance than China's.[166]

In 2018, Taiwanese government sites were scanned 200 million times and suffered 30 million attacks per month, mainly from China. These cyberattacks increased during Taiwan's January 2020 presidential and legislative elections, along with an unprecedented disinformation campaign seeking to discredit Tsai and Green candidates. And attacks against Taiwanese government's agencies have intensified since then, amounting to five million per day in 2021.[167] They constitute warnings intended to demonstrate the Chinese government's—especially PLA cyber specialists'—ability to potentially paralyze Taiwan's economy. It is well known that for many years similar attacks were mounted for the same purpose against the United States.

Taiwan has long been aware of these risks. In 2001, the Executive Yuan (government) adopted a security plan and established both a dedicated structure (National Information & Communication Security Taskforce) and a National Center for Cyber Security Technology.[168] In 2016, Taiwan contended with increasing threats, so it created a new Cyber Security Department which supervises all activities in the field and promotes them in economic and academic circles and among people at large.[169]

In order to better protect themselves, Taiwan and the United States have strengthened their cooperation in this area. In November 2019, they coorganized for the first time a multinational exercise called CODE (Cyber Offensive and Defensive Exercise), including Australia, Indonesia, Japan, Malaysia, and the Czech Republic as well as six other observer countries.[170] Taiwan is cooperating with other Western countries, including the Netherlands, on cybersecurity.[171] Through its own experience and different forms of cooperation, Taiwan has acquired expertise which it is considering exporting, especially by creating in 2022 a cybersecurity center of excellence.[172]

As for disinformation, threats have intensified since 2016. Using the web extensively, Chinese propaganda services have sought to spread fake news intended to discredit Tsai's government and strengthen the Pan-Blue camp, particularly the KMT. While these offensives have become constant, they are focused around election periods. For example, an online disinformation campaign erupted before the November 2018 local elections, helping the victory of opposition candidates, including Han Kuo-yu in Kaohsiung (he was recalled from his post by popular vote in June 2020).

Taiwan has since learned to better protect itself. A major difficulty in this fight stems from a lack of public and irrefutable proof of these disinformation operations' origin, in other words here again a lack of attribution. As in other countries, Taiwan's government and society are forced to trust data from intelligence services. Recent studies have attested to these disinformation campaigns' Chinese origin, especially during the January 2020 Taiwanese elections.[173] Not all originate in China. In order to cover their tracks, some are launched from Malaysia, for example. But the language used is the CCP's. Others aimed to falsely show reprehensible information emerging from Taiwan, such as racist remarks against the controversial WHO director general Tedros Adhanom Ghebreyesus after the COVID-19 outbreak.

Attacks around the January 2020 elections focused on the Anti-Infiltration Act (*fan shentou fa*) the Legislative Yuan passed in December 2019, despite KMT boycott. Backed by a majority of Taiwanese (about 80%),[174] this new law aims to combat disinformation companies likely to seriously distort the island's debates and democratic life. The CCP has good reason to oppose the law, which seeks to thwart its united front strategy intended to gradually win over Taiwan's elites and society at large (cf. infra).

Taiwanese officials overseeing the fight against disinformation remain calm. To control its destabilizing effects, they rely on the society's open and democratic nature. They have also adopted major protective measures. It is likely that Taiwan will thereby be able to continue protecting itself. In any case, the January 2020 election results showed it has indeed acquired such means.

United Front Strategy

Beijing is not without current and potential allies in Taiwan. Some newspapers like the *Zhongguo shibao* (China Times) belong to groups (*Wangwang* in this case) close to Beijing. Many firms are economically dependent on the mainland where approximately 400,000 Taiwanese live (against one million ten years ago). In recent years this dependence has tended to decrease and a number of Taiwanese businesses have, for primarily commercial reasons, moved their production lines from China, where production costs have risen rapidly, to Southeast Asia and South Asia or even Taiwan itself, where life has paradoxically remained inexpensive. The COVID-19 pandemic has accelerated this migration. But economic dependence on China is set to remain significant, as it is still the island's leading trading partner far ahead of the United States (42% compared to 15% of exports in 2021) and the primary first destination of its foreign investments although China's share fell from 83 percent to 33 percent between 2010 and 2020.

Added to this is a geographical and above all cultural proximity on which the CCP relies to try and win over a greater number of Taiwanese to the "reunification" cause. As noted earlier, this united front strategy has so far borne little fruit. However, Beijing is not going to give it up. Too many members of the party and state apparatus depend on it. Moreover, this strategy goes beyond the "rebel island" and aims to rally, neutralize, or isolate all forces worldwide that are a priori hostile to the Chinese Communist Party and the PRC. Beijing's White Paper on Taiwan published in August 2022 and Xi's report to the 20th Party Congress in October have confirmed that the united front strategy toward Taiwan will not be abandoned.[175] It is thus likely to remain a pillar of its Taiwan policy, even if its relative importance in relation to military threats and intimidations, cyberattacks, and disinformation has notably diminished.

CONCLUSION: THE IMPACT OF THE UKRAINE WAR AND ITS LIMITS

Taiwan is clearly in a more perilous state than twenty years ago. The risks, if not of total war, of armed incidents or even limited confrontations in the strait are growing and will force the three parties involved—Beijing, Taipei, and Washington—to better prepare to manage difficult, even insoluble, crises.

These incidents and crises could have worrying economic and social consequences for Taiwan. They may be perceived in Beijing as effective means to frighten the Taiwanese and make them feel more acutely the growing asymmetry of forces and the inevitability of opening political talks with the mainland and finally accept a form of unification. But will they be enough to make the island's authorities bend? In the foreseeable future, any new crisis would have the immediate result of tightening the already close Taipei–Washington ties and perhaps also convincing Tokyo and even Canberra to shed its reserve.

Ahead of any crisis, Taiwan has been striving to adapt to any new China-imposed military-strategic scenario. It has been investing more in armed forces to improve conventional deterrence capability, protecting itself more effectively against cyberattacks and disinformation. And democracy protects it from the strongest pulls of the CCP's united front strategy.

But its double dependence on China and the United States requires caution, regardless of the party in power in Taipei. As for Beijing, Taipei must avoid any move toward formal independence; while trying hard to reduce its dependence upon the mainland, it must bear in mind its economic interests there. Simultaneously, it must remain in tune with the US administration, regardless of whichever party is in office, to be assured of support in all circumstances. The strategic importance of Taiwan's electronics industry, especially the TSMC company, for US industry strengthens Taipei's hand in this equation but it is far from being an absolute guarantee against a future war, especially as the United States is working actively at developing its own semi-conductor industry and moving TSMC and others to its soil.

The real question for any "Green" government is whether its position is tenable in the long term or whether the CCP will succeed, through threats, in forcing the DPP to subscribe to the "92 consensus," or One China. Growing PLA pressures may have no other purpose, even if this concession is made only to renew intimidations in order to force Taipei to continue giving ground and accept the unification idea.

Taiwan's geographical position paradoxically places it not only at the fore-front, but also at the heart of the new Sino–US cold war. It is simultaneously a source of protection but also of danger.

Each of the three parties is aware of the famous Thucydides Trap risks. And the war in Ukraine has clearly made them more aware of the danger of trespassing the threshold of an armed conflict. China may be tempted to conduct more aggressive gray zone tactics and coercion. But it has been taken aback by all the negative and unintended consequences of the Russian invasion and is now trying actively to address them both from a military and economic standpoint. If there is one lesson the PLA has learned from this war is the need for speed: the only way forward for the PLA is to be able to move fast and combine various types of aggression, for example under the guise of a naval exercise—missile strikes, blockade, and landing at several points on the island—to impose on both Taipei and Washington a fait accompli and raise the stakes, including a nuclear threat, in case of any US intervention.[176]

Beijing is also aware of the need to reduce its economic dependence upon the West and is working actively to achieve it. Although far from Taiwan, the Ukraine war has contributed to waking up the Taiwanese, arguably to a larger extent than the post-Pelosi visit PLA exercise, to the real dangers that the ROC is facing today, leading to an unprecedented investment in national defense and a better preparation of the society for war. Putin's Ukraine invasion has confirmed to Washington as well as Taipei how quicky and easily such a decision can be made, particularly in an authoritarian country, convincing the Biden Administration to move closer to strategic clarity in its support of the status quo and invest more in Taiwan's defense, turning the island into essentially a large weapon depot. The Ukraine war has also led the US government to reducing US economic dependence on China, particularly in technologies and products used in military and national security.[177] While it has increased the prospect of an armed conflict in the Taiwan Strait, the Ukraine war has also shown how different the geography, context, and strategies of the three actors involved may be, compelling all of them to think twice before starting a kinetic confrontation.[178]

Meanwhile, possible causes of conflict are ever present: fear, honor, and interests. If interests continue outweighing the other two, war may yet be avoided.[179] Otherwise, Beijing could find itself compelled to use the slightest pretext to start hostilities, at great risk to itself, given that even ten years from now, despite the progress likely to be made by the PLA and the additional operational speed it may acquire, it will have to face stronger and more resolute American and Taiwanese armed forces, probably supported by Japanese and perhaps Australian militaries.

In this chapter, I have not sought to consider the future of cross-strait relations, both because it lies beyond the discussion's scope and as it remains unresolved except for the ROC's disappearance, which is unacceptable to any civilized and rational human being.[180] I believe that only China's democratization can change the balance. A Chinese researcher said in September 2020: "I don't think Taiwan can go against the tide of time, . . . if the Taiwanese don't reunite and if they don't declare independence, where will they go?"[181] In fact, it's been more than seventy years since the island's residents have answered this question in their own way by adhering to the status quo in the strait. Is there a better solution? Probably not.

Notes

1. *Chine-Taiwan: la guerre est-elle concevable?* (China-Taiwan: Is war conceivable?), Paris: Economica, 2004.

2. For a good analysis of recent evolution in China–Taiwan relations, cf. J. Michael Cole, *Cross-Strait Relations since 2016: The End of the Illusion*, London and New York: Routledge, 2020.

3. Mainland Affairs Council, "Over 80% of the Public Oppose CCP's Hong Kong National Security Law and Military and Diplomatic Suppression of Taiwan," August 6, 2020, https://www.mac.gov.tw/en/News_Content.aspx?n=2BA0753CBE348412&sms=E828F60C4AFBAF90&s=B7E13A0DE0617343; *Yahoo News*, "Poll: Almost 9 in 10 Taiwanese oppose China's 'one country, two systems' policy," November 23, 2021, https://news.yahoo.com/poll-almost-9-10-taiwanese-184348279.html?fr=yhssrp_catchall; "Public Opinion in Taiwan Supports the Government's 'Four Commitments' and 'Four Resiliences' Position and Resolutely Opposes the CCP's Political Stands and Military Coercion against Taiwan," Mainland Affairs Council, October 27, 2022, https://www.mac.gov.tw/en/News_Content.aspx?n=2BA0753CBE348412&sms=E828F60C4AFBAF90&s=7DE2B04B14A025E3.

4. Mainland Affairs Council, "Percentage Distribution of the Questionnaire for the Survey on 'Public Views on Current Cross-Strait Issues,'" June 2, 2022, https://ws.mac.gov.tw/001/Upload/297/relfile/8010/6112/9f7cb24e-07ae-45e9-b940-bfe0e75202e4.pdf.

5. Itamar Waksman, "Opposition Leader: '92 Consensus' Example of 'Creative Ambiguity,'" *Radio Taiwan International*, June 7, 2022, https://en.rti.org.tw/news/view/id/2007663.

6. "203. Joint Statement Following Discussions with Leaders of the People's Republic of China," *Office of the Historian*, Department of State, United States of America Foreign Relations of the United States, 1969–1976, Vol XVII, China, 1969–1972, Shanghai, February 27, 1972, https://history.state.gov/historicaldocuments/frus1969-76v17/d203.

7. Ibid, https://history.state.gov/historicaldocuments/frus1977-80v01/d104.

8. "Zhongguohua renmin gongheguo he Meilijianhezhongguo guanyu jianli waijiao guanxi de lianhe baogao (1979nian 1yue 1ri)" (Joint Communiqué on the establishment of diplomatic relations between the People's Republic of China and the United States of America," January 1, 1979), http://www.gov.cn/ztzl/zmdh/content_624348.htm.

9. White House Diary, p. 265, cited in "104. Address by President Carter to the Nation," *Office of the Historian*, op. cit. ,https://history.state.gov/historicaldocuments/frus1977-80v01/d104. He was referring to the 1952 US-Taiwan Mutual Defense Treaty and which could only be scrapped a year after informing the other party, that is, January 1, 1980.

10. "When touching on the question of Taiwan, Vice Premier Deng said that China was willing to solve the Taiwan question in a peaceful way but will not undertake to use force because that will be a disservice to a peaceful settlement of the question." In The Establishment of Sino-U.S. Diplomatic Relations and Vice Premier Deng Xiaoping's visit to the United States, https://www.fmprc.gov.cn/mfa_eng/ziliao_665539/3602_665543/3604_665547/200011/t20001117_697797.html (accessed September 23, 2022).

11. "H.R.2479 - Taiwan Relations Act," 96th Congress (1979–1980), *US Congress* https://www.congress.gov/bill/96th-congress/house-bill/2479.

12. Public Law 96–8 April 10, 1979, 96th Congress, https://www.govinfo.gov/content/pkg/STATUTE-93/pdf/STATUTE-93-Pg14.pdf#page=1; US archives recording these engagements with Taiwan were declassified in August 2020; cf. "Declassified Cables: Taiwan Arms Sales & Six Assurances (1982)," American Institute in Taiwan, https://www.ait.org.tw/our-relationship/policy-history/key-u-s-foreign-policy-documents-region/six-assurances-1982/.

13. Richard Haass and David Sacks, "American Support for Taiwan Must Be Unambiguous. To Keep the Peace, Make Clear to China that Force Won't Stand," *Foreign Affairs*, September 2, 2020, https://www.foreignaffairs.com/articles/united-states/american-support-taiwan-must-be-unambiguous?utm_medium=newsletters&utm_source=press_note&utm_campaign=&utm_content=20200902&utm_term=FAPressNoteHaassSacksSept22020.

14. In January 2018, Trump asked an adviser: "What do we get from protecting Taiwan, say?" cited by Bob Woodward, *Fear: Trump in the White House*, New York: Simon & Schuster, p. 305. This idea of abandoning Taiwan was also made public by John Bolton, former national security adviser, in his book, *The Room Where It Happened: A White House Memoir*, New York: Simon & Schuster, 2020.

15. "The United States Strategic Approach to the People's Republic of China," May 26, 2020, https://trumpwhitehouse.archives.gov/wp-content/uploads/2020/05/U.S.-Strategic-Approach-to-The-Peoples-Republic-of-China-Report-5.24v1.pdf.

16. Nike Ching, "US Adjusts Taiwan Policy, Declassifies Cables," *Voice of America*, September 1, 2020, https://www.voanews.com/a/east-asia-pacific_voa-news-china_us-adjusts-taiwan-policy-declassifies-cables/6195286.html.

17. See above, footnote 12, cf. also Shirley Kan, "US Rebuts China on 'Six Assurances,'" *Taipei Times*, September 5, 2020, https://www.taipeitimes.com/News/editorials/archives/2020/09/05/2003742827.

18. John Xie, "Will US Make Clear-cut Commitment to Defend Taiwan From China?" *Voice of America News*, August 21, 2020, https://www.voanews.com/east-asia-pacific/voa-news-china/will-us-make-clear-cut-commitment-defend-taiwan-china.

19. Ruchir Sharma, "Pound for Pound, Taiwan Is the Most Important Place in the World," *The New York Times*, December 14, 2020, https://www.nytimes.com/2020/12/14/opinion/taiwan-computer-chips.html#click=https://t.co/1DayDqYbhx.

20. Randall G. Schriver, "Memo to the Next President: The Inheritance in the Indo-Pacific and the Challenges and Opportunities for Your Presidency," *Project 2049*, December 1, 2020, https://project2049.net/2020/12/01/memo-to-the-next-president-the-inheritance-in-the-indo-pacific-and-the-challenges-and-opportunities-for-your-presidency/.

21. Interim national Security Strategic Guidance, op. cit., p. 21. Cf. also State Department statement, January 23, 2021, https:www.state.gov/pre-military-pressure-against-taiwan-threatens-regionalpeace-and-stability/; the expression "rock-solid" has since been repeated many times.

22. Josh Wingrove, "Biden Says US Would Defend Taiwan in 'Unprecedented Attack,'" *BNNBloomberg*, September 18, 2022, https://www.bnnbloomberg.ca/biden -says-us-would-defend-taiwan-in-unprecedented-attack-1.1820512.

23. Cf. interview of Joe Biden by CBS *60 minutes*, *CBS News*, September 19, 2022, https://www.cbsnews.com/video/president-biden-on-taiwan-60-minutes/.

24. *National Security Strategy*, The White House, Washington, October 12, 2022, https://www.whitehouse.gov/wp-content/uploads/2022/10/Biden-Harris -Administrations-National-Security-Strategy-10.2022.pdf.

25. David Brunnstrom and Michael Martina, "Strategic clarity on Taiwan policy carries 'significant downsides' - U.S.," *Reuters*, May 5, 2021, https://www.reuters.com/world /asia-pacific/significant- downsides-strategic-clarity-over-taiwan-us-2021-05-04/.

26. Like European states, the United States favours Taiwan's WHO participation as observer.

27. Xinhua Headlines: Xi says "China must be, will be reunified" as key anniversary marked, *Xinhua*, January 2, 2019, http://www.xinhuanet.com/english/2019-01 /02/c_137714898.htm.

28. "China Releases White Paper on Taiwan Question, Reunification in New Era," *Xinhua*, August 10, 2022, "The Taiwan Question and China's Reunification in the New Era," The Taiwan Affairs Office of the State Council and The State Council Information Office, August 2022, https://english.www.gov.cn/archive/whitepaper /202208/10/content_WS62f34f46c6d02e533532f0ac.html.

29. Xi Jinping, "Hold High the Great Banner of Socialism with Chinese Characteristics and Strive in Unity to Build a Modern Socialist Country in All Respects," Report to the 20th National Congress of the Communist Party of China, October 16, 2022, p. 51.

30. China's National Defence in 2010, Information Office of the State Council, The People's Republic of China, March 2011, Beijing: English and Chinese versions (Annotated by Andrew S. Erickson: China analysis from original sources), http:// www.andrewerickson.com/wp-content/uploads/2019/07/China-Defense-White-Paper _2010_English-Chinese_Annotated.pdf.

31. "Full Text of 2019 Defence White Paper: 'China's National Defence in the New Era'" (English & Chinese Versions), Andrew S. Erickson: China analysis from original sources, July 24, 2019, https://www.andrewerickson.com/2019/07/full -text-of-defense-white-paper-chinas-national-defense-in-the-new-era-english-chinese -versions/.

32. Cf. footnote 10.

33. "Changes in Taiwan/Chinese Identity of Taiwanese as Tracked in Surveys by the Election Study Center, NCCU (1992–2022.06)," Election Study Center, National Chengchi University, https://esc.nccu.edu.tw/upload/44/doc/6961/People202206.jpg (accessed September 23, 2022).

34. Annual Report to Congress, Washington, DC: Office of the Secretary of Defense, November 29, 2022, https://media.defense.gov/2022/Nov/29/2003122279/ -1/-1/1/2022-MILITARY-AND-SECURITY-DEVELOPMENTS-INVOLVING-THE -PEOPLES-REPUBLIC-OF-CHINA.PDF, pp. 123–30. Joel Wuthnow, Derek Grossman, Phillip C. Saunders, Andrew Scobell, and Andrew N. D. Yang, eds., *Crossing*

the Strait. China's Military Prepares for War with Taiwan, Washington, DC, National Defense University Press, 2022, https://ndupress.ndu.edu/Portals/68/Documents/Books/crossing-the-strait/crossing-the-strait.pdf?ver=VFL9qlF8Flii9svD4EI31g%3d%3d.

35. Eric Heginbotham, Michael Nixon, Forrest E. Morgan, Jacob L. Heim, Jeff Hagen, Sheng Tao Li, Jeffrey Engstrom, Martin C. Libicki, Paul DeLuca, David A. Shlapak, David R. Frelinger, Burgess Laird, Kyle Brady, and Lyle J. Morris, *The U.S.-China Military Scorecard: Forces, Geography, and the Evolving Balance of Power, 1996–2017*, Santa Monica, CA: RAND Corporation, RR-392-AF, 2015, pp. 28–35.

36. Michael Chase, Cristina L. Garafola, and Nathan Beauchamp-Mustafaga, "Chinese Perceptions of and Responses to US Conventional Military Power," *Asian Security*, Vol. 14, No. 2, 2018, pp. 1–15.

37. Liu Xuanzun, "China's 10,000 Ton-Class Destroyer Equipped with Long-Range Land Attack Missiles," *Global Times*, December 22, 2019, https://www.globaltimes.cn/content/1174437.shtml; *South China Morning Post (SCMP)*, September 11, 2020, https://sg.news.yahoo.com/china-upgrade-destroyers-carrier-killer-121938414.html; "China Commissions 8th Quasi-Stealthy, High-Tech, Missile-Armed Type 055 Destroyer," Warrior Maven, Center for Military Modernization, January 23, 2023, https://warriormaven.com/china/china-commissions-8th-quasi-stealthy-high-tech-type-055-destroyer.

38. Kristin Huang, "Chinese State Broadcaster Reveals Details of New Airborne Weapon Tianlei 500 as Tensions Simmer with Taiwan," *SCMP*, August 17, 2020, https://www.scmp.com/news/china/military/article/3097709/chinese-state-broadcaster-reveals-details-new-airborne-weapon.

39. "PLA Holds Joint Drills in Waters to the East of Taiwan Island," *PLA Daily*, April 4, 2019, http://english.chinamil. com.cn/view/2019-04/16/content_9479909.htm.

40. Liu Xuanzun, "PLA Army's Attack Helicopters Conduct Sea-Crossing Assault Drills on Navy Warship," *Global Times*, August 5, 2020, https://www.globaltimes.cn/content/1196799.shtml.

41. Derek Grossman, Nathan Beauchamp-Mustafaga, Logan Ma, and Michael S. Chase, *China's Long-Range Bomber Flights: Drivers and Implications*, Santa Monica, CA: Rand, 2018, https://www.rand.org/pubs/research_reports/RR2567.html; Bates Gill, Adam Ni, and Dennis Blasko, "The Ambitious Reform Plans of the People's Liberation Army: Progress, Prospects and Implications for Australia," *Australian Journal of Defence and Strategic Studies*, Vol. 2, No. 1, June 25, 2020, https://www.defence.gov.au/adc/publications/AJDSS/documents/volume2-number1/Gill.pdf.

42. Minnie Chan, "US-China relations: Chinese submarines put through their paces in promotional video," *SCMP*, August 22, 2020, https://www.scmp.com/news/china/military/article/3098424/us-china-relations-chinese-submarines-put-through-their-paces.

43. The article does not specify whether the DF17 and DF26 are conventional or nuclear, probably the former; cf. Liu Xuanzun, "Frequent Operations Near China

Related to Each Other, Reveal New Threats: Experts," *Global Times*, August 24, 2020, https://www.globaltimes.cn/content/1198725.shtml.

44. (Updated August 31 [2022]), *China Power*, https://chinapower.csis.org/tracking -the-fourth-taiwan-strait-crisis/ (accessed September 26, 2022).

45. Liu, "Frequent Operations," op. cit.

46. Bonny Lin and Joel Wuthnow, "Pushing Back against China's New Normal in the Taiwan Strait," War on the Rocks, August 16, 2022, https://warontherocks.com /2022/08/pushing-back-against-chinas-new-normal-in-the-taiwan-strait/.

47. *Military and Security Developments Involving the People's Republic of China 2021*, op. cit., pp. 116, 121.

48. "Qian guoTaiban fuzhuren: Heping tongyi Taiwan de kenengxing yi yuelai yuexiao" (Former Deputy Director of the Taiwan Affairs Office of State Council: The possibility of peaceful reunification of Taiwan is getting smaller and smaller), *Huanqiu shibao* (Global Times), December 17, 2016, https://taiwan.huanqiu.com/ article/9CaKrnJZTHG.

49. "Zhou Zhihuai: Jiuzhi jiang man yinian, Cai Yingwen renzhuang shui weixing" (Zhou Zhihuai: Tsai Ing-wen still pretends not to wake up one year after her inaugura- tion), *Huanqiu shibao* (Global Times), May 18, 2017, https://opinion.huanqiu.com/ article/9CaKrnK2Qy8.

50. "Sheping: 2018nian, Zhongguo gongzhong qitai shenme?" (Editorial: What does the Chinese public expect in 2018?), *Huanqiuwang* (Global Times online), Janu- ary 1, 2018, https://opinion.huanqiu.com/article/9CaKrnK6cqN.

51. "Lan yiyuan: 'Qi Tai lun' baifenbai cunzai Telangpu shangtai hui jiasu liang'an tongyi" (Blue Legislator: "Abandoning Taiwan" exists 100%, Trump's inauguration will accelerate cross-Strait reunification), *Huanqiu shibao* (Global Times), January 22, 2017, https://taiwan.huanqiu.com/article/9CaKrnJZXeB.

52. Peter Gries and Tao Wang, "Will China Seize Taiwan? Wishful Thinking in Beijing, Taipei and Washington Could Spell War in 2019," *Foreign Affairs*, February 15, 2019, https://www.foreignaffairs.com/articles/china/2019-02-15/will-china-seize -taiwan.

53. Wang Zhiyao, "Liang'an hui bu hui baofa zhanzheng? Jiefangjun zhong jiang he taiwan lujun tuiyi shang jiang ge you jiedu" (Will there be a cross-Strait war? PLA Lieutenant General and retired Taiwanese general have their own interpretations), *Guancha.cn*, March 12, 2020, https://user.guancha.cn/main/content?id=259934&s =fwrmhtycwz. The Taiwanese general deemed a war unlikely (cf. infra).

54. Luo Qingsheng, "Taiwan jiang bei boda dailiren zhanzheng" (Taiwan will be forced into a proxy war), *Taihai wang* (Taihainet.com) published sina.com, August 17, 2020, http://k.sina.com.cn/article_2730765330_a2c42c1202000uk7l.html?from —news&subch=onews.

55. Lu Zhenhua, Wang Zili, and Xu Heqian, "China and US to Fight for Tech Primacy, Not War," *Caixin*, May 18, 2020, https://www.caixinglobal.com/2020 -05-14/china-and-the-us-wont-go-to-war-but-will-fight-for-tech-supremacy-tsinghua -professor-says-101554127.html; https://asia.nikkei.com/Spotlight/Caixin/China-and -US-to-fight-for-tech-primacy-not-war-Tsinghua-expert.

56. Minnie Chan, "'Too Costly': Chinese Military Strategist Warns Now Is Not the Time to Take Back Taiwan By Force," *SCMP*, May 4, 2020, https://www.scmp.com/news/china/military/article/3082825/too-costly-chinese-military-strategist-warns-now-not-time-take.

57. "Has the Wind Changed? PLA Hawks General Dai Xu and General Qiao Liang Release Odd Articles," *GNews*, July 11, 2020, https://gnews.org/257994/.

58. Gries and Wang, "Will China Seize Taiwan?" op. cit.

59. "Mei haijun guanfang kanwu: Jiefangjun hen keneng mingnianchu dui Tai dongwu. 3 tian jiejue wenti" (Official publication of the US Navy: The People's Liberation Army is likely to use force against Taiwan early next year and solve the problem in three days), *Huanqiu shibao*, August 15, 2020, https://taiwan.huanqiu.com/article/3zTvkWMXZPw?bsh_bid=5540016044.

60. "Jin Canrong: Zhong Mei yao jili bimian rezhan huo 'xin lengzhan,' dan yao da mingpai" (Jin Canrong: China and the US should try their best to avoid a hot war or a "new Cold War," but they need to "play clear cards"), Fudan Daxue Zhongguo Yanjiuyuan (Fudan University, China Institute), April 2, 2022, http://www.cifu.fudan.edu.cn/b6/d8/c413a440024/page.htm.

61. "Zhang Weiwei 'Zhe jiushi Zhongguo 158 qi': Zuguo tongyi jinru kuai chedao" (Zhang Weiwei 'This is China No. 158': The reunification of the motherland enters the fast lane), *Guanchazhe* (The Observer), September 4, 2022, https://www.guancha.cn/ZhangWeiWei/2022_09_04_656475_1.shtml.

62. Cf. Jin Canrong's comments in "Zhang Weiwei 'Zhe jiushi Zhongguo 158 qi,'" op. cit.

63. "PLA's Post 'Preparing for War' Draws Wide Support from Netizens ahead of Army Day," *Global Times*, July 29, 2022, https://www.globaltimes.cn/page/202207/1271742.shtml.

64. Staff Reporter, "PLA Drills around Taiwan Continue to 'Rehearse Reunification Operation' after Pelosi's Visit, 'Exercises Blockading Island to Become Routine,'" *Global Times*, August 3, 2022, https://www.globaltimes.cn/page/202208/1272108.shtml.

65. Wang Qi, "Taiwan Straits Has Entered a More Dangerous and Fragile New Stage Featuring Long-Term Confrontation, But Windows of Peaceful Reunification Are Not Completely Closed: Experts," *Global Times*, August 24, 2022, https://www.globaltimes.cn/page/202208/1273805.shtml.

66. Cf. interview of Zhu Feng, Director of the International Relations Institute of Nanjing University, "Yaowen/Xuezhi: Xu zuohao changqi douzheng, shenyan 'wutong' maojin," *Xingdao Huanqiu* (Xingdao Global), August 4, 2022, https://www.stnn.cc/c/2022/0804/3748056.shtml.

67. Rachel Sharp, "US 'Would Lose a War with China Fought in the Pacific, Is Unable to Defend Taiwan from an Invasion and Fears the Guam Military Base Is at Risk NOW,' Pentagon Sources Warn," *Daily Mail*, May 16, 2020, https://www.msn.com/en-au/news/world/us-would-lose-a-war-with-china-fought-in-the-pacific-is-unable-to-defend-taiwan-from-an-invasion-and-fears-the-guam-military-base-is-at-risk-now-pentagon-sources-warn/ar-BB14aJO2; Michael Evans, "US Would Lose Pacific War with China," *The Times*, May 16, 2020, accessible via *The Australian*,

https://www.theaustralian.com.au/world/the-times/us-would-lose-any-war-with
-china-in-pacific/news-story/989d5832d6460e3bd7bbab4ca983967b.

68. Sydney J. Seedberg, "US 'Gets Its Ass Handed To It' In Wargames: Here's A $24 Billion Fix," *Breaking Defense*, March 7, 2019, https://breakingdefense.com /2019/03/us-gets-its-ass-handed-to-it-in-wargames-heres-a-24-billion-fix/.

69. Ibid.

70. This is why Michael O'Hanlon's analyses that I had used in my previous book have become obsolete. Michael E. O'Hanlon, "Why China Cannot Conquer Taiwan," *International Security*, Vol. 25, No. 2, Autumn 2000, pp. 51–86; Cabestan, *Chine–Taiwan: la guerre est-elle concevable?* (China-Taiwan: is a war likely?), op. cit.

71. Richard Bernstein, "The Scary War Game Over Taiwan That the U.S. Loses Again and Again," *RealClearInvestigations*, August 17, 2020, https://www .realclearinvestigations.com/articles/2020/08/17/the_scary_war_game_over_taiwan _that_the_us_loses_again_and_again_124836.html.

72. James A. Winnefeld and Michael J. Morell, "The War that Never Was?" *Proceedings*, Vol. 146/8, August 2020, U.S. Naval Institute, https://www.usni.org/ magazines/proceedings/2020/august/war-never-was.

73. Mark F. Cancian, Matthew Cancian, and Eric Heginbotham, *The First Battle of the New War: Wargaming a Chinese Invasion of Taiwan*, Washington, DC: CSIS, Center for Strategic and International Studies, A Report of the CSIS International Security Program, January 2023, https://csis-website-prod.s3.amazonaws .com/s3fs-public/publication/230109_Cancian_FirstBattle_NextWar.pdf?VersionId =WdEUwJYWIySMPIr3ivhFolxC_gZQuSOQ.

74. Cited by Evans, "US Would Lose Pacific War with China," op. cit. Bonnie Glaser joined the German Marshall Fund of the United States in May 2021.

75. Nadia Schadlow, "The End of American Illusion," *Foreign Affairs*, September-October 2020, https://www.foreignaffairs.com/articles/americas/2020-08 -11/end-american-illusion.

76. Ian Easton, *The Chinese Invasion Threat: Taiwan's Defense and American Strategy in Asia*, Washington, DC: Eastbridge Books, 2017. Easton is with 2049 Institute, a think tank long headed by Randall Schriver, who was assistant secretary of defense for Asian and Pacific Security Affairs, 2018–2019. Cf. also Tanner Greer, "Taiwan Can Win a War with China," *Foreign Policy*, September 25, 2018, https:// foreignpolicy.com/2018/09/25/taiwan-can-win-a-war-with-china/.

77. Michael Beckley, "The Emerging Military Balance in East Asia. How China's Neighbors Can Check Chinese Military Expansion," *International Security*, Vol. 42, No. 2, Autumn 2017, pp. 78–119 and on Taiwan, pp. 83–95; cf. review of Ian Easton's book by William S. Murray, *Naval War College Review*, Vol. 72, No. 1, 2019, Article 10, pp. 1–3, https://digital-commons.usnwc.edu/nwc-review/vol72/iss1/10.

78. Peng Guangqian and Yao Youzhi, eds., *The Science of Military Strategy*, Beijing: Military Science Publishing House, 2005, p. 327. English version of *Zhanlüexue* by the same authors published in 2001.

79. *Military and Security Developments involving the People's Republic of China 2022*, op. cit., pp. 59–60, 64–65, 167.

80. Beckley, "The Emerging Military Balance in East Asia," op. cit., p. 86.

81. Ian Easton, "Able Archers: Taiwan Defense Strategy in an Age of Precision Strike," Arlington, VA: Project 2049 Institute, 2014, pp. 35–45.

82. For a good discussion of the pros and cons of such an objective, cf. Mathieu Duchâtel, "An Assessment of China's Options for Military Coercion of Taiwan," in Wuthnow et al., *Crossing the Strait*, op. cit., pp. 103–4.

83. Joshua Arostegui, "PLA Army and Marine Corps Amphibious Brigades in a Post-Reform Military," in Wuthnow et al., *Crossing the Strait*, op. cit., p. 1.

84. Joel Wuthnow, "System Overload: Can China's Military be Distracted in a War over Taiwan?" *China Strategic Perspectives*, No. 15, Center for the Study of Chinese Military Affairs, Institute for National Strategic Studies, National Defense University, June 2020.

85. Beckley, "The Emerging Military Balance in East Asia," op. cit., pp. 94–95.

86. Michael A. Glosny, "Strangulation from the Sea? A PRC Submarine Blockade of Taiwan," *International Security*, Vol. 28, No. 4, Spring 2004, pp. 125–160. Cf. also Michael Casey, "Firepower Strike, Blockade, Landing: PLA Campaigns for a Cross-Strait Conflict," in Wuthnow et al., *Crossing the Strait*, op. cit., pp. 123–27.

87. Lyle J. Goldstein, "How China Sees the U.S. Navy's Sea Hunter Drone," *National Interest*, January 31, 2017, https://nationalinterest.org/feature/how-china-sees-the-us-navys-sea-hunter-drone-19264.

88. Ryan Browne and Barbara Starr, "Pentagon Reveals Some Details of Trump's 'Super Duper' Hypersonic Missile," *CNN*, July 16, 2020, https://edition.cnn.com/2020/07/16/politics/pentagon-hypersonic-missile/index.html.

89. Wajahat Khan and Ken Moriyasu, "US Preps Midrange Missile to Pierce China's 'Anti-Access' Shield Army Chief of Staff Vows to Strengthen Partnerships in First Island Chain," *Asia Nikkei*, August 1, 2020, https://asia.nikkei.com/Politics/International-relations/South-China-Sea/US-preps-midrange-missile-to-pierce-China-s-anti-access-shield.

90. Lloyd J. Austin III, speech, Reagan National Defense Forum, Department of Defense, December 4, 2021, https://www.defense.gov/News/Speeches/Speech/Article/2861931/remarks-by-secretary-of-defense-lloyd-j-austin-iii-at-the-reagan-national-defen/, quoted by Wuthnow et al., *Crossing the Strait*, op. cit., p. 12.

91. Denny Roy, "A Chinese Attack on Taiwan Is Not Imminent," *Asia Times*, August 19, 2020, https://asiatimes.com/2020/08/a-chinese-attack-on-taiwan-is-not-imminent/.

92. Kenji Minemura, "Ian Easton: Crisis over Taiwan Coming in Next Few Years," *The Asahi Shimbun*, August 30, 2020, http://www.asahi.com/ajw/articles/13666742; cf. also, Ian Easton, *The Final Struggle: Inside China's Global Strategy*, London: Camphor Press and Eastbridge Books, 2022.

93. Testimony before the Senate Armed Service Committee, March 9, 2021, https://www.armed-services.senate.gov/imo/media/doc/ 21–10_03-09-2021.pdf.

94. Testimony before the Senate Armed Service Committee, March 23, 2021, https://www.armed-services.senate.gov/imo/media/doc/21-14_03-23-2021.pdf.

95. "U.S. General Warns Troops that War with China Is Possible in Two Years," *The Washington Post*, January 27, 2023, https://www.washingtonpost.com/national-security/2023/01/27/us-general-minihan-china-war-2025/.

96. Bernstein, "The Scary War Game Over Taiwan," op. cit.

97. Cf. Ankit Panda and James Acton, "Why the Pentagon Must Think Harder about Inadvertent Escalation," *Defense News*, December 2, 2020, https://www.defensenews.com/opinion/commentary/2020/12/02/why-the-pentagon-must-think-harder-about-inadvertent-escalation/.

98. Michael Swaine, "Threat Inflation and the Chinese Military," *Qincy Papers*, No. 7, June 2022, pp. 45–47 and 71–73, https://quincyinst.org/report/threat-inflation-and-the-chinese-military/.

99. Minnie Chan, "US-China Relations: Chinese Submarines Put through Their Paces in Promotional Video," *SCMP*, August 22, 2020, https://www.scmp.com/news/china/military/article/3098424/us-china-relations-chinese-submarines-put-through-their-paces.

100. On the risks of nuclearization of an armed conflict in the Taiwan Strait, cf. Wuthnow et al., *Crossing the Strait*, op. cit., pp. 80, 129. Cf. also Michael J. Mazarr, Nathan Beauchamp-Mustafaga, Timothy R. Heath, and Derek Eaton, *What Deters and Why? The State of Deterrence in Korea and the Taiwan Strait*, Washington, DC: Rand, 2021, pp. 67, 71–72, https://www.rand.org/pubs/research_reports/RR2451.html. Cancian et al., *The First Battle of the War*, op. cit., pp. 70–72.

101. George F. Will, "The Eroding U.S. Military Dominance," *The Washington Post*, September 10, 2020, https://www.washingtonpost.com/371d00ca-f207-11ea-999c-67ff7bf6a9d2_story.html.

102. Oriana Skylar Mastro, "The Taiwan Temptation: Why Beijing Might Resort to Force," *Foreign Affairs* 100, No. 4, July/August 2021, pp. 58–67. Rachel Esplin Odell and Eric Heginbotham, "Don't Fall for the Invasion Panic," *Foreign Affairs* 100, No. 5, September/October 2021, pp. 216–20. Bonny Lin and David Sacks, "Force Is Still a Last Resort," *Foreign Affairs,* 100, No. 5, September/October 2021, pp. 222–26. For a good discussion of the US debate, cf. Wuthnow et al., *Crossing the Strait*, op. cit., pp. 12–20.

103. Hal Brands, "Does the U.S. Need to Fear That China Might Invade Taiwan?" *Bloomberg*, August 20, 2020, https://www.bloomberg.com/opinion/articles/2020-08-20/does-the-u-s-need-to-fear-that-china-might-invade-taiwan.

104. U.S.–Japan Joint Leaders' Statement: "U.S.–Japan Global Partnership for a New Era," April 16, 2021, The White House, https://www.whitehouse.gov/briefing-room/statements-releases/2021/04/16/u-s-japan-joint-leaders-statement-u-s-japan-global-partnership-for-a-new-era/.

105. Gries and Wang, "Will China Seize Taiwan?" op. cit.

106. He Yicheng, "'Lian Mei kang Zhong' baobuliao Taiwan! Meiguo hui wei Taiwan da yichang bishu de zhanzheng ma?" ('The United States against China: cannot protect Taiwan! Will the United States wage a war for Taiwan it is sure to lose?'), *Taihaiwang*, August 25, 2020, https://baijiahao.baidu.com/s?id=1675946251489296003&wfr=spider&for=pc.

107. Wang, "Liang'an hui bu hui baofa zhanzheng? . . ." ("Will there be a cross-Strait war? . . . ,"), op. cit.

108. Kelvin Chen, "Former President of Taiwan Says US Will Not Engage in Cross-Strait Conflict," *Taiwan News*, August 11, 2020, https://www.taiwannews.com .tw/en/news/3985012; Aaron Tu, Su Yung-yao, and Dennis Xie, "Majority Disagrees with Ma's War Statement: Poll," *Taipei Times*, August 25, 2020, https://taipeitimes .com/News/taiwan/archives/2020/08/25/2003742251.

109. Su Chi, "Taiwan's Strategic Shift: From Defensive to Offensive," *United Daily News*, August 15, 2020, https://udn.com/news/story/7339/4785084, English version: http://taiwansecurity.org/files/archive/593_1f732080.pdf.

110. "'1992 consensus' key to KMT's engagement with Beijing: Eric Chu," *Focus Taiwan CNA English News*, June 7, 2022, https://focustaiwan.tw/cross-strait /202206070019.

111. William S. Murray, "Revisiting Taiwan's Defense Strategy," *Naval War College Review*, Vol. 61, No. 3, Summer, https://digital-commons.usnwc.edu/cgi/ viewcontent.cgi?article=1814&context=nwc-review.

112. Drew Thompson, "Hope on the Horizon: Taiwan's Radical New Defense Concept," *War on the Rocks*, October 2, 2018, https://warontherocks.com/2018/10/hope -on-the-horizon-taiwans-radical-new-defense-concept/.

113. "Information, Communication and Electronic Warfare Command Formed," *Focus Taiwan*, June 29, 2017, https://focustaiwan.tw/politics/201706290027.

114. *Taiwan National Defense Report 2019*, Ministry of National Defense, Taipei, ROC, pp. 68–69.

115. "Navy to spend NT$470bn on 12 shipbuilding projects," *Taipei Times*, June 21, 2016, http://www.taipeitimes.com/News/taiwan/archives/2016/06/21/2003649127.

116. Yimou Lee and Ben Blanchard, "Taiwan Says China Still Lacks Ability for Full Assault on Island," *Reuters*, August 31, 2020, https://www.reuters.com/article/us -taiwan-china-security/taiwan-says-china-still-lacks-ability-for-full-assault-on-island -idUSKBN25R1C0.

117. "Geography a Tactical Edge: Defense Report," *Taipei Times*, August 25, 2020, https://www.taipeitimes.com/News/taiwan/archives/2020/08/25/2003742252.

118. Lawrence Chung, "Beijing 'fully able' to invade Taiwan by 2025, island's defence minister says," *SCMP*, October 2021, https://www.scmp.com/news/china /military/article/3151340/beijing-capable-taiwan-invasion-2025-islands-defence -minister.

119. Matt Yu and Sean Lin, "Missile Production to More Than Double with Completion of New Facilities," *Focus Taiwan*, August 13, 2022, https://focustaiwan .tw/sci-tech/202208130014.

120. Michael Mazza, "Taiwan's High-End and Low-End Defense Capabilities Balance," *Taiwan Global Institute*, October 23, 2019, https://www.aei.org/ articles/taiwans-high-end-and-low-end-defense-capabilities-balance/; Dave Makichuk, "Taiwan to Boost 'Invasion' Defenses with US Weapons," *Asia Times*, August 14, 2020, https://asiatimes.com/2020/08/taiwan-to-boost-invasion-defenses-with-us -weapons/; Lo Tien-pin, Wu Su-wei, and Jake Chung, "Military Eyeing Defense

against 'Drone Swarm,'" *Taipei Times*, July 27, 2020, https://www.taipeitimes.com/News/taiwan/archives/2020/07/27/2003740631.

121. Brian Sung, "Han Kuang Showcases Progress," *Taipei Times*, August 6, 2020, https://www.taipeitimes.com/News/editorials/archives/2020/08/06/2003741193.

122. Huizhong Wu, "Military Reserves, Civil Defense Worry Taiwan as China Looms," *AP*, September 5, 2022, https://apnews.com/article/russia-ukraine-taiwan-china-taipei-0ac81227d1fe37822b8a1d084119e248.

123. Kelvin Chen, "Taiwan Conducts Multiple Counterattack Drills around Nation," *Taiwan News*, September 17, 2021, https://www.taiwannews.com.tw/en/news/4289770; Keoni Everington, "Photo of the Day: Taiwan Artillery Sends Strong Signal to China," *Taiwan News*, July 27, 2022, https://www.taiwannews.com.tw/en/news/4608388.

124. John Van Trieste, "Cabinet Ok's 11.1% Hike in Defense Spending as Part of 2021 Budget," *Radio Taiwan International*, August 13, 2021, https://en.rti.org.tw/news/view/id/2003785.

125. Yimou Li and Ben Blanchard, "Taiwan Aims for Big Rise in Defence Spending Amid Escalating China Tension," *Reuters*, August 25, 2022, https://www.reuters.com/business/aerospace-defense/taiwan-proposes-129-on-year-rise-defence-spending-2023-2022-08-25/.

126. "China's Might Is Forcing Taiwan to Rethink its Military Strategy," *The Economist*, January 26, 2019, https://www.economist.com/asia/2019/01/26/chinas-might-is-forcing-taiwan-to-rethink-its-military-strategy.

127. "Taipei Economic and Cultural Representative Office in The United States (Tecro)—155mm M109a6 Paladin Medium Self-Propelled Howitzer System," *Defense Security Cooperation Agency*, August 4, 2021, https://www.dsca.mil/press-media/major-arms-sales/taipei-economic-and-cultural-representative-office-united-states-20.

128. Briant Harris, "US Approves $1.1 Billion Taiwan Arms Sale," *Defense News*, September 6, 2022, https://www.defensenews.com/pentagon/2022/09/06/us-approves-11-billion-taiwan-arms-sale/.

129. Michael Hunzeker and Brian Davis, "The Defense Reforms Taiwan Needs," *Defense One*, August 10, 2020, https://www.defenseone.com/ideas/2020/08/defense-reforms-taiwan-needs/167558/; Tanner Greer, "Why I Fear for Taiwan," *The Scholar's Stage*, September 11, 2020, https://scholars-stage.blogspot.com/2020/09/why-i-fear-for-taiwan.html.

130. Phillip Charlier, "Retired Submarine Officer's New Book Criticizes Taiwan's Indigenous Submarine Building Project," *Taiwan News*, June 22, 2020, https://taiwanenglishnews.com/retired-submarine-officers-new-book-criticizes-taiwans-indigenous-submarine-building-project/.

131. Daniel Darling, "Taiwan Dispatching Teams to Europe, U.S. as Indigenous Submarine Program Readies Launch," *Defense Security Monitor*, September 10, 2019, https://dsm.forecastinternational.com/wordpress/2019/09/10/taiwan-dispatching-teams-to-europe-u-s-as-indigenous-submarine-program-readies-launch/; Tso-Juei Hsu, "Taiwan to Complete IDS Submarine Pressure Hull Assembly By

June," *Naval News*, January 31, 2022, https://www.navalnews.com/naval-news/2022 /01/taiwan-to-complete-ids-submarine-pressure-hull-assembly-by-june/.

132. Yimou Lee and Ann Wang, "Taiwan to Extend Conscription to One Year, Citing Rising China Threat," *Reuters*, December 27, 2022, https://www.reuters.com /world/asia-pacific/taiwan-extend-compulsory-military-service-official-media-2022 -12-27/

133. Chen Dingyu, "Taiwan minyi jijin hui min diao: gong jun wuli fan Tai 65% minzhong mei bawo guojun bao Tai lan zhichizhe bi lü geng mei xinxin (Taiwan Public Opinion Foundation Poll: The Communist Army invades Taiwan by force, 65% of the people are not sure that the national army will protect Taiwan, and the blue supporters are less confident than the green ones), *Fengchuanmei* (The Storm Media), April 23, 2018, https://www.storm.mg/article/428123.

134. William E. Sharp, "Taiwan's Floundering Military Needs to Up its Game," *National Interest*, August 10, 2016, https://nationalinterest.org/blog/the-buzz/taiwans -floundering-military-needs-its-game-17303.

135. Ben Blanchard, "Ukraine War Gives Taiwan's Military Reservist Reform New Impetus," *Reuters*, March 12, 2022, https://www.reuters.com/world/asia-pacific /ukraine-war-gives-taiwans-military-reservist-reform-new-impetus-2022-03-12/.

136. Wayne Chang, "Taiwan to Allow Women into Military Reserve Force Training as China Fears Grow," *CNN*, January 18, 2023, https://edition.cnn.com/2023/01/18/ asia/taiwan-women-military-reserve-intl-hnk-ml/index.html.

137. Chang Chien-chung and Frances Huang, "Controversial IC Tycoon to Donate NT$3 Billion for Taiwan's Security," *Focus Taiwan*, August 5, 2022, https:// focustaiwan.tw/politics/202208050010.

138. Mark Stokes, Yang Kuang-shun, and Eric Lee, "Preparing for the Nightmare: Readiness and *Ad hoc* Coalition Operations in the Taiwan Strait," Washington, DC: Project 2049 Institute, September 1, 2020, https://project2049.net/wp-content/uploads /2020/09/Preparing-for-the-Nightmare_Readiness-and-Ad-hoc-Coalition-Operations -in-the-Taiwan-Strait_Stokes_Yang_Lee_P2049_200901.pdf.

139. *L'esprit de défense de Taiwan face à la Chine. La jeunesse taiwanaise face à la tentation de la Chine* (Taiwan's defensive against China: Taiwanese youth facing China's baits), Paris: L'Harmattan, 2009.

140. Press Release, "2019 TFD Survey on Taiwanese View of Democratic Values and Governance," July 19, 2019, The Taiwan Foundation for Democracy, http://www .tfd.org.tw/export/sites/tfd/files/news/pressRelease/0719_press-release_web.pdf.

141. "ET mindiao/liang'an ruo baofa chongtu 40.9% yuanyi shang zhan-chang,75.2% rentong huifu zhibing zhi" (ET Poll/If there is a conflict between the two sides of the Taiwan Strait, 40.9% are willing to go to the battlefield, 75.2% agree with the restoration of the conscription system), *ETtoday Xinwenyun*, July 20, 2020, https://www.ettoday.net/news/20200720/1764795.htm.

142. Chinese Association of Public Opinion Research (CAPOR), report of an August 2020 study, https://drive.google.com/file/d/19qgKiF3Mrj5yK1PCIiqxLr6Fk uog11wb/view.

143. Jake Chung, "Majority would go to war for Taiwan," *Taipei Times*, May 1, 2022, https://www.taipeitimes.com/News/front/archives/2022/05/01/2003777507.

144. Lin Shixiang, "Yuanjian diaocha/junyan weiji hao jiuxin! 63.6% mínzhong you liang'an kaizhan, 65.4% jianshao dui zhengfu xinren du" (The Foresight investigation/military exercise crisis is so worrying! 63.6% of people worry about war between the two sides of the strait, 65.4% reduce their trust in the government), *Lianhebao* (United Daily News), September 16, 2022, https://udn.com/news/story /6842/6615096.

145. Matthew Strong, "Taiwan Poll: 51.2% See China Win after Invasion, 29.6% Expect Taiwan to Win," *Taiwan News*, September 20, 2022, https://www.taiwannews .com.tw/en/news/4663330.

146. Pau Huang, "If Invaded, Will the Taiwan Public Fight? Don't Look to Polls for an Answer," *Blog*, The Chicago Council of Global Affairs, March 28, 2022, https: //www.thechicagocouncil.org/commentary-and-analysis/blogs/if-invaded-will-taiwan -public-fight-dont-look-polls-answer.

147. "2022nian 12 yue '2022 xuanju hou Taiwan zhengju yu liang'an guanxi'" (December 2022 "Taiwan political situation and relations across the Strait after the 2022 elections"), Taiwan Minyi Jijinhui (Taiwan Public Opinion Foundation), December 2022, https://www.tpof.org/精選文章/2022年12月20日「2022選後台灣 政局與兩岸關係」/.

148. Cancian et al., *The First Battle of the War*, op. cit.

149. Charlie Vest, Agatha Kratz, and Reva Goujon, "The Global Economic Disruption from a Taiwan Conflict," *Note*, Rhodium Group, December 14, 2022, https://rhg .com/research/taiwan-economic-disruptions/. David Santoro and Ralph Cossa, eds., "The World After Taiwan's Fall", Pacific Forum International, *Issues & Insights*, Vol. 23, SR2, February 2023, https://pacforum.org/wp-content/uploads/2023/02/ Issues_and_Insights_Vol23_SR2.pdf.

150. Kinling Lo, "US Presidential Election: China, Donald Trump and Red Lines on Taiwan," *SCMP*, September 13, 2020, https://www.scmp.com/news/china/diplomacy/ article/3101363/us-presidential-election-china-trump-and-red-lines-taiwan.

151. Charles Parton, "Taiwan in the Next Decade: No War, but Much Tension," Council on Geostrategy, May 2021, https://www.geostrategy.org.uk/research/taiwan -in-the-next-decade-no-war-but-much-tension/.

152. Kerry K. Gershaneck, *Political Warfare: Strategies for Combating China's Plan to "Win Without Fighting,"* Quantico, VA: Marine Corps University Press, 2020.

153. Mathieu Duchâtel, "Anticipating China's Military Coercion of Taiwan," *Blog*, Institut Montaigne, September 15, 2020, https://www.institutmontaigne.org/en/blog/ anticipating-chinas-military-coercion-taiwan; Duchâtel, "An Assessment of China's Options for Military Coercion of Taiwan," in Wuthnow et al., *Crossing the Strait*, op. cit., pp. 87–112.

154. Thomas J. Shattuck, "Assessing the Patterns of PLA Air Incursions into Taiwan's ADIZ," *Global Taiwan Brief*, Vol. 6, No. 7, https://globaltaiwan.org/2021/04/ vol-6-issue7/?mc_cid=166795d63a&mc_eid=39b0511b94#ThomasShattuck0; Lin et al. "Tracking the Fourth Taiwan Strait Crisis," op. cit.

155. "Does China's Softer Tone Extend to Taiwan," *The Economist*, January 26, 2023, https://www.economist.com/china/2023/01/26/does-chinas-softer-tone-extend -to-taiwan.

156. Kathrin Hille, "Taiwan Claims 'Severe Provocation' after China Military Drill," *Financial Times*, September 10, 2020, https://www.ft.com/content/9bf1c039 -3222-4aa7-be37-6f01afc41ef2.

157. Thomas Newdick, "Troops Throw Rock at Drones Over Taiwan Island Close to Chinese Coast," The Drive, *The War Zone*, August 24, 2022, https:// www.thedrive.com/the-war-zone/troops-throw-rocks-at-drone-over-taiwanese-island -close-to-chinese-coast; Koeni Everington, "Taiwan Fires Flares at Chinese Drone Flying over Outer Island," *Taiwan News*, July 29, 2022, https://www.taiwannews.com .tw/en/news/4610321; Lin et al. "Tracking the Fourth Taiwan Strait Crisis," op. cit.; "Taiwan Shoots Down Drone off Chinese Coast for First Time," *NBC News, Reuters*, September 1, 2022, https://www.nbcnews.com/news/world/taiwan-china-drone-shot -down-first-time-xi-jinping-rcna45813.

158. "Chinese Warplanes Fly First Night-Time Mission Near Taiwan: MND," *Focus Taiwan*, March 17, 2020, https://focustaiwan.tw/politics/202003170009; Duchâtel, "Anticipating China's Military Coercion of Taiwan," op. cit.

159. Li Ning, "Jiefangjun lianxu 2 tian zai Tai xinan kongyu yan xun min jin dang dangju jinji kai jizhe hui" (The People's Liberation Army exercises in the airspace of southwest Taiwan for two consecutive days, the DPP authorities hold an emergency press conference), *Zhongguo Taiwanwang* (www.taiwan.cn), September 11, 2020, http://www.taiwan.cn/taiwan/jsxw/202009/t20200911_12295186.htm.

160. Lu Li-shih, "Changing the Rules of Engagement," *Taipei Times*, February 28, 2020, http://taipeitimes.com/News/editorials/archives/2020/02/28/2003731740.

161. Lawrence Chung, "Taiwan Military to Allow Forces to Fire Back after Mainland Chinese Air Incursions," *SCMP*, September 21, 2020, https://www.scmp.com /news/china/military/article/3102419/taiwan-military-redefines-rules-engagement -allow-forces-fire.

162. Koeni Everington, "Chinese Dredger Forced to Return Sand to Taiwan's Matsu," *Taiwan News*, October 5, 2020, https://www.taiwannews.com.tw/en/news /4023609.

163. Louise Watt, "Line in the Sand: Chinese Dredgers Are Stealing Taiwan, Bit By Bit," *Nikkei Asia*, June 16, 2021, https://asia.nikkei.com/Spotlight/The-Big -Story/Line-in-the-sand-Chinese-dredgers-are-stealing-Taiwan-bit-by-bit; Elizabeth Braw, "China Is Stealing Taiwan's Sand," *Foreign Policy*, July 11, 2022, https:// foreignpolicy.com/2022/07/11/china-stealing-taiwan-sand/.

164. Shen Ming-shih, "Gong junji jian biandui rao Tai yitu, yingxiang ji Taiwan yinying zuowei" (The purposes and implications of PLA aircraft and boat circumnavigations around Taiwan and the responses the island should make), *Zhanwang yu tansuo* (Prospective and exploration), Vol. 16, No. 7, July 2018, pp. 21–27, https://www .mjib.gov.tw/FileUploads/eBooks/a8a7e952bdbf419ba34182889fcb664c/Section _file/9b5cea00e4664a018468824a3dfc2e12.pdf; Lee Guan-cheng, "Zhonggong dui Tai junshi donghe yu huyu kezhi de liangshou celuë " (The Chinese dual strategy against Taiwan of military intimidation and calls for restraint), *Guofang anquan shuangzhoubao* (Defence and security bi-weekly), No. 11, September 11, 2020, https: //indsr.org.tw/Content/Upload/files/4_中共對台軍事恫嚇與呼籲克制的兩手策略 .pdf, cited by Duchâtel, "Anticipating China's Military Coercion of Taiwan," op. cit.

165. Yimou Lee, David Lague, and Ben Blanchard, "China Launches 'Gray-Zone' Warfare to Subdue Taiwan," *Reuters*, December 10, 2020, https://www.reuters.com/investigates/special-report/hongkong-taiwan-military/.

166. Duchâtel, "An Assessment of China's Options for Military Coercion of Taiwan," in Wuthnow et al., *Crossing the Strait*, op. cit., pp. 104–5.

167. "Taiwan Government Faces 5 Million Cyber Attacks Daily: Official," *France 24/AFP*, October 11, 2021, https://www.france24.com/en/live-news/20211110-taiwan-government-faces-5-million-cyber-attacks-daily-official.

168. "National Center for Cyber Security Technology—Taiwan," https://www.cybersecurityintelligence.com/national-center-for-cyber-security-technology-nccst-taiwan-5956.html (accessed October 18, 2022).

169. "About NCCST," *National Center for Cyber Security Technology*, https://www.nccst.nat.gov.tw/About?lang=en; "National Cyber Security Program of Taiwan (2017–2020)," National Information and Communication Security Taskforce, Executive Yuan, Republic of China (Taiwan), November 2017, https://nicst.ey.gov.tw/File/3BF304D39EA91236.

170. Mike Yeo, "In First, America Co-Hosts Cyber War Game 'CODE' with Taiwan," *Fifth Domain*, November 7, 2019, https://www.fifthdomain.com/international/2019/11/07/in-first-america-co-hosts-cyber-war-game-with-taiwan/.

171. Ministry of Foreign Affairs of the Netherlands, *Research of Cyber Security Industry in Taiwan*, Industrial Technology Research Institute, June 2020, https://www.rvo.nl/sites/default/files/2020/07/Research-of-Cyber security-in-Taiwan.pdf.

172. Huang Tzu-ti, "Taiwan Works to Create Cybersecurity Excellence Center," *Taiwan News*, September 15, 2020, https://www.taiwannews.com.tw/en/news/4009162; "Zi'an Zhuoyue zhongxin guihua jianzhi jihua" (Cybersecurity Center of Excellence's establishment plan), https://ccoe.narlabs.org.tw/CTI/training/main/index.html (accessed October 18, 2022).

173. Nick Monaco, Melanie Smith, and Amy Studdart, *Detecting Digital Fingerprint. Tracing Chinese Desinformation in Taiwan*, Institute for Future's Digital Intelligence Lab, Graphika, The International Republican Institute, June 2020, https://public-assets.graphika.com/reports/detecting_digital_fingerprints-tracing_chinese_disinformation_in_taiwan.pdf.

174. Press Release, "2019 TFD Survey on Taiwanese View of Democratic Values and Governance," Taiwan Foundation For Democracy, Press Release, July 19, 2019, http://www.tfd.org.tw/export/sites/tfd/files/news/pressRelease/0719_press-release_web.pdf.

175. "China releases white paper on Taiwan question, reunification in new era," op. cit.; Xi Jinping, "Hold High the Great Banner of Socialism with Chinese Characteristics and Strive in Unity to Build a Modern Socialist Country in All Respects," Report to the 20th National Congress of the Communist Party of China, October 16, 2022, pp. 51–52.

176. Stacie Pettyjohn, Becca Wasser, and Chris Dougherty, "Dangerous Straits: Wargaming a Future Conflict over Taiwan," Center for New American Security, *Defense*, June 2022, https://s3.amazonaws.com/files.cnas.org/CNAS+Report-Dangerous+Straits-Defense-Jun+2022-FINAL-print.pdf; "What Taiwan can learn

from Russia's invasion of Ukraine," *The Economist*, August 23, 2022, https://www
.economist.com/briefing/what-taiwan-can-learn-from-russias-invasion-of-ukraine
/21808850.

177. Michèle Flournoy and Michael Brown, "Time Is Running Out to Defend
Taiwan: Why the Pentagon Must Focus on Near-Term Deterrence," *Foreign Affairs*,
September 14, 2022, https://www.foreignaffairs.com/china/time-running-out-defend
-taiwan.

178. Kevin Rudd, *The Avoidable War: The Dangers of a Catastrophic War between
the US and Xi Jinping's China*, New York: Public Affairs, 2022. Cf. also Kevin
Rudd's "CLM Insight Interview," *China Leadership Monitor*, Issue 73, September
2022, https://www.prcleader.org/rudd-september-2022.

179. Wuthnow et al., *Crossing the Strait*, op. cit., pp. 15, 23–26.

180. On this issue, Cf. Richard C. Bush, *Difficult Choices: Taiwan's Quest for
Security and the Good Life*, Washington, DC: Brookings Institution Press, 2021.

181. Lo, "US Presidential Election: China, Donald Trump and Red Lines on Taiwan," op. cit.

4

War Risks in the South China Sea

The South China Sea situation is particularly complex, primarily as it involves several countries: not only six States which claim part or all of the land features there (in addition to China, Brunei, Malaysia, the Philippines, Taiwan, and Vietnam) but also the United States and other countries such as Australia, Japan, India, France, and the United Kingdom which intend to enforce freedom of navigation. A complicating fact is the effective occupation by these six states of part of the land features each claims and the great diversity of the claims. The various parties have different interpretations of the law of the sea, especially the United Nations Convention (UNCLOS) signed in Montego Bay (Jamaica) in 1982, which entered into force in 1994. For instance, China ratified the convention in 1996 but attached significant reservations, pointedly refusing any settlement of maritime and territorial disputes by an arbitration tribunal. The United States signed the convention but has never ratified it; however, the US administration says it respects and applies it.

What has added the most to the situation's complexity and dangerousness is Beijing's desire from 2012 to transform the disputed area into a "fundamental interest" (*hexin liyi*), the same as Taiwan or Tibet and its ambition to gradually modify the status quo in its favor. Claiming all of the land features and 90 percent of the waters of the South China Sea, Beijing has long expressed its desire to gradually take control of both.[1] In 1974, just before Saigon fell, it annexed all of the Paracels (Xisha), evicting the South Vietnamese from the part they had occupied since France's departure in 1954. In 1988, it dislodged *manu militari* Vietnamese soldiers from five islets in the Spratlys (Nansha) archipelago, the Socialist Republic of Vietnam having administered them since the country's 1975 reunification. And in 1995, it added the Mischief Reef (Meiji jiao) claimed by the Philippines but left unoccupied, to its hunting list. Nonetheless, it was from the April 2012 Sino–Philippines face-to-face around the Scarborough Shoal (*Huangyan dao*) that the situation fundamentally changed[2] (cf. map 2).

Following an unsuccessful attempt at US mediation, China took control of a lagoon the Philippines had long occupied before neglecting it.[3] Some Obama Administration members declared that Washington was not going to risk "starting a third world war" for Scarborough Shoal.[4] Now, some Americans regret the Democrats' caution then and seek to correct it (cf. infra). Beijing has since undertaken land reclamation on the Spratlys rocks and shoals it controls, turning them into artificial islands and forward PLA bases, despite the "non-militarization" promises Xi made to Obama in 2015.[5]

In order to thwart Chinese ambitions as much as possible, the US Navy has boosted operations to enforce freedom of navigation throughout the South China Sea. But they failed to persuade Beijing to stop building artificial islands there. These are now equipped with ports, airstrips capable of accommodating all types of aircrafts, civil and military, radar systems, and even missile ramps. Developments adding a little more to the complex situation and contributing to rising tensions, especially between the PLA and the US Seventh fleet.

Having no other options, Manila in 2013 decided to lodge a case against China before the international Court at The Hague. In its July 2016 judgment the Permanent Court of Arbitration (PCA) ruled for the Philippines on almost all the issues raised.[6] While it did not pronounce on the sovereignty of the South China Sea islands, it deemed "extinct" the historical rights on the sea and its resources which China claimed since the establishment by the Nationalist government in 1947 of the Nine-dash line (originally eleven) that Beijing adopted. These rights and thus the nine-dash line, the PCA held, were incompatible with the exclusive economic zones (EEZ) provided for by UNCLOS. Moreover, Chinese fisherfolk have never been the only ones present in these waters and using the islets. However, crucially, the PCA also declared that none of the Spratly land features could claim island status, given the impossibility of them all to sustain human habitation or economic life. The verdict had significant consequences on the validity and especially the extent of parties' maritime rights. Reduced to the status of "rock," none of the land features could claim EEZs of 200 nautical miles. If they are artificial islands built on rocks previously submerged at high tide (such as Mischief or Johnson South), they cannot claim territorial waters of twelve nautical miles because only their "natural state" would count. Finally, the PCA accused China of infringing the Philippines's economic rights (fishing, oil exploration) and damaging the marine environment through land reclamation. Of course, Beijing rejected this accusation but, as shall be seen, cannot totally ignore it.

It is undoubtedly this growing complexity which has contributed, since the 1988 Sino–Vietnamese skirmishes until now, to avoiding any armed conflict between the parties. Disregarding the borderline case of Scarborough Shoal, without seeking to dislodge other countries from their islets and thus while formally respecting the status quo, China has been able to decisively increase since 2012 its effective presence in a sea bigger than the Mediterranean. This strategy change coincides with Xi's rise to power and specifically his taking charge of the South China Sea issue from mid-2012. Like vis-à-vis Taipei, Beijing aims to exploit gray areas between war and peace, in order to boost its advantage and position.

This new strategy is not without risks, partly as it is increasingly contested by the United States and other maritime powers which intend to enforce UNCLOS. After taking office in 2017, the Trump Administration more actively countered China by increasing its military presence around the Spratlys and Paracels, openly criticizing Beijing's claims and by providing, since 2020, support to other claimants. In 2020, then Secretary of State Mike Pompeo released a statement that not only supported the PCA's decision and denounced Beijing's bullying of its neighbors but also rejected most of its territorial, maritime, and thus economic claims in the area.[7] Biden has stuck to the same line. Beijing' strategy is also risky because other claimants see it as a source of instability and insecurity and, as a result, seek to better protect their interests, when possible with US help.

Such rise in tensions multiplies conflict risks, particularly Sino–US ones. But can it escalate to provoke a war? Could it spark other conflicts, such as between China and Vietnam or the Philippines? I consider these questions in this chapter.

VARIOUS PARTIES' CLAIMS AND CONTROLS

My purpose here is not to discuss the validity of the littoral states' claims but to briefly state them in order to better understand the changes in the land features they control and where risks of armed conflicts are concentrated.

China

China remains much attached to the nine-dash line which roughly delimits both its historical rights and maritime territory. The line not only ignores the claims of the four other littoral countries (Brunei, Malaysia, Philippines, and Vietnam) but straddles their EEZ as well as Indonesia's around the Natuna archipelago, albeit without claiming the latter. Beijing considers the sea's land features as a set of four archipelagos to be considered in their entirety: Paracels (Xisha qundao), Pratas (Dongsha qundao), Macclesfield Bank (Zhongsha qundao), although it is submerged at high tide except Scarborough which is now part of it, and Spratlys (Nansha qundao). In 2009, the Foreign

Ministry submitted a map to the United Nations making this claim, prompting protests from the five states mentioned above.[8]

While China agreed to sign with ASEAN in 2002 in Phnom Penh a declaration for establishing a South China Sea Code of Conduct, it much prefers negotiating bilaterally with each party.[9] The negotiations sought and undertaken since by China and ASEAN parties to adopt a Code of Conduct do not cover the land features' sovereignty, which in Beijing's view, all belong to it undisputedly, a bit like the Senkaku in Japan's eyes (cf. chapter 5). It covers methods of cooperation and dispute settlement between the parties over rights to exploit marine resources (fishing, oil), environmental protection, or military activities. While a "framework agreement" was adopted in 2017, the "negotiating text" approved the following year constitutes a "living document" or rather an incoherent patchwork to which each party contributed adhering to its own interests and concerns. China seeks, with little success thus far, to persuade other parties to agree to joint exploitation of resources and to notify in advance any military exercise in the area.[10] Beijing was optimistic, hoping that a Code of Conduct could be adopted in 2021. However, too many disagreements have so far remained, preventing the conclusion of a Code of Conduct, let alone a binding one.[11] One wonders if China is not more interested in a negotiation process that obliges ASEAN to remain on good terms with it, while highlighting their internal divisions, and thus strengthening its own hand, rather than any outcome.

Since at least 2008, Beijing has favored another objective: establishing what experts call greater "strategic depth" along its coasts in order to improve the security of its strategic submarines and their undetected access to the Pacific Ocean or the Indian Ocean. To this end, China has decided to strengthen its presence comprehensively in the South China Sea and to establish a ratio of military forces favorable to it, including vis-à-vis the United States. Contrary to its 2002 commitment, China has since been far from showing "restraint," directly contradicting the letter and spirit of the Phnom Penh declaration. China says it abides by the law of the sea; has maintained consultations and cooperation with ASEAN; and formally avoided resorting to non-peaceful means. But it has multiplied faits accomplis, in much greater proportion than neighbors such as Vietnam and the Philippines, which have themselves consolidated their presence on the land features they control. As noted, in 2012 China took control of the Scarborough shoal; it has reclaimed the seven islets it controls in the Spratlys, creating 3,200 acres of new land, and militarized them: in addition to Mischief reef, those of Cuarteron, Fiery Cross, Gaven, Hughes, Johnson, and Subi[12]; meanwhile, it has expanded several of the twenty Paracels land features, including Woody, Palm/Duncan, Triton, Tree, Pattle, Money, Drummond, and Antelope, boosting military presence there[13]; it has reduced or sought to reduce third power warships' freedom of navigation; it has intensified threats of the use of force against parties seeking to exploit resources in the EEZ they claim; the PLA has boosted anti-submarine warfare exercises, and, testing its new medium-range anti-ship missiles, has demonstrated from 2019 its ability to destroy foreign vessels, especially US (or other countries') aircraft carriers venturing into the area.[14] In August 2020, the PLA tested two missiles, a DF-26B, fired from Qinghai, and a DF-21D, fired from Zhejiang, in the South China Sea to protest US carrier groups' maneuvers in the zone. The missiles splashed in the sea between Hainan and the Paracels. Four months later, obviously warning the United States, the PLA claimed that the missiles fired had managed to hit moving targets (which has not been confirmed by the US side).[15] In April 2020, Beijing created two new administrative districts (*xian*), Xisha (Paracels and Macclesfield) and Nansha (Spratlys), within the prefectural level municipality of Sansha established in 2012 and announced the names of fifty-five formations submerged at high tide (thus with no value under UNCLOS) and located on the Vietnamese continental shelf. Another sign that it eventually intends controlling all the South China Sea land features and 90 percent of its waters, in short, to transform it into a Chinese lake.

Meanwhile, using threats to deter neighbors from exploiting the area's resources, China has managed to develop its own economic activities there with total impunity. To achieve this, it applied what the PLA calls "cabbage tactics" (*baicai zhanluë*) mobilizing fishing vessels, coastguards, maritime militia, and the PLA Navy to intimidate neighbors and gradually advance its interests. Thus, each year, citing scarcity of fishery resources for which China itself is largely responsible, it unilaterally prohibits between May 1 and August 16 all fishing north of the Spratlys.[16] Protected by powerful coast guards, Chinese vessels go down to the Natuna (Indonesia) to fish, while those of other countries' fisherfolk are boarded by these same coast guards in the vast areas Beijing claims, such as around the Paracels where a Vietnamese vessel was sunk in April 2020 or the Spratlys where the same happened to a Filipino one in 2019. Until 2016, China managed to prohibit any oil exploration or exploitation by neighbors in these areas by exerting pressure on the oil companies involved. Since then, to achieve its ends, it threatens countries concerned with military intervention. This was the case in Vietnam in 2017 where General Fan Changlong, then the Central Military Commission number two, went to successfully convince it to cancel the contract it had signed with Spanish oil company Repsol; in 2020, under Chinese pressure, Russian company Rostnef abandoned all cooperation with PetroVietnam. In 2017, Duterte admitted that Xi had threatened the Philippines with an armed attack if it carried out gas projects in the Reed Bank area in western Palawan.[17]

On February 1, 2021, a new coast guards law took effect, authorizing them to more frequently use force, in other words, their weapons, in the event of a violation or "imminent threat of violation" of China's sovereign rights (art. 22).[18] Criticized by the United States and many countries in the region, particularly Japan and the Philippines, this new law increases the risk of incidents. Pushing its advantage further, in March 2021, China decided to park more than 200 fishing vessels, some actually belong from maritime militia, near Whitsun Reef, north of the Spratlys, causing a faceoff with the Philippines, which claims the EEZ around this reef (cf. infra).

It is thus clear that Beijing has turned its back on the Phnom Penh declaration and directly contributed to breaking the "confidence" it sought to build through increasing intimidation and seeking to dominate the South China Sea by its physical and armed presence. Becoming the zone's policeman is the condition for creating the famous strategic depth China seeks.

Ignoring the 2016 arbitration decision, such power projection can only encourage other stakeholders to harden their position, as we will see. It can only complicate any negotiations for a truly binding code of conduct with ASEAN. And it can only provoke a reaction from the United States and its allies or partners (such as India), not only because they are attached to freedom of navigation but also because they are increasingly inclined to contest China's excessive claims in the area.

Vietnam

Seeing itself as heir to French colonial occupation of the Paracels and Spratlys in the 1930s, Vietnam is the country whose claims are the broadest and most directly in conflict with China's. It is also the largest Spratly occupant in terms of the number of rocks and reefs it administers: some 50 outposts spread across 27 land features. These include facilities built on 21 rocks and reefs and 14 "economic, scientific and technological (DK1)" platforms built on 6 sand banks submerged at high tide. Since 2014, like China, Vietnam too has reclaimed some of its land features, expanding eight of the ten rocks it occupies, including Spratley "Island" now equipped with an airstrip, and building a greater number of DK1 stations, but in much more modest proportions than its bigger neighbor.[19]

Recall that France had integrated these archipelagos into Indochina because Vietnam already claimed them. If today the latter respects the status quo and does not seek, for obvious reasons, to reconquer the islands which it lost control of, it regularly tries to fish or explore for oil in the part of its EEZ which overlaps the Chinese nine-dash line, with the frustrations noted earlier. In recent years several incidents have occurred in what Hanoi calls the East Sea. In 2014, Vietnam's coast guard challenged China's installation of an oil rig in the Paracels. After a tense faceoff and tough negotiations, the platform was dismantled. On several occasions Chinese coast guard have boarded Vietnamese fishing vessels.

In 2009, Vietnam and Malaysia submitted to the UN Commission on the Limits of the Continental Shelf a Joint Submission indicating their respective claims in the South China Sea. These included part of the Spratly and surrounding waters. Having been approached by its Southeast Asian neighbors, the Philippines refused to join in this process. Instead, it sided with China in officially disputing the claims. Yet, having already decided in 1992 to set aside their disputes over their respective EEZs' delimitation in the Gulf of Thailand to exploit oil, Vietnam and Malaysia reached broad understanding on a distribution of their respective possessions in the South China Sea.[20] This was an important step toward a common ASEAN position on the issue. Moreover, although Vietnamese and Filipino claims partly overlap in the Spratly, they coexist peacefully now and have even established various confidence-building measures since 2012. Since 2014, they regularly organize cultural events or sports competitions between soldiers posted on neighboring islets.[21]

Finally, Vietnam positively welcomed the US statement of July 13, 2020. It hinted that it would be tempted, like the Philippines in 2013, to open arbitration proceedings against China. But the close ties between the Vietnamese and Chinese communist parties could continue to prevent Hanoi from doing so.[22]

The Philippines

The Philippines' demands are more recent. They only date back to the late 1970s, leaving aside the Scarborough Shoal where Manila had a lighthouse installed in the 1960s but abandoned it, although Filipino fishermen continued to use it uninterruptedly until 2012.

While the occupation of some rocks began in 1968, it was only ten years later that the Philippines officially annexed Kalayaan island group located in the eastern part of the Spratlys. The Philippines now control nine land features there. China is increasingly contesting the occupation, boosting its military pressure around these islets and reefs. In 2014, the latter tried several times to prevent the resupply of the dozen Filipino marines posted inside the *Sierra Madre*, an old warship stranded on Second Thomas Shoal, a lagoon located about 200 km west of Palawan, after unsuccessfully asking Manila to withdraw the vessel. Since then, China has sought mainly to prevent any Filipino construction of a more lasting infrastructure by maintaining a maritime presence nearby. Its harassment has extended since 2018 to other Philippine islets, including Thitu (Pagasa), the only one with an airstrip (cf. infra).[23]

In 2012 the Philippines lost control of the Scarborough shoal located 200 km west of Luzon, north of the Spratlys, following the arrival of an increasing number of Chinese fishermen and a tense standoff between Philippine and Chinese navies and coast guards (*Zhongguo haijian*). Washington, acting as mediator, asked the two sides' coast guards to withdraw, which they apparently did, despite communication problems and ambiguities that surrounded the negotiations. However, soon thereafter PLA vessels returned, roped off the lagoon, and barred access to Filipino fishermen. Unable to mobilize a divided ASEAN, Manila decided to approach the PCA.

The 2016 PCA decision caused a deep but temporary deterioration in Beijing–Manila ties. The election shortly earlier of Rodrigo Duterte as the Philippines president led to a reassessment of China's policy, the new administration deciding to accept Chinese offer to resume bilateral negotiations in exchange for significant economic aid. In November 2018, the two sides signed a Memorandum of Understanding concerning energy cooperation in the Philippines EEZ located inside the nine-dash line. However, Beijing's activism in the Spratlys and rising Sino–US tensions gradually persuaded Duterte to harden his stance and play the ASEAN card more broadly. As a result, no joint development agreement has yet been signed with China.[24] And since then, the Philippines' attempt to conduct oil exploration west of Palawan has been stopped by Chinese coast guard, for example in April 2022.[25] More generally, evolution in the US position from 2020 has led the Philippines to move closer to its historical ally, a move that Duterte's successor Ferdinand Marcos Jr. has deepened after he came into office in June 2022 (cf. infra).[26]

In the spring of 2021, the Whitsun Reef incident (Julian Felipe Reef for the Philippines, Niu'e jiao in Chinese) confirmed this evolution. Located north of the Spratlys, 320 km west of Palawan, and almost submerged, including at low tide, until the late twentieth century, this reef has since become more visible: a sandbank has formed there, arousing various claimants' greed: China, whose vessels began to berth there in 2019 and more regularly from early 2020, but also Vietnam. However, under UNCLOS, as this reef consists of "low tide land features," it generates no territorial rights. The Philippines claims this area under its EEZ and the extension of its continental shelf. In March 2021, some 220 Chinese fishing vessels anchored there, officially to protect themselves from bad weather. Suspected of belonging to the maritime militia, they prolonged their presence there, sparking protests by Manila, which asked they vacate, by Hanoi and also Washington. Fearing a new Scarborough incident, and with less ambiguous US support, the Philippines sent coast guards and then naval ships to dislodge the Chinese vessels. Meanwhile, the US Navy moved some of its own closer to the area. Moreover, a few days later, the State Department spokesperson declared "an armed attack on the Philippines armed forces, public vessels or aircraft in the Pacific, including the South China Sea, will trigger our [US–Philippines] treaty obligations."[27] Given such pressure, Beijing partly gave in: in April that year, there were around twenty Chinese vessels left, mainly maritime militia ones, illustrating again how much it favors the gray areas strategy as also Washington's likely commitment to stabilize the situation.[28] Nonetheless, a year later, in April 2022, a few days before Duterte and Xi Jinping held a telesummit, over 100 Chinese vessels returned to the area, triggering protests from Manila.[29] President Marcos Jr.'s state visit to China in January 2023 allowed both countries to restore a high-level dialogue on the South China Sea and establish a communication mechanism between both foreign ministries. But it is likely that the Philippines will continue to invest more in coast guards and military equipment to better protect the land features it occupies and its EEZ.[30] The decision made by Marcos in January 2023 to give the US military access to four more bases, including in Northern Luzon, 200 km south of Taiwan, and in Palawan, underscores the deepening strategic Filipino–American strategic proximity in a context of growing China–US tensions.

Finally, what complicates the Philippines' position is its difficulty in finding common ground with Malaysia, Manila claiming not only land features the latter occupies in the Spratlys but also reviving occasionally its claims on Northern Borneo (or eastern Sabah).

Malaysia

Malaysia too announced its South China Sea claims only in the 1970s. Since 1983, it has gradually occupied five land formations there (Swallow, Ardaiser, Erica, Mariveles, and Investigator reefs), located in the north of Borneo and claims a dozen of them, two of which are occupied by Vietnam and two others by the Philippines. It has a C-130 airstrip on Swallow (or Layang-Layang) and a small military presence on other reefs. Malaysia has long kept a low profile on this issue so as not to annoy China.

Rising Chinese presence in the area has led Malaysia to gradually shed its reserved attitude. In 2016, it reacted cautiously to the PCA's decision. In September 2019, after having long favored multilateral negotiations through ASEAN, it agreed to open bilateral talks with China. However, since 2018, it has raised its voice more often, especially challenging the nine-dash line. In December 2019, it submitted to the UN its continental shelf limits in the South China Sea, provoking protests from China and also Vietnam. Through this unilateral approach, Kuala Lumpur indirectly called into question the consensus forged in 2009 with Hanoi and thereby weakened ASEAN's position.

This development was motivated by Malaysia's desire to explore for oil in its EEZ. In early 2020, Malaysian oil company Petronas dispatched the drilling vessel *West Capella* there, triggering a short but unexpected faceoff between the US Navy and a PLA ship, accompanied by Chinese coast guards and maritime militia ships. It was the first time the United States had gone to the aid of Malaysia through a naval presence operation near the drilling area. The operation involved not only three US Seventh Fleet ships and bombers based in Guam, but also an Australian Navy ship, highlighting US desire to associate its allies more broadly with securing the South China Sea.[31] Shortly thereafter, at the end of its exploration activity, the *West Capella* left the disputed area. Despite the lack (voluntarily on Malaysia's part) of coordination with the Malaysian Navy, this intervention constituted a turning point in the US posture, confirmed by Pompeo in July 2020 and pregnant with multiple consequences (cf. infra).[32] This led Kuala Lumpur to doubt the usefulness of bilateral talks with Beijing.

Brunei

Brunei's claims are the most recent. They are not territorial but maritime. In 1984, two years after the adoption of the Montego Bay Convention, Brunei delimited its EEZ and included in it three land features of the Spartly archipelago: Louisa Reef, Owen Shoal, and Rifleman. Since then, these reefs have remained uninhabited although Louisa Reef, half submerged at low tide, is on the continental shelf. For a long time, Brunei remained the "silent claimant" among countries with South China Sea claims. In July 2016, Brunei endorsed with Laos and Cambodia, two ASEAN states without claims in this area and close to China, a four-point declaration proposed by the latter and according to which territorial and maritime disputes were not a matter to be resolved by ASEAN but through "dialogues and consultations between the parties directly concerned," that is, bilaterally. This stand coincided with a rise in Chinese investment in the Sultanate at a time when it was seeking to diversify its economic activities, which were too dependent on oil, and Beijing was developing its Belt and Road Initiative.[33] By 2020, China had already invested more than six billion US dollars in Brunei, representing half the latter's GDP (US$12 billion).

In 2020, Brunei partly changed its stand. Now, it favors a dual approach: to continue bilateral negotiations and to adopt an ASEAN-China code of conduct. This followed a rise in the South China Sea tensions, a greater US commitment as aforementioned and a hardening of Vietnamese and Philippine positions ahead of the finalization of this code of conduct. Since Brunei's 1984 independence, Britain has maintained a modest military presence there. But the British Navy could be called upon to conduct more freedom of navigation operations in Brunei's EEZ if China continues to increase its presence there.[34]

Taiwan

Taiwan, as the Republic of China's heir, appears at first glance to align itself with Beijing's stand. In reality, occupying all of the Pratas (Dongsha) east of the Paracels since 1945 and Itu Aba or Taiping, the main Spratly land feature since the following year, Taipei favors the status quo. Today, it no longer refers to Chiang Kai-shek's eleven-dash line and declares commitment to UNCLOS, freedom of navigation and peaceful settlement of disputes.[35] It welcomed the July 2020 US declaration. Meanwhile, the three Pratas atolls, having become a national park in 2007, are only claimed by China.

Permanently occupied since 1956, Itu Aba has a C-130 airstrip. A new wharf was built there in 2015. In 2000, coast guards replaced the 500 marines stationed there before. Taipei protested part of the 2016 arbitration award, saying that having a natural fresh water source and thus able to support independent life, Itu Aba was entitled to island status. For the rest, Taiwan keeps a low profile, not seeking to exercise its maritime rights beyond the twelve nautical mile zone. The main problem for Taiwan is that it is not recognized by China—nor, for that matter, officially by the other claimants, although they maintain unofficial relations that are often courteous and close: Vietnam in opposition to China, Malaysia because of the close ties between its Chinese community, partly originating in Fujian, and the Philippines, partly for similar reasons but also given the intensity of trade and human exchanges with its northern neighbor. Consequently, Taiwan cannot claim to participate in talks for establishing a binding code of conduct aimed at reducing tensions and preventing any future war.

Since 2016, rising tensions in the Taiwan Strait have fueled speculation about Beijing's intention to challenge this status quo. In September 2020, the PLA held major aeronaval maneuvers inside Taiwan's Air Defense Identification Zone (ADIZ), halfway between Kaohsiung and the Pratas. The following month, a Taiwanese civilian plane had to abandon attempt to reach the Pratas, after Hong Kong refused permission to cross its airspace on the pretext of "dangerous activities" in the area. And in April 2021, Chinese drones circled the Pratas, leading the Taiwanese military to contemplate shooting drones that enter Taiwan's airspace, including in the South China Sea.[36] Since 2000, only coast guards have been stationed on the Pratas, but since August 2020, a significant number of marines (the 99th brigade) have gone to support them.[37] Any Chinese takeover of the Dongsha would constitute a *casus belli*, with incalculable consequences for cross-strait relations (cf. chapter 3).

Indonesia

Indonesia does not claim any land feature in the South China Sea but its EEZ around the Natuna archipelago, northwest of Borneo, overlaps the nine-dash line and thus the historical rights Beijing claims. In recent years, Indonesia has increased maritime patrols and boosted control over this area, for instance not hesitating to burn Chinese fishing vessels it has been able to board. It has been planning since January 2020 to establish a military base on the archipelago. China wants peaceful dispute settlement. But not only does it continue to let Chinese fishermen go to the Natuna EEZ, but it also sends coast guards there quite often to protect them. In September 2020, Jakarta upped the ante, officially protesting against the intrusions and asking its maritime security to expel Chinese coast guards; they left the area two days after entering it.[38] In June 2021, another standoff occurred, this time between an Indonesia oil rig drilling 140 nautical miles north of Natuna Besar and Chinese coast guards which claimed the area as "Chinese territory." This time again, Jakarta refused to back down.[39] In December 2022–January 2023, China's largest coast guard, CCG 5901, penetrated in Indonesia's EEZ north of Natuna after this country had concluded an accord with Vietnam delineating their respective EEZ. Beijing clearly wanted to send a signal as this pact will facilitate the exploitation of gas in Tuna Field, which is part of Indonesian EEZ but overlaps with China's nine-dash line.[40] In coming years more such incidents could well occur, perhaps with US involvement (cf. infra). But Indonesia's economic dependence on China has persuaded it to remain cautious.[41]

By pushing its advantage, China has contributed to "internationalizing" and "militarizing" territorial and maritime disputes that it claimed to keep peaceful. The other parties present still remember the remarks by the then Chinese foreign minister Yang Jiechi at the 2010 ASEAN summit in Hanoi: "China is a big country, the other countries are small countries. That's a fact!" This begs the question, why, in these conditions, would Beijing not take advantage of this asymmetry? Then again, why, given its own responsibilities and ambitions in the area, would Washington not seek to mitigate this asymmetry?

PROLIFERATING SINO–US CONFLICTS

Over the past decade, tension has been rising in the South China Sea mainly pitting Beijing and Washington against each other. In the name of freedom of navigation and given the fragile and questionable legal status of the islets, rocks, and other sandbanks, the US Navy has been conducting operations since 2012 intended to enforce both this principle and UNCLOS.

In reality, Sino–US confrontation in the South China Sea is older. It first manifested itself around US surveillance operations at the PLA naval base in Sanya, south of Hainan Island, and Chinese submarines' activities in the area. The aforementioned 2001 EP-3 affair was one of the first illustrations of this. Already the United States contested the restrictions China wanted to impose on any passage through its EEZ, deeming the space as international and free to all maritime or air traffic. Obviously, it also intended to continue espionage activities, especially monitoring Chinese strategic submarines' movements. Other incidents caused by such disagreement over interpreting UNCLOS, this time in the Yellow Sea, took place during the same period. In 2002, Chinese fishing vessels blocked the USNS *Bowditch*, an unarmed military hydrographic survey vessel in the EEZ Beijing claims. Subsequently, for several years, following the establishment of a more direct and closer relationship between the Chinese and US militaries, the situation seemed to stabilize. But from 2008 on, China's power assertion and the PLA's signifi-cant resource boost have reignited Sino–US confrontation in the region. Since then, incidents between China's Navy and the Seventh Fleet have multiplied. Among the most notable was that of the *Impeccable* in 2009, a surveillance ship surrounded by Chinese fishing vessels off Hainan; more seriously, in 2013 of the *Cowpens*, a missile-launch cruiser which, in the same area, that watched a little too closely, according to the PLA (than the 45 km perimeter it had imposed), the first deployment of its new and then only aircraft car-rier, the *Liaoning*: intercepted perilously by a Chinese amphibious vessel, the *Cowpens* had to maneuver hastily to avoid a collision.

As noted, the Beijing–Washington tension had already increased after US mediation's failure around Scarborough in 2012. However, starting the fol-lowing year, the vast reclamation work on Chinese-controlled Spratly reefs greatly fueled the rise in Sino–US confrontation.

At first, the Americans were content to closely observe the artificial islands' construction, contesting the new status China claimed to give them, by flying over them regularly. These overflights have caused several incidents, includ-ing the dangerous interception in August 2014 by a Chinese Su-27 of a US Navy *P-8 Poseidon* surveillance plane. A few months later, in May 2015, the same type of American plane ferried a CNN team which was able to testify to the repeated requests made by the PLA Navy to immediately leave the area of the Spratlys it was flying over, especially Fiery Cross, a reef now equipped with a 3,000m airstrip. This second incident gave Beijing an excuse to signal its right to establish an air security zone (ADIZ) in the area but that "prevail-ing conditions" did not require to invoke it.[42]

From 2015, the United States decided to intensify its so-called freedom of navigation operations (FONOPs). The US government has often said it has conducted such operations since 1979 to ensure respect for UNCLOS by all countries, regardless of their relationship with the United States. Nevertheless, from 2015, its FONOPs in the South China Sea have become more intrusive and specifically target China. In October 2015, the USS *Lassen* passed within the twelve nautical mile zone surrounding Subi (Zhubi jiao) to demonstrate, not the absence of rights generated by this ancient reef submerged at high tide, but the right of "innocent passage" or transit of any warship in the territorial waters of another country. Shortly afterward, the *Lassen* passed close to Philippines- and Vietnamese-controlled land features.[43] It was accompanied by two surveillance planes, a P-8 Poseidon and a P-3 Orion, to demonstrate to China the freedom to fly over the area. However, the US Navy respects a 500-meter security zone around the new Chinese artificial islands.

Beijing's reaction is worth noting: two PLA boats followed the *Lassen* asking it to leave the "waters surrounding" Subi which it had entered "without authorization from the Chinese government," making clear not so much that it now considered these reefs as islands and therefore could claim such a right, but rather that it had always considered the Nansha as an archipelago (*qundao*), and therefore a set of islands where any foreign passage was subject to such authorization. Indeed, this has been China's stand after promulgating its territorial sea law in 1992. Shortly earlier, China's foreign ministry had said it did not "condone infringement of China's territorial sea and airspace by any country under the pretext of maintaining freedom of navigation and overflight."[44]

After Trump took office, US FONOPs increased (four in 2017, five in 2018, eight in 2019, and ten in 2020), causing further incidents. The most dangerous occurred in October 2018 when a Chinese destroyer tried to intercept the USS *Decatur* near Gaven coral reef (Nanxun jiao) in the Spratlys, risking collision and forcing it to hastily change course, as only forty meters separated the two vessels.[45] Interestingly, however, the Chinese government remained discreet about this incident, as if it wished to distance itself from it, doubtless fearing the consequences of a real confrontation.[46]

These FONOPs aim not only to remind and attempt to impose on Beijing the majority interpretation of UNCLOS, but also to respond to the growing concerns of Hanoi, Manila, and even Kuala Lumpur given the increasingly oppressive PLA presence in the South China Sea. Washington has long been committed to displaying total neutrality on various claimants' territorial and maritime claims. But since 2020, given Chinese desire for domination, this neutrality has gradually given way to support for the most vulnerable claimants and above all those most opposed to Beijing, at least with regard to their maritime rights.

In March 2020, US Secretary of State Pompeo declared in Manila that any attack on a Philippine vessel or aircraft in the South China Sea would oblige the United States to react as per article 4 of the 1951 mutual defense treaty with the Philippines.[47] This shift in Washington's position was a reaction to mounting Chinese intimidation, from December 2018, against infrastructure improvement projects—including repairing the airstrip and building an unloading ramp for vessels—on Thitu islet, the largest Philippines-controlled land feature in the Spratlys.[48] It also followed an incident in June 2019 around Reed Bank, near Palawan, in a disputed and oil-rich area Manila claims as part of its EEZ. Then, a Chinese fishing vessel, from the maritime militia according to some sources, rammed a Filipino fishing boat and left the scene without going to the aid of the crew (who were rescued by Vietnamese fishermen). President Duterte initially, unlike his defense minister, downplayed the incident so as to maintain good relations with Beijing, but came round to strengthening security ties with Washington.[49]

As aforementioned, the July 13, 2020, US declaration confirms this development. Preceded by a Trump Administration letter to the UN,[50] it deems "most" of Beijing's claims to the South China Sea natural resources "illegal"; criticizes China's "might makes right" attitude; denies the legal basis of the nine-dash line, and recalls its support for the arbitration decision favorable to the Philippines; in this regard, it denounces Beijing's EEZ claims around Scarborough and the Spratlys, especially those infringing Manila's rights; it rejects both the idea that the new artificial islands would generate territorial waters (twelve nautical miles) and the Chinese claims on the surrounding waters of Vietnamese and Malaysian land features as well as on Brunei and Indonesia EEZs in the Natuna region; it particularly attacks the statement that James Shoal (Zengmu ansha), a sandbar submerged in twenty-two meters of water at low tide and located 83 km from Borneo and 1,800 km from Hainan, constitutes "the southernmost Chinese territory"; finally, it adds: "America stands with its allies and partners in Southeast Asia in protecting their sovereign rights over their resources at sea, which are in accordance with their rights and obligations under international law."[51]

Shortly thereafter, on August 26, 2020, the US State Department announced sanctions against an unknown number of Chinese citizens "responsible for or complicit in the construction or militarization of outposts in the South China Sea." Simultaneously, the Department of Commerce blacklisted twenty-four Chinese state companies engaged in building the seven artificial islands of the Spratlys, including the vast China Communications Construction Company (CCCC) and the China Shipbuilding Group.

Meanwhile, the Pentagon reinforced hypersonic anti-ship missiles capable of weakening the PLA's anti-access strategy (A2/AD) in the area.[52]

After taking office, Biden did not relax the pressure on China: The State Department quickly confirmed backing for all the statements and actions taken by Pompeo;[53] the Department of Defense has continued regularly organizing FONOPs in the South China Sea.[54] Thus, the United States persists in seeking to prevent Chinese domination of the area. Besides, since 2020, Washington has shed its neutrality and decided by words and actions to go to the aid of other South China Sea claimants. This new context—Chinese militarization of incidents and evolution in the US stand—obviously raises the risks of crisis, even of war in the region.

Gray Zones Tactics and War Risks

On the diplomatic and legal fronts, the territorial and maritime disputes among the parties involved remain unresolved. Taking advantage of COVID, Beijing further pushed its advantage in 2020. Even if China and ASEAN eventually manage to agree on a code of conduct in the South China Sea, it will have little effect on the nature of disagreements between the parties and Beijing's desire to impose itself as the policeman of this sea.

Clearly, China will persist with efforts to dominate and it has the means. Now, especially, it can mass a greater number of warships or coast guards than all other countries in the South China Sea, including the United States. Sure of its overall military preeminence and deterrent capacity, the latter will probably not abandon FONOPs, perhaps even intensifying them as they enjoy bipartisan support.[55] In future, Washington might even be tempted to strengthen its support for the positions of Hanoi, Manila, and Kuala Lumpur. Other capitals feeling they have to remind Beijing of UNCLOS, such as Paris, London, Delhi, Tokyo, or Canberra, will continue their crossings while avoiding venturing inside the twelve-nautical-mile zones around the artificial islands controlled by China, or the other countries.

But these gestures are unlikely to fundamentally upset the South China Sea situation. The last few years have shown how, although suspicious, ASEAN countries with interests in the area remain measured vis-à-vis China.[56] This attitude is the expression of a new balance of power the United States is struggling to counter without taking additional risks and no doubt deemed prohibitive, particularly given the PLA's new missile capabilities. Some US strategists believe Washington must prevent any new Scarborough-type incident, that is, an effective and non-combat takeover by Beijing of a land feature it does not already administer. But, contrary to the bleakest predictions, this does not mean recapturing Scarborough, which to my knowledge is not an option unless China militarizes the lagoon.[57] The new US commitment is limited to making China better respect the maritime rights of neighboring countries. Even if a showdown did occur, it is not certain that Washington would intervene militarily.

Increasing Use of Gray Zones Tactics

As noted, China has thus far used, not without great shrewdness, what are called the gray zones tactics between war and peace, to defend its interests and increase its advantage.[58] Pressure, intimidation, harassment, showdowns, taking advantage of the opponent's slightest weakness or hesitation, these are the methods Beijing favors, whether under Hu Jintao or since Xi's rise to power. Even if China's risk-taking is now greater and more frequent, its intention is not to trigger an armed conflict with the United States, which, as in the Taiwan Strait, could quickly turn nuclear. Some optimists also believe that as China develops into a naval power, its interests will evolve and thus its interpretation of UNCLOS will get closer to the US one. Citing reciprocity, the PLA Navy began in 2013 to enter the EEZs of the United States and Japan without informing their authorities.

Nonetheless, China shows no signs of changing in terms of its compliance with the Montego Bay Convention, and the well-known limits it places. Its rise to power pushes it on the contrary to affirm more confidently the nine-dash line's validity and its "historic rights" in the South China Sea. The PLA and various facets of Chinese naval armada by their simple and constant presence have created a new power balance that the older militarization of the Paracels and more recent of the Chinese artificial islands in the Spratlys have consolidated. It could therefore become increasingly perilous for any foreign navy to venture inside the nine-dash line without Beijing's consent. For now, China is content to protest and send PLA vessels to monitor, track, and shadow any non-Chinese warships. But relying on a power balance that will be increasingly favorable to it, China may well decide to raise the stakes. For instance, following the June 2020 border incidents between China and India in the Himalayas (cf. chapter 6), in late August Beijing threatened to expel Indian Navy vessels crossing the South China Sea.[59] Eventually, the PLA merely intercepted the ships on way to join a US destroyer. It is this greater India–US strategic proximity, and more broadly within the Quad (with Australia and Japan) and their joint activities in the area that worry China.[60] What will its reaction be next time? If it threatens to use force, possibly most countries will give in, except perhaps the United States with which the risks of war could only increase.[61]

However, is it in China's interest to go that far? Its elbow room is narrower than generally believed. Certainly, no power, not even the United States, could envisage dislodging China from its artificial islands or even forcing it to demilitarize them. However, one should not exaggerate these islands' importance: in the event of war, they are vulnerable and of little strategic value.[62] And, by its more frequent or regular presence, the United States and its allies can partly rebalance the new power equation Beijing has imposed and contribute to everyone respecting the status quo, at least in terms of the various land features' occupation. By backing ASEAN capitals striving to enforce their respective EEZs, Washington contributes even more directly to this rebalancing. Faced with this, China tends to tense up, but it cannot react too strongly without alienating other claimants and thus endangering the negotiations it is committed to on a code of conduct with ASEAN. More importantly, it cannot react militarily without risking a war with the United States. The fear of such a conflict is perceptible in Beijing.[63] Such that in August 2020, it became known that the PLA was instructed not to fire first in case of a confrontation with the Seventh Fleet.[64] In other words, although those like Wang Jisi advocating the area's demilitarization remain a minority in Beijing,[65] Washington has already adopted many actions the 2019 Rand report recommended it should take, regaining some "strategic advantage."[66]

However, in this new context, the risks of military incidents and even of a Sino–US military crisis can only increase. Such crises' eruption depends on these two capitals: how far can the Americans guarantee and defend the status quo, including with regard to Taiwan's possessions? How far are they willing to support the maritime claims of Malaysia, the Philippines, Vietnam, or even Brunei? To what extent and with what means are the Chinese ready to thwart such support? So many variables and uncertainties that need close observation in the coming years.

A Better Way to Handle Crises

Right now, as many American and Chinese experts suggest, the two countries must be better prepared to manage such crises and, if possible, to strengthen confidence-building measures.[67] Consultation mechanisms already exist, such as Military Maritime Consultative Agreement (MMCA) concluded in 1998 or the US-China Memorandum of Understanding on the Rules of Behavior for the Safety of Air and Maritime Encounters, signed in 2014. A hotline was set up between the Chinese and American presidents as early as in 1998, between the Chinese Foreign Ministry and the State Department in 2001, and between the PLA and the Pentagon (more particularly PACOM, today INDOPACOM) in 2007. The problem is that based on past experience (EP-3, *Impeccable*, *Decatur*, etc.), when a crisis erupts, China is more apt to freeze these mechanisms than to use them to lower tensions. This is why it is possible that with each crisis, ad hoc communication channels will be opened, preferably between diplomats than between soldiers, in order to more quickly and effectively reduce tensions and organize an exit from the crisis. The lengthy telephone conversation between Chinese Defense Minister Wei Fenghe and his US counterpart, Mark Esper, in August 2020 shows that a preemptive dialogue is useful. In October 2020, the two countries' militaries held the first teleconference of the Crisis Communications Working Group. On the US side, the group includes representatives of the Defense Department, the Joint Chiefs of Staff and INDOPACOM; the Chinese side includes members of the Central Military Commission's Office for International Military Cooperation, the chief of General Staff, and PLA's Southern Theater Command. According to the Pentagon, "the two sides agreed on the importance of establishing mechanisms for timely communication during a crisis, as well as the need to maintain regular communication channels to prevent crisis and conduct post-crisis assessment."[68] But such an initiative is far from being able to prevent any future crisis and points on the contrary to an increase in risk taking.

Risks of war with other countries bordering the South China Sea also cannot be ruled out. For China, an armed conflict with Vietnam, Malaysia, or even the Philippines presents far less risk than a military crisis with the United States. Conversely, for Hanoi and Manila, rise in regional tensions is their primary security concern.[69] Of course, Washington began in March 2020 to strengthen its obligations vis-à-vis Manila. It clearly wants to avoid another "Scarborough." But its language remains cautious and if the Philippine armed forces were not directly attacked, any change Beijing imposes on the status quo, for example the destruction of fishing vessels or the takeover of a Philippine islet, might not provoke ipso facto a US military reaction. It would much rather prevent than intervene.

China's strategy vis-à-vis Southeast Asian claimants is twofold. On the one hand, it consists of threatening them with armed attacks if they do not comply. But will the PLA take action if these countries, now with US backing, persist? In 2014, China protected its oil exploration platform in the Paracels area with water cannons against Vietnamese coast guards who sought to contest the presence. Chinese maritime surveillance went so far as to ram a vessel. But, on the other hand, the confrontation ended there and the crisis was settled through diplomatic channels and withdrawal of the platform. During the Scarborough crisis, China imposed economic sanctions against the Philippines, for example by limiting the import of bananas. These examples show how much China favors pressure tactics that let it stay below the war threshold and push its interests by making more systematic use of gray area operations. Its desire to maintain stable relations with all ASEAN countries in a context of growing strategic competition with the United States and Japan also explains this relative caution.[70] Doubtless such caution has also led Beijing to postpone establishing an ADIZ in the South China Sea. Such a difficult to define ADIZ would not only complicate relations with all riparian countries but would have even less chance of being respected than the one it established in the East China Sea in 2013 (cf. chapter 5).

For these reasons, an armed conflict in the South China Sea seems unlikely but skirmishes will continue. Beijing will carry on consolidating its presence there while trying to delegitimize Washington's, or its allies,' which it portrays as the main factor of instability and insecurity. The United States for its part has no reason to disengage. Countering as much as possible Chinese ambitions in a sea strategically placed between the Malacca and Taiwan Straits is likely to remain at the heart of its priorities. Observing PLA Navy movements there will also remain a priority for the United States, especially its submarines, although this task today presents greater risks.

CONCLUSION

In the South China Sea, Beijing has clearly favored the indirect strategy, that is, gray area tactics and operations. Without calling into question the respective occupations' status quo except in the borderline Scarborough case, this has consisted of massively increasing its civilian and military presence, especially through the creation and militarization of artificial islands in the Spratlys. It has also consisted of reinforcing its pressures and threats on the other parties so that they end up acknowledging, if not recognizing, its interests. Without declaring war on its neighbors, China has clearly challenged the status quo and thus seems to have come to dominate the South China Sea and become its policeman.

This Chinese desire for domination is contested. It has provoked, especially after 2012, well reported reactions from neighboring countries, the United States and, to a lesser extent, from its allies. US presence has a dissuasive character, persuading China a little more to respect the status quo. But when it comes to maritime rights, the fight has continued and even intensified.

Risks of war, and more so of military crises, are thus far from being eliminated. Although China does not yet seem to desire taking advantage of its military, and particularly naval, superiority to change the status quo vis-à-vis its neighbors, it is likely to use the slightest weakness or opening to consolidate its position. But this will be more difficult now that Washington has multiplied military, diplomatic, legal, informational, and economic means to stem Beijing's gray areas strategy; also since the United States has agreed to take more risks to curb Chinese ambitions.

The longer-term question is whether US presence and counterweight are sustainable. For the foreseeable future, most ASEAN countries will continue seeing this presence as a stabilizing factor, capable of containing Chinese adventurism. In the more distant future, the PLA's naval and air dominance will only increase the risks for the Seventh Fleet, probably prompting it to weigh its support for other parties' claims.[71]

For now, two things are certain. One, despite China's insistence, riparian countries are likely to remain committed to the majority interpretation of

UNCLOS and their EEZs. They will continue to refuse any "joint development" with China in disputed areas. They will also continue fighting on diplomatic and legal grounds, with the obvious limits of this weak vs. strong strategy. Two, while being tempted to flex its muscles more frequently, Beijing intends to continue cultivating its image as a responsible great power eager to find common ground, if not with Washington, at least with Southeast Asian capitals. So many parameters that limit war risks, without eliminating the risks of military crises.[72]

Notes

1. Sébastien Colin, "China's Policy in the China Seas: Sovereignty, Security, and Cooperation," Special Feature, *China Perspectives*, 2016/3, https://journals .openedition.org/perspectiveschinoises/7409.

2. Bill Hayton, *The South China Sea: The Struggle for Power in Asia*, Newhaven, CT: Yale University Press, 2014.

3. Michael Green, Katahleen Hicks, Zack Cooper, John Schaus, and Jake Douglas, "Counter-Coercion Series: Scarborough Shoal Standoff," *Asia Maritime Transparency Initiative*, Washington, DC: CSIS, May 22, 2017, https://amti.csis.org/counter -co-scarborough-standoff/.

4. Lyle J. Goldstein, "The South China Sea Showdown: 5 Dangerous Myths. Why 'Asia's Cauldron' May Only Get More Dangerous in the Years to Come," *National Interest*, September 29, 2015, http://nationalinterest.org/feature/the-south-china-sea -showdown-5-dangerous-myths-13970.

5. Ankit Panda, "It's Official: Xi Jinping Breaks His Non-Militarization Pledge in the Spratlys," December 16, 2016, *The Diplomat*, https://thediplomat.com/2016/12/ its-official-xi-jinping-breaks-his-non-militarization-pledge-in-the-spratlys/.

6. Decision's full text, *The Diplomat*, July 12, 2016: http://thediplomat.com/wp -content/uploads/2016/07/thediplomat_2016-07-12_09-15-50.pdf.

7. Michael R. Pompeo, "U.S. Position on Maritime Claims in the South China Sea," Press Statement, U.S. State Department, July 13, 2020, https://2017-2021.state .gov/u-s-position-on-maritime-claims-in-the-south-china-sea/index.html.

8. A recent reminder of these claims, cf. the note verbale CML/14/2019 of December 12, 2019, https://www.un.org/Depts/los/clcs_new/submissions_files/mys85_2019 /CML_14_2019_E.pdf; cf. also United State Department of State, Bureau of Oceans, International Environmental and Scientific Affairs, *Limits in the Sea, No. 150, People's Republic of China: Maritime Claims in the South China Sea*, January 2022, https://news.usni.org/2022/01/13/state-department-report-on-chinese-claims-in-the -south-china-sea.

9. "Declaration on the Conduct of Parties in the South China Sea," November 4, 2002, https://asean.org/?static_post=declaration-on-the-conduct-of-parties-in-the -south-china-sea-2.

10. Carl Thayer, "A Closer Look at the ASEAN-China Single Draft South China Sea Code of Conduct," *The Diplomat*, August 3, 2018, https://thediplomat.com/2018/08/a-closer-look-at-the-asean-china-single-draft-south-china-sea-code-of-conduct/.

11. Viet Hoang, "The Code of Conduct for the South China Sea: A Long and Bumpy Road," *The Diplomat*, September 28, 2020, https://thediplomat.com/2020/09/the-code-of-conduct-for-the-south-china-sea-a-long-and-bumpy-road/.

12. For more information not only on the construction of these artificial islands but also on all the emerging lands in the South China Sea, cf. the interactive, well documented, and constantly updated site of the CSIS, *Asia Maritime Transparency Initiative*, https://amti.csis.org.

13. "Update: China's continuing reclamation in the Paracels," August 9, 2017, *Asia Maritime Transparency Initiative*, https://amti.csis.org/paracels-beijings-other-buildup/.

14. Kristin Huang, "Chinese Military Fires 'Aircraft-Carrier Killer' Missile into South China Sea in 'Warning to the United States,'" *South China Morning Post* (*SCMP*), August 27, 2020, https://www.scmp.com/news/china/military/article/3098972/chinese-military-launches-two-missiles-south-china-sea-warning.

15. Kristin Huang, "China's 'Aircraft-Carrier Killer' Missiles Successfully Hit Target Ship in South China Sea, PLA Insider Reveals," *SCMP*, November 14, 2020, https://www.scmp.com/news/china/military/article/3109809/chinas-aircraft-carrier-killer-missiles-successfully-hit-target.

16. Sébastien Colin, "Le mythe de la coopération halieutique entre la Chine et les Etats d'Asie du Sud-Est en Mer de Chine du Sud" (Myth of fisheries cooperation between China and Southeast Asian states in the South China Sea), in Nathalie Fau and Benoît de Tréglodé, eds., *Mers d'Asie du Sud-Est: coopérations, intégration et sécurité* (Southeast Asia's seas: cooperation, integration and security), Paris: CNRS Editions, 2018, pp. 147–74.

17. Manuel Mogato, "Duterte Says China's Xi Threatened War if Philippines Drills for Oil," *Reuters*, May 19, 2017, https://www.reuters.com/article/us-southchinasea-philippines-china-idUSKCN18F1DJ.

18. Law in Chinese: https://zh.wikisource.org/wiki/中华人民共和国海警法; In English: "Coastguard Law of the People's Republic of China" https://www.airuniversity.af.edu/Portals/10/CASI/documents/Translations/2021-02-11%20China_Coast_Guard_Law_FINAL_English_Changes%20from%20draft.pdf?ver=vrjG35ymdOsmid0NF66uTA%3D%3D; a comparative analysis of the law: "Force Majeure: China's Coast Guard Law in Context," *Asia Maritime Transparency Initiative*, March 30, 2021, https://amti.csis.org/force-majeure-chinas-coast-guard-law-in-context/.

19. "Vietnam Island Tracker," *Asia Maritime Transparency Initiative*, https://amti.csis.org/island-tracker/vietnam/#Spratly%20Islands; For an account of transformations, "Vietnam Builds Up Its Remote Outposts," *Asia Maritime Transparency Initiative*, https://amti.csis.org/vietnam-builds-remote-outposts/.

20. According to the then Malaysian Prime Minister Najib Razak, "Hanoi and KL reach broad understanding on sea claims," *The Star*, June 2, 2009, https://www

.thestar.com.my/news/nation/2009/06/02/hanoi-and-kl-reach-broad-understanding
-on-sea-claims/.

21. Prashanth Parameswaran, "Vietnam-Philippines South China Sea Activity in Focus With Naval Exchange," November 16, 2018, https://thediplomat.com/2018/11/vietnam-philippines-south-china-sea-activity-in-focus-with-naval-exchange/.

22. Bill Hayton, "The South China Sea in 2020," Statement before the U.S.-China Economic and Security Review Commission hearing on "U.S.-China Relations in 2020: Enduring Problems and Emerging Challenges," September 9, 2020, https://www.uscc.gov/sites/default/files/2020-09/Hayton_Testimony.pdf.

23. Cf. "Update: China Blocks Another Philippine Resupply Mission," *Asia Maritime Transparency Initiative*, July 27, 2022, https://amti.csis.org/three-rounds-of-coercion-in-philippine-waters/.

24. Aaron Rabena, "The Challenges Facing Philippines-China Joint Development in the South China Sea," *Asia Maritime Transparency Initiative*, October 16, 2020, https://amti.csis.org/the-challenges-facing-philippines-china-joint-development-in-the-south-china-sea/.

25. "Update: China Blocks Another Philippine Resupply Mission," op. cit.

26. Richard Javad Heydarian, "Marcos Jr. and ASEAN: Minilateralism in the South China Sea," *AMTI Update*, Washington, DC: CSIS, October 18, 2022, https://amti.csis.org/marcos-jr-and-asean-minilateralism-in-the-south-china-sea/.

27. Tweet by U.S. Asia Pacific Media Hub @eAsiaMediaHub, April 8, 2021, https://twitter.com/eAsiaMediaHub/status/1380038416373444609.

28. Ryan D. Martison and Andrew S. Erickson, "Manila's Images are Revealing the Secrets of China's Maritime Militia," *Foreign Policy*, April 19, 2021, https://foreignpolicy.com/2021/04/19/manilas-images-are-revealing-the-secrets-of-chinas-maritime-militia/; David Axe, "China Blinks as American, Philippine Fleets Challenge Possible Reef Seizure," *Forbes*, April 15, 2021, https://www.forbes.com/sites/davidaxe/2021/04/15/china-blinks-as-american-philippine-fleets-challenge-reef-seizure/?sh=173a41085531.

29. "Statement: On The Return of Illegal Chinese Vessels in Julian Felipe Reef," Republic of the Philippines, Department of Foreign Affairs, June 9, 2022, https://dfa.gov.ph/dfa-news/statements-and-advisoriesupdate/30637-statement-on-the-return-of-illegal-chinese-vessels-in-julian-felipe-reef.

30. Lucio Blanco Pitlo III, "The Significance of President Marcos's Visit to China," *China US Focus*, January 31, 2023, https://www.chinausfocus.com/foreign-policy/the-significance-of-philippine-president-marcos-visit-to-china.

31. Ben Werner, "Maritime Standoff Between China And Malaysia Winding Down," *USNI News*, May 13, 2020, https://news.usni.org/2020/05/13/maritime-standoff-between-china-and-malaysia-winding-down.

32. Blake Herzinger, "Earning in the South China Sea: The U.S. Response to the West Capella Standoff," *War on the Rocks*, May 18, 2020, https://warontherocks.com/2020/05/learning-in-the-south-china-sea-the-u-s-response-to-the-west-capella-standoff/.

33. Michael Hart, "Brunei Abandons South China Sea Claim for Chinese Finance," *Geopolitical Monitor*, April 4, 2018, https://www.geopoliticalmonitor.com/brunei-abandons-south-china-sea-claim-for-chinese-finance/.

34. Joshua Espeña and Chelsea Uy Bomping, "Brunei, ASEAN and the South China Sea," *The Interpreter*, August 3, 2020, https://www.lowyinstitute.org/the-interpreter/brunei-asean-and-south-china-sea.

35. Taiwanese Foreign Ministry statement, July 14, 2020, https://www.mofa.gov.tw/en/News_Content_M_2.aspx?n=1EADDCFD4C6EC567&s=C36D37156BF4FB62.

36. Yimou Lee, "Taiwan Says It May Shoot Down Chinese Drones in the South China Sea," *Reuters*, April 7, 2021, https://www.businessinsider.com/taiwan-may-shoot-down-chinese-drones-in-south-china-sea-2021-4?IR=T, quoted by Duchâtel, "An Assessment of China's Options for Military Coercion of Taiwan," in Wuthnow et al., *Crossing the Strait*, op. cit., p. 102.

37. Lo Tien-pin and William Hetherington, "PLA Drill Spurs Deployment of Troops to Pratas," *Taipei Times*, August 5, 2002, https://www.taipeitimes.com/News/front/archives/2020/08/05/2003741143.

38. Amy Chew, "South China Sea Heats Up as Indonesia Shadows Chinese Ship Near Natuna Islands," *SCMP*, September 14, 2020, https://www.scmp.com/week-asia/politics/article/3101519/south-china-sea-heats-indonesia-shadows-chinese-ship-near-natuna.

39. Sebastian Strangio, "China Demanded Halt to Indonesian Drilling Near Natuna Islands: Report," *The Diplomat*, December 2, 2021, https://thediplomat.com/2021/12/china-demanded-halt-to-indonesian-drilling-near-natuna-islands-report/.

40. Maria Siow, "China 'Sending a Signal' by Deploying Largest Coast Guard Vessels Near Indonesia's Natuna," *South China Morning Post (SCMP)*, January 2023, https://www.scmp.com/week-asia/politics/article/3206445/china-sending-signal-deploying-largest-coastguard-vessels-near-indonesias-natunas.

41. Evan A. Laksmana, "Indonesia Getting 'Gray Zoned' by China," *Asia Times*, August 30, 2022, https://asiatimes.com/2022/08/indonesia-getting-grey-zoned-by-china/.

42. David Brunnstrom, "U.S. Vows to Continue Patrols after China Warns Spy Plane," *Reuters*, May 21, 2015, https://www.reuters.com/article/us-southchinasea-usa-china-idUSKBN0O60AY20150521.

43. "A Freedom of Navigation Primer for the Spratly Islands," *Asia Maritime Transparency Initiative*, November 2, 2015, https://amti.csis.org/fonops-primer/.

44. Michael Green, Bonnie Glaser, and Gregory Poling, "The U.S. Asserts Freedom of Navigation in the South China Sea," *Asia Maritime Transparency Initiative*, October 27, 2015, https://amti.csis.org/the-u-s-asserts-freedom-of-navigation-in-the-south-china-sea/.

45. Luis Martinez, "Chinese Warship Came within 45 Yards of USS Decatur in South China Sea: US," *ABC*, October 2, 2018, https://abcnews.go.com/Politics/chinese-warship-45-yards-uss-decatur-south-china/story?id=58210760.

46. Liu Xiaobo, "How Can China Resolve the FONOPs Deadlock in the South China Sea," *Asia Maritime Transparency Initiative*, March 1, 2019, https://amti.csis.org/how-china-can-resolve-fonop-deadlock/.

47. Pia Ranada, "South China Sea Covered by PH-U.S. Mutual Defense Treaty— Pompeo," *Rappler*, March 1, 2019, https://www.rappler.com/nation/pompeo-says -south-china-sea-covered-philippines-us-mutual-defense-treaty.

48. "The Long Patrol: Staredown at Thitu Island Enters its Sixteenth Month," *Asia Maritime Transparency Initiative*, March 5, 2020, https://amti.csis.org/the-long-patrol -staredown-at-thitu-island-enters-its-sixteenth-month/.

49. Richard Javad Heydarian, "The Reed Bank Crisis: A Call For Upgrading The Philippine-US Alliance," *Asia Maritime Transparency Initiative*, July 10, 2019, https://amti.csis.org/the-reed-bank-crisis-a-call-for-upgrading-the-philippine-u-s-alliance/.

50. Letter dated June 1, 2020, https://usun.usmission.gov/wp-content/uploads/sites /296/200602_KDC_ChinasUnlawful.pdf.

51. Pompeo, "U.S. Position on Maritime Claims in the South China Sea," op. cit.

52. Wajahat Khan and Ken Moriyasu, "US Preps Midrange Missile to Pierce China's 'Anti-Access' Shield," *Nikkei*, August 1, 2020, https://asia.nikkei.com/Politics/ International-relations/South-China-Sea/US-preps-midrange-missile-to-pierce-China -s-anti-access-shield.

53. Ned Price, State Department Spokesman, Press Briefing, February 19, 2021, https://www.state.gov/briefings/department-press-briefing-february19-2021.

54. The latest report (October 1, 2020 to September 30, 2021) of the Department of Defense, *Annual Freedom of Navigation Report, Fiscal Year 2021*, Washington, DC: Report to Congress, https://policy.defense.gov/Portals/11/Documents/FON %20Program%20Report_FY2021.pdf.

55. Michèle A. Flournoy, "How to Prevent a War in Asia? The Erosion of American Deterrence Raises the Risk of Chinese Miscalculation," *Foreign Affairs*, June 18, 2020, https://www.foreignaffairs.com/articles/united-states/2020-06-18/how-prevent -war-asia; Flournoy was Under-Secretary of Defense in the Obama Administration.

56. If they had to choose between China and the United States, a small majority (54%) of Southeast Asians surveyed would opt for the latter; but 79 percent of them believe the former is the most influential economic power (United States: 8%) and 52 percent the most influential political and strategic power (US: 27%); China's economic domination worries 72 percent of them while its political-strategic domination worries 85 percent of them, ISEAS, *The State of Southeast Asia: 2020 Survey Report*, Singapore: ASEAN Studies Centre at ISEAS-Yusof Ishak Institute, https://www.iseas.edu.sg/wp-content/uploads/pdfs/TheStateofSEASurveyReport_2020.pdf.

57. Lawrence A. Franklin, "China: Military Experts Urge Beijing to Prepare for War with U.S.," Gatestone Institute, August 12, 2020, https://www.gatestoneinstitute.org/16336/china-military-war; Zhou Bo, "The Risk of China-US Military Conflict Is Worryingly High," *Financial Times*, August 24, 2020, https://www.ft.com/content /0f423616-d9f2-4ca6-8d3b-a04d467ed6f8.

58. Lyle J. Morris, Michael J. Mazarr, Jeffrey W. Hornung, Stephanie Pezard, Anika Binnendijk, and Marta Kepe, *Gaining Competitive Advantage in the Gray Zone: Response Options to Coercive Aggressions Below the Threshold of Major*

Wars, Washington, DC: Rand, Corporation, 2019, pp. 27–42; Ketian Zhang, "Cautious Bully. Reputation, Resolve and Beijing's Use of Coercion in the South China Sea," *International Security*, Vol. 44, No. 1, Summer 2019, pp. 119–59. Anthony H. Cordeman, *Chronology of Possible Chinese Gray Area and Hybrid Warfare Operations*, Working Draft, Washington, DC: CSIS, September 28, 2020, https://csis-website-prod.s3.amazonaws.com/s3fs-public/publication/200702_Burke_Chair _Chinese_Chronology.pdf.

59. Editor's Note, "Is S. China Sea card useful to New Delhi?" *Global Times*, August 31, 2020, https://www.globaltimes.cn/content/1199461.shtml.

60. For instance, US and Japanese navies held a joint exercise in the South China Sea in June 2020.

61. Michael T. Klare, "A New Tonkin Gulf Incident in the Making?" *The Nation*, July 7, 2020, https://www.thenation.com/article/world/south-china-sea-military/.

62. Andrew Scobell, Edmund J. Burke, Cortez A. Cooper III, Sale Lilly, Chad J. R. Ohlandt, Eric Warner, and J. D. Williams, *China Grand Strategy Trends Trajectories and Long-term Competition*, Santa Monica, CA: Rand, 2020, p. 40.

63. Franklin, "China: Military Experts Urge Beijing to Prepare for War with U.S.," op. cit.; Zhou Bo, "The Risk of China-US Military Conflict Is Worryingly High," op. cit.

64. Wendy Wu and Minnie Chan, "South China Sea: Chinese Military Told Not to Fire First Shot in Stand-Off with US Forces," *SCMP*, August 11, 2020, https://www.scmp.com/news/china/diplomacy/article/3096978/south-china-sea-chinese -military-told-not-fire-first-shot; International Crisis Group, *Competing Visions of International Order in the South China Sea*, Brussels: Asia Report No. 315, November 29, 2021, https://www.crisisgroup.org/asia/north-east-asia/china/315-competing -visions-international-order-south-china-sea#:~:text=Competing%20Visions%20of %20International%20Order%20in%20the%20South,rivalry%2C%20meanwhile%2C %20loads%20the%20dissension%20with%20geopolitical%20significance.

65. Wang Jisi, "Light at the End of a Bumpy Tunnel?" *China-US Focus*, June 18, 2020, https://www.chinausfocus.com/foreign-policy/light-at-the-end-of-a-bumpy -tunnel.

66. Morris et al., *Gaining Competitive Advantage in the Gray Zones*, op. cit., pp. 129–87.

67. Dialogue between He Yafei and Michael Swaine, October 17, 2020, https://justworldeducational.org/transcript-the-u-s-china-dialogue-with-dr-michael-swaine -and-amb-he-yafei/.

68. "U.S. Department of Defense Hosts First Crisis Communications Working Group With the People's Republic of China People's Liberation Army," US Department of Defense, October 29, 2020, https://www.defense.gov/Newsroom /Releases/Release/Article/2398907/us-department-of-defense-hosts-first-crisis -communications-working-group-with-t/; Catherine Wong, "China-US Tension: Military Officials Meet to Discuss How to Avoid All-Out Conflict Amid Rising Temperature," *SCMP*, October 30, 2020, https://www.scmp.com/news/china/diplomacy/ article/3107852/china-us-tension-military-officials-meet-discuss-how-avoid-all.

69. ISEAS, *The State of Southeast Asia*, op. cit., p. 7.

70. David Shambaugh, *Where Great Powers Meet: America and China in Southeast Asia*, Oxford: Oxford University Press, 2020.

71. Joe Sestak, "The U.S. Navy Loss of Command of the Seas to China and How to Regain it," *The Strategist*, Vol. 4, No. 1, Winter 2020–2021, https://tnsr.org/2020/11/the-u-s-navys-loss-of-command-of-the-seas-and-how-to-regain-it/.

72. Ian Storey, "As US-China Tensions Rise, What Is the Outlook on the South China Sea Dispute in 2020–21?" *SCMP*, 8 September 2020, https://www.scmp.com/week-asia/opinion/article/3100563/us-china-tensions-rise-what-outlook-south-china-sea-dispute-2020.

5

War Risks over the Senkaku (Diaoyu) Islands

The Senkaku (Diaoyu) islands issue is simpler than the South China Sea's. First, it is essentially bilateral between Japan, which annexed them in 1895 and has controlled them since, and China, which has claimed them since the early 1970s. It is thus more recent. Occupied after 1945 by the US military, which was testing some new weapons there, these few islets—five "islands" and three rocks—were returned to Japan in 1972 along with Okinawa, forming part of the Ryukyu archipelago in Washington's and Tokyo's view. It was this restitution that roused Chinese nationalist feelings, dormant for nearly seventy-five years, in Beijing as well as in Taipei and Hong Kong. This territorial dispute served as fertile ground for fostering a new generation of politicians in Taiwan, including former president Ma Ying-jeou, then a student, as well as in Hong Kong.[1]

But for a long time, China and Japan chose to set aside the issue since it lacked a solution acceptable to either side. The 1972 normalization of Sino–Japanese relations followed by the signing of a peace and friendship treaty six years later persuaded Deng Xiaoping to leave its settlement to, in his view, a "probably wiser" future generation.[2] From time to time, usually when Beijing wanted to show its displeasure—for example over a Japanese prime ministerial visit to the Yasukuni shrine which contains the tablets of fourteen Class A war criminals—the Diaoyu hit the front pages. Chinese fishing vessels appeared nearby. But not for long.

The rise in tension around the Senkaku can be linked to China's power assertion from 2008, the Hu Jintao era. Since then, starting before Xi's rise to power in 2012, China's actions to weaken Japan's sovereignty over the islets and thus challenge the status quo have multiplied. Incursions by fishing vessels, coast guards, and PLA ships into their territorial waters (12 nautical miles) or contiguous zone (24 miles) have become more frequent. In 2013 China established in the East China Sea an ADIZ (Air Defense Identification

Zone) that included this small archipelago. Thus, Hu's and now Xi's China embarked around these islands on a veritable and undeclared "war of attrition" taking advantage of the gray zone between peace and armed conflict, such that Tokyo and Washington are greatly concerned about Beijing's true intentions.

Does China intend resorting to the use of force to (re-)take the Diaoyu? Some think so, believing the question now is not whether but when it will take place.[3] But is the PLA ready to face the Japanese Self-defense Forces and perhaps also US forces to achieve it? More seriously, would such an operation not risk triggering a much larger war, engulfing the entire region?[4] Is it Beijing's real objective? Isn't its aim rather to use gray zone tactics and operations to compel Japan, through increased presence and intimidation, to accept not only the existence of a territorial dispute, which it continues to reject, but also gradually a form of co-sovereignty, then of Chinese sovereignty over these islands? Isn't its goal more broadly to extend dominance over the East China Sea? Can this strategy succeed? If it fails, is war the only left option for Beijing? Unclear.

CHINESE AND JAPANESE STANDS ON THE DISPUTE

As in the previous chapter, I take no sides on the territorial and maritime dispute between China and Japan over the Senkaku, although the former's legal claim would seem weaker than the latter's. This brief historical reminder is just intended to explain the nature of the disagreement and the reason for nationalist passions it arouses, especially in China.

China is categorical: since 1971, it has consistently declared that the Diaoyu is part of China "from ancient times." In reality, identified in the fifteenth century by Ming cartographers who included them in the Ryukyu archipelago, the islands were never occupied by the successive Chinese regimes, although Chinese fishermen, like those of the Ryukyu or later Japan, often visited it. As in the South China Sea, naming an island often leads in Beijing's official discourse to appropriating it; a non-exclusive fishing area becomes a title deed.[5]

In the late nineteenth century, Empress Dowager Ci Xi gifted her herbalist a Diaoyu islet. But it is doubtful that she knew where it was. Some Chinese historians rely on the existence for several centuries of tributary links between the Ryukyu kingdom and the Chinese Empire to claim the Diaoyu. After the invasion of the Ryukyu by the Satsuma clan in the early seventeenth century, at the time of the Tokugawa, Japan set up its own tributary relations with this kingdom. In 1879, at the Meiji era's dawn, Tokyo simply annexed the Ruykyu, ending any special link between Okinawa and the Chinese Empire.

In 1895, amid the Sino–Japanese war, Tokyo took possession of the Senkaku, which it deemed terra nullius, or uninhabited land. Fearing Beijing's reaction, Japan initially kept it secret. It was only after hostilities ended, the Treaty of Shimoneseki, and Taiwan's annexation that it was made public. This claim as well as the occupation and development of the islets for more than a century favor Japan, which from the late nineteenth century was more familiar than the Chinese Empire with Western-imported international law.[6]

The name Senkaku does not come from Diaoyu, which is the main islet's name (Uotsuri shima in Japanese), but from Pinnacle, the name given to this string of islands (shotô) by an English navigator in the eighteenth century. Between 1900 and 1940, an entrepreneur exploited the bonito there but thereafter these islands remained uninhabited, although owned privately. Japan believes it was the revelation in 1969 of potential natural gas and oil reserves around the Senkaku that aroused Chinese and Taiwanese claims, to which it attaches no value. Even today, Japan denies the very existence of a territorial dispute with China on this issue, a stand identical to the latter on the Paracels.

It was Taiwan which first claimed, in 1971, the islands which it constantly called the Diaoyutai (tai meaning terrace, alluding to the main island's topography). Washington then found some merit in Taipei's legal arguments, recognizing the existence of a territorial dispute and encouraging discreetly but with little hope bilateral negotiation with Tokyo. However, the United States preferred to remain neutral as it was preparing for rapprochement with China and let it replace Taiwan in the United Nations.[7] Since then, it has stuck to its position, stating that it only transferred the islands' "administration" to Tokyo. As of now, Washington's stand remains the same. For its part, Taiwan persists in claiming the islands, with much more vigor in "blue" circles (the Kuomintang or KMT) than in "green" or pro-independence circles, often close to Japan. In reality, maintaining only informal relations with Japan since 1972, Taiwan seeks mainly to protect traditional fishing rights in the area, formally recognized by the latter in 2013, during the presidency of Ma Ying-jeou, who worked hard for it.[8]

It was only in 1971 that China made public its claim to the Diaoyu in the form of a formal protest against the islands' return to Japan by the United States at the same time as Okinawa's. Since then, Beijing (like Taipei) declares that the Diaoyu, having been administratively dependent on Taiwan and not Okinawa during the Japanese era, were returned to China in 1945 under the Cairo Declaration's (1943) and the Potsdam Treaty's (1945) terms but that they were arbitrarily integrated into the Ryukyu by the Americans. But none of these documents nor the San Francisco Peace Treaty (1951) mention these islands.

After the launch of reforms in 1979, Beijing gradually included the Diaoyu in official documents and laws relating to its territorial waters

(1992), protection of its remote islands (2009 law), and the baselines gener-ated (2012). It was only in the early 2010s, through a 2012 white paper, that China began asserting its jurisdiction over the waters surrounding the Diaoyu, and challenging the status quo, thereby multiplying the sources of tension with Japan.

The White Paper states:

> China has maintained routine presence and exercised jurisdiction in the waters of Diaoyu Dao. China's marine surveillance vessels have been carrying out law enforcement patrol missions in the waters of Diaoyu Dao, and fishery adminis-tration law enforcement vessels have been conducting regular law enforcement patrols and fishery protection missions to uphold normal fishing order in the waters of Diaoyu Dao. China has also exercised administration over Diaoyu Dao and the adjacent waters by releasing weather forecasts and through oceano-graphic monitoring and forecasting.[9]

While deeming the Diaoyu as "undisputed Chinese territory," it acknowl-edged having agreed with Japan that the issue be settled later. Crucially, it accuses Japan of having taken unilateral measures, such as the "nationaliza-tion" of three of the Senkaku in 2012 (cf. infra), which obliges it to react and, more importantly, weaken Japan's sovereignty over the islands through various actions.

CHINESE ACTIONS AIMED AT UNDERMINING JAPANESE SOVEREIGNTY OVER THE SENKAKU

These Chinese actions around the Senkaku since early 2010s point to one objective: challenging the status quo. Their immediate objective is to force Tokyo to acknowledge the territorial dispute, so far without success; second to prevent any human activity on these islands and therefore a fortiori any repopulation; third to establish a form of surrounding waters' co-management and broadly a new power balance favorable to Beijing in the East China Sea; fourth to create such insecurity around the Diaoyu that, tired of conflict, so to speak, Japan accepts a form of co-sovereignty of the islands; the ultimate aim is to force Japan to cede or "return" the Diaoyu to China. Can this strategy succeed without an armed conflict? Probably not. This is why only the first three objectives are likely to be achieved and why a military confrontation cannot be excluded.

As the quote above perfectly shows, Beijing has also decided vis-à-vis Tokyo to risk venturing into gray zone operations between war and peace. It all started with a 2010 fishing incident. Since then, China has increased incursions into contiguous or territorial waters around the Senkaku as well as violations of Japanese airspace above the islands. Of course, China contests these waters and space. By establishing an ADIZ in November 2013 including the Diaoyu, Beijing has sought to boost its challenge to Tokyo's administration of the islands. Such actions forced Tokyo to react, thereby rendering it responsible for any escalation.

In retrospect, the September 7, 2010, incident constituted a premeditated provocation by China. That day a Chinese fishing boat not only entered the twelve nautical mile zone around the Senkaku, but also deliberately rammed two Japanese coast guard vessels. The Chinese trawler was boarded, its crew and inebriated captain taken into custody, and the Japanese government asked for financial compensation. China protested and immediately placed economic and diplomatic sanctions against Tokyo, such as suspending all rare earth exports to the archipelago. Japan's cabinet, then led by Naoto Kan, an inexperienced prime minister of the centrist Democratic Party that had come to power a year earlier, rapidly caved in, freeing the crew and the captain, who returned home triumphantly.

Chinese policy toward Japan had changed by then. Attempts to compromise on the EEZ between the two sides, sought by Hu Jintao in May 2008, were strongly criticized in Beijing power circles.[10] Although accepted by both sides during Hu's May 2008 Tokyo visit, any idea of co-management and exploitation of the Shirakaba (Chunxiao in Chinese) disputed area in the East China Sea had been abandoned. Situated outside of the Senkaku, the Shirakaba (Chunxiao) zone is located southeast of the median line between the two countries' shores, the line recognized by Japan, and northwest of the continental shelf limit, the EEZ border China claims. Thus, under nationalists' pressure, Beijing had gone on the offensive, now openly challenging Japan's Diaoyu Administration and seeking to assert its power against Tokyo.

This new strategy was confirmed two years later when Japan's government, still in the Democratic Party's hands, now led by Yoshihiko Noda, decided in September 2012 to nationalize three Senkaku islands in order to prevent the then conservative Tokyo governor Shintaro Ishihara from buying them from their private owners to probably repopulate them, and annoy Beijing. Presented by China as a violation of status quo ante, this "nationalization" ignited matters as the term's use was perceived by Chinese authorities and a part of society, as negating their own claim. Fueled in China by sometimes violent nationalist demonstrations, the tension between the two countries intensified, while paradoxically Japan's cabinet was controlled by a political formation initially better disposed than the conservative Liberal Democratic Party (LDP) toward China. Since then, Chinese vessels' incursions into the Senkaku territorial waters or contiguous zone have become regular, escalating from 2016.

It is China's coast guards that operate in priority (cf. chapter 1). Over four years, incursions were organized around the so-called 3-3-2 model: three times a month, three coast guard vessels entered Senkaku territorial waters for two hours. The pace increased to four vessels, including a larger tonnage one (3-4-2), in 2016. Since the Japanese coast guards do not challenge the Chinese vessels, such as with water cannons, but just order them to leave the area, as the latter only spend a limited time there, it is difficult for them to compel the intruders to comply, except through use of force. The Chinese brief presence is thus tolerated.

China's coast guard aren't the only ones entering the Senkaku. Probably in coordination with them as well as with the maritime militia and the PLA Navy, fishing boats are also often spotted there. Although in civvies, the Chinese fishermen are suspected to be from the militia. Such violations of Japanese territorial waters tend to increase each time Beijing wants to express its displeasure. Thus, in August 2016, obviously reacting to the Hague court's July verdict which the Japanese government had endorsed, 200 to 300 Chinese fishing vessels, escorted by several dozen coast guard ships, entered the contiguous zone, and some of them the Senkaku territorial waters. Beijing thus showed Tokyo its ability to saturate the maritime space around the islands.

Finally, albeit more cautious as only entering the contiguous Senkaku zone, the PLA Navy has also participated in such demonstrations of force since 2013. In January that year a Chinese frigate went so far as to lock its fire-control radar on a Japanese Maritime Self-Defense Force destroyer that was keeping an eye on it. Five years later, a PLA nuclear submarine passed through the area. Although legal internationally, Tokyo deems such passages near the disputed islands as provocative.

Similar caution is shown by the Chinese Air Force, despite the ADIZ's establishment in November 2013. Actually, Chinese aircraft do not overfly the Senkaku, where they risk being immediately intercepted, but the area close to the airspace Japan claims, especially the Tsushima or Miyako strait since 2017, while trying to reach the Western Pacific. The only aircraft that have passed over the islands belong to the Oceanic Administration (a Y-12 in December 2012) or the coast guard (a drone in May 2017). However, the number of Japanese Air Force interceptor take-offs involving PLA aircraft has steadily increased since 2012: they rose to almost 700 (675 out of a total of 947 foreign aircraft interceptions, or 71%) in fiscal year (FY) 2019 (April 1, 2019, to March 31, 2020), compared to fewer than 100 in 2010. Most of these interceptions (581 in FY2019) take place in Japan's Southwest Defense Zone of Japan, in the East China Sea near the Senkaku and Okinawa. Probably due to the pandemic the following year (FY2020), the number of incursions and thus interceptions decreased (725), but the southwestern area

(404) and Chinese aircrafts (458) continue to dominate.[11] And in the first half of 2022, scrambles increased again (446), especially against Chinese aircraft (340, + 20% compared to a year before).[12]

Through all such actions, China intends both to assert its sovereignty over the Diaoyu and test Japanese surveillance and defense means. To this end, as in the South China Sea, it increasingly uses gray zone tactics. Admittedly, given Japan's relative strength and its alliance with the United States (cf. infra), it uses them more measuredly. But its goal is clear: weakening the claims of countries contesting its territorial or maritime claims.

Has Beijing achieved its goals? Yes, if its intention is limited to contesting Tokyo's sovereignty over the Senkaku through regular presence and incursions. No, if its intention is to seize the islands, including by military means. In any event, such gestures by the Chinese have caused a hardening of the Japanese and American positions. They forced Tokyo to negotiate on the issue, but the 2014 agreement is far from having brought convincing benefits to Beijing.

HARDENING OF JAPANESE AND US STANDS AND THE 2014 AGREEMENT

The reason for this relative Chinese caution is the hardening from 2013 of Japan's stand, with LDP leader Shinzo Abe in charge of the government between December 2012 and September 2020. To recap, it was during Abe's first term as prime minister that in January 2007 Japan's Defense Agency was transformed into the Ministry of Defense. Noted for his desire to strengthen Japan's defense capabilities and revise Article 9 of the Constitution— renouncing war as a means of settling international disputes—Abe quickly drew his own red line: he made it clear to China that any landing on the island would be repelled militarily.[13] More generally, with Abe, China, even more than North Korea, became the focus of Japan's defense policy (cf. infra).

Meanwhile, Chinese incursions in the Senkaku area have caused a change in the US position. As noted, its position has always been ambiguous. However, rising Beijing–Tokyo tensions over the Senkaku have forced Washington to draw its own red line: in 2010, it officially included this small archipelago in the perimeter covered by the US–Japan Security Treaty, a position President Obama stated with greater vigor in April 2014.[14] Meaning, if China attacked the Senkaku, the United States would be obliged, as per Article 5 of the treaty, to render aid to Japan.

Thus, the Abe government saw its position buttressed ahead of bilateral talks on a compromise over the Diaoyu, China's condition for any resumption of high-level relations. In fact, in the four-point agreement signed just before the November 2014 APEC summit in Beijing during which Abe and Xi had a brief and icy meeting, Japan does not recognize the existence of a territorial dispute. The joint declaration made public just before that meeting was highly ambiguous. It stated: "the two sides recognize that they have different points of view ["position" in the Chinese version] on the emergence of a tense situation in recent years in the East China Sea, including around the Senkaku Islands" ("Diaoyu" in the Chinese version). Their disagreement is not strictly speaking about the dispute over sovereignty, but about rising tensions. In exchange, satisfying a repeated request from Tokyo, Beijing agreed to adopt crisis management mechanisms, in order to keep incidents under control that could occur in disputed waters or airspace.

However, the effectiveness and especially the purpose of these new crisis management mechanisms are questionable.

CRISIS MANAGEMENT MECHANISMS
AND THEIR LIMITATIONS

Negotiated since 2007, a Maritime and Aerial Communication Mechanism (MACM) was finally established in May 2018 during Premier Li Keqiang's Japan visit and meeting with Abe. It took effect the following month and was intended to avoid accidental collisions between Chinese and Japanese ships and warplanes. This mechanism was inspired by precedents established during the Cold War between NATO and the Warsaw Pact. The two sides have implemented rules for direct communication between Japan's Self-defense Forces and the PLA if their vessels or planes got near each other: they are called upon to use frequencies, signals, and abbreviations established by the Code for Unplanned Encounters at Sea (CUES) adopted in 2014 by twenty-one countries and the International Civil Aviation Convention. The two sides' defense authorities—Japan's General Staff and China's CMC—have established a hotline. The two governments have also decided to hold annual meetings to review the agreement's implementation.[15] Long a bone of contention, no geographical area for the mechanism's implementation is mentioned in the agreement (Beijing wanted to include the Diaoyu while Tokyo hoped to exclude its territorial waters and space, including around these islands).[16]

This initial crisis management mechanism has three major limitations. First, it does not apply to the two sides' coast guards although they are known to hunt each other regularly around the Senkaku. Then, blocked several times, given the vagaries of bilateral ties, its negotiation was designed on the Chinese side as a means of pushing its advantage over the territorial dispute: guarantee that the islands will remain uninhabited, with no new construction nor even visits; demilitarize them by avoiding any deployment in their vicinity; and impose co-management of the waters and the surrounding space by asking their coast guards to keep a certain distance between each other. Laid out by Zhang Tuosheng, one of China's best-known crisis management proponents, these goals have largely been achieved, especially since the 2014 four-point agreement was struck.[17] Finally, this modest mechanism does not oblige the Chinese side to reduce risk-taking. Rather, it is likely to encourage Beijing to test Tokyo's reaction capacities soon as it needs to exert pressure on the latter. In any event, it is only in the spring of 2023 that a hotline under the MACM has been put in place between both defense ministries.

This mechanism therefore has solved nothing. In 2018, during Abe's Beijing visit, the two sides made progress on maritime issues. Restoring the policy Hu Jintao had promoted, they reaffirmed, according to Tokyo, their support for the 2008 agreement on joint development of resources in the East China Sea, calling for a rapid resumption of negotiations leading to its implementation.[18] The two sides also signed an agreement which took effect in February 2019, establishing a legal framework intended to promote, under a 2009 agreement, cooperation in Search and Rescue (SAR) between the Japanese coast guards and the Chinese sea rescue center.[19] And in June 2019, when they met on the sidelines of the G20, Xi and Abe recognized, according to Tokyo, that there could be no "real improvement in" bilateral relations "without stability in the East China Sea."[20] Beijing speaks rather of the shared will "to make joint efforts to preserve peace and stability in the East China Sea."[21] Xi and Abe also favored quickly establishing a hotline.

But this improved climate has not moderated at all Chinese authorities' attitude around the Diaoyu. In its defense white paper published in July 2020, Japan said it was "seriously concerned" about developments, indicating that China continued "relentlessly" to try to change the status quo "by coercion" in waters around the Senkaku."[22] In 2019, Chinese coast guard entered the islands' contiguous seas 1,097 times, spending 283 days there, compared to 819 incursions over 232 days in 2013. They seek not only to "normalize" their presence there but exercise a policing role, increasingly excluding Japanese fishermen from the area. In response to this, the Ishigaki municipality, the southern island of the Ryukyu on which the Senkaku depend, decided in June 2020 to change the administrative area to which they belong from Tonoshiro to Tonoshiro Senkaku (the reason was to put an end to confusion with an Ishigaki district also named Tonoshiro). An annoyed Beijing reacted promptly: the next day, the Chinese Ministry of Natural Resources published a list of fifty names of seabeds, including in the Diaoyu area.

These administrative skirmishes heralded a more offensive Chinese strategy, a war of attrition: on July 5, 2020, two Chinese coast guards spent not two but forty hours in the islands' territorial waters. Between January and

October 2020, as many as twenty-one Chinese coast guards entered the twelve nautical mile zone.[23] In November 2020, China announced a bill to authorize its coast guard to open fire on any foreign vessel engaged in illegal activities in Chinese territorial waters and that refuses to comply with instructions. In December 2020, Chinese and Japanese Defense Ministers, Wei Fenghe and Nobuo Kishi, had a telephone conversation which resolved nothing: while they sought to make progress on the hotline implementation, Wei offered to exclude all fishing boats from the Diaoyu area, which Kishi could only reject.[24] Consequently, while Beijing might continue exercising greater restraint with Japan than with other South China Sea claimants, the risk of an incident has increased instead of receding.

This leads us to try and understand China's real intentions under Xi. Does it really want to take control of the Diaoyu, as well as Taiwan and all the Spratlys land features? This depends on the evolution of Japanese defense policy and US posture toward its ally's security.

ENHANCED SENKAKU MILITARIZATION

We have seen how much of a threat China poses since the early 2010s to Japan's security (cf. chapter 1). Consequently, Tokyo has strengthened its defense effort, the Self-defense Forces have improved coordination with INDOPACOM and US military deployment on the archipelago. The 2015 guidelines facilitate this coordination. Moreover, as far as the Senkaku (and the other remote islands) are concerned, and in the event of an external attack, such as from the Chinese, they establish a new division of labor between the Japanese and US forces, the former being mainly responsible relying on the Dynamic Joint Defense Force, the latter playing a supporting role by providing a strategic strike capability.[25]

Meanwhile, Japan has boosted its military and civilian surveillance measures around the Senkaku. Of course, so-called saturation operations can temporarily put Japan's coast guard in difficulty. But the latter's number of vessels and workforce have risen sharply in recent years. And Japan has an Air Force and a Navy capable of blocking any landing on the islands. Since at least 2014, the Self-Defense Forces have regularly trained, either by themselves or in coordination with the Americans, to retake an enemy-conquered remote island.

Japanese coast guards are a civil unit under the supervision of the Ministry of Land, Infrastructure, Transport and Tourism. As their Japanese name suggests, the coast guards are responsible for protecting maritime safety (*Kaijô Ho'an Chô*, name retained after the 2000 reform). With about 14,500 employees, it is equipped with 474 boats, including 145 patrol boats and 238 patrol crafts, and 90 aircraft, including 35 planes and 55 helicopters.[26] Between 2015 and 2021 FY, its budget grew from 1,880 billion to 2,25 billion yen (then $2.231 billion).

Since 2012, a greater number of coast guards have been assigned to the Okinawa area, based in Naha from where they operate around the Senkaku (12 large patrol boats in 2015). More importantly, from 2015, they were integrated into the US–Japan coordination mechanisms, facilitating responses to Chinese incursions in the area.[27] Nevertheless, it is impossible for Japan to seek numerical parity with Chinese coast guards, especially as the latter can add innumerable fishing boats that the maritime militia can mobilize anytime[28] (cf. chapter 1). Moreover, Japan's maritime space, EEZ included, is not negligible (4 million km2), stretching its coast guards somewhat thin.[29] This is why Japanese forces have in recent years boosted deployment, including in terms of surface-to-sea and surface-to-air missiles, on the southern islands of Ryukyu, especially on Ishigaki and Miyako, closest to the Senkaku.[30]

But can this greater awareness of the rise in risks and strengthening of the Japan–US alliance stem a China-initiated war of attrition? Are new red lines needed? Is this situation not conducive to more dangerous risk-taking? Isn't this precisely the trap Beijing is trying to set for Tokyo? So many questions that have led to a clarification of positions but also greater uncertainty about the longer-term.

CLARIFICATIONS AND UNCERTAINTIES

US and Japanese clarifications made public in the early 2010s have been noted above. However, these did not end the doubts among certain segments of the Japanese society and elites as to any US military commitment in the event of a Chinese attack over the Senkaku. Balance of power changes especially in the East China Sea; US mobilization in other theaters, the latter's failed mediation in the Scarborough crisis, and the disproportion between the territorial issue and the risks of an armed conflict that would pit Beijing and Washington against one another have fueled these doubts.

This is also the reason for the Obama, Trump, and Biden Administrations repeating many times the promise of US involvement if the PLA lands on the Senkaku. In February 2017, during the first US–Japan summit after Trump took office, this commitment found mention for the first time in a joint press release, provoking China's acerbic reaction. In October 2020, due to a further escalation in Chinese intimidation, the Trump Administration went further. US forces commander in Japan, Lieutenant General Kevin Schneider, then raised the possibility of deploying US combat troops to the Senkaku to defend them or respond to a crisis. This declaration was made public as US and

Japanese armed forces undertook biennial maneuvers, including amphibious landings that year on isolated islands of the archipelago.[31]

In a sign of the importance for the United States of China's attrition war, no sooner was the Democratic candidate Joe Biden elected as president than did he confirm on November 12 in a telephone conversation with Prime Minister Suga that for his administration too the US–Japan security treaty would apply in case of Chinese aggression against the Senkaku. At least, that is what Suga told the press, when the absence of explicit reference to the islands on the US side fueled suspicions.[32] But this was clarified shortly after Biden took office: on January 27, 2021, it was made clear to Suga that Article 5 of the treaty applied to the Senkaku, a commitment renewed during Suga's Washington visit in April of the same year.[33] It was also an occasion for the two allies to go further and to demonstrate their shared interest in maintaining peace and stability in the Taiwan Strait and the peaceful resolution of "Cross-Strait issues."[34] A few months later, Biden's commitment was made again to Fumio Kishida, Japan's incoming prime minister.[35] Thus, the Chinese intimidations have strengthened rather than weakened the US–Japan alliance.

Until a showdown takes place, it will be difficult to predict what the US reaction will be. As noted earlier, Japanese forces will in any case be the first to react. What role the US advanced deployment might play remains relatively undetermined.

Several US analysts are concerned about the aforementioned disproportion between the effective control of these islets and world war risks any Chinese military engagement entails. Some advise Washington to prepare more appropriate military responses to promote de-escalation rather than risk an escalation to extremes, or even the conflict's nuclearization.[36] Beijing's strategy is to persuade Tokyo and Washington that "the game is not worth the candle," to use a colloquial expression. But is that the reality? If Japan caved in on the Senkaku, wouldn't it open the door to other faits accomplis, other Chinese attempts to dominate its maritime perimeter, or even the Western Pacific?

This is why the Senkaku (Diaoyu) conflict is so sensitive, revealing both the ambitions of Xi's China, its new strategy, and the various tactics it favors. Ahead of any open and generalized war, Xi seems rather to be pushing his advantage gradually, such as by first threatening Japanese fishermen and then the coast guards, using force against them, and to wait for reactions from Tokyo and Washington before going further. In short, to make more muscular use of gray zone tactics without crossing the conflict threshold.

This strategy can succeed if Tokyo and Washington do not draw sharper red lines—including the use of force against any Chinese vessel or aircraft entering Senkaku territorial waters or airspace—and give in to Beijing's threats, or rather its blackmail. As it has often done in the past to achieve its ends, Beijing is seeking to leverage the Japanese business community that needs a stable and predictable relationship with China, Japan's first trade partner. And they are far from deaf to its arguments.[37] But can Japan really abandon the Senkaku, which it has administered for almost 130 years? This is where nationalism comes in (cf. chapter 1). Which Japanese government or even industrial leader can accept responsibility for the islands' loss? If Tokyo is resolute, Beijing will not dare to use force. For all these reasons, it is more likely that for the foreseeable future Japan will hold its own and Xi's China will not prevail.

But what of the long-term? If the PLA manages to dominate East Asia and if the US–Japan alliance is no longer able to counter this domination, would it not be in Japan's interest to question this alliance and get closer to China, of which it is, for better or for worse, a close and most important neighbor? Already some in Japan are worried about the consequences of the alliance growing stronger, especially in the event of a military crisis or war between China and Taiwan. Indeed, given the PLA's superiority, why should Japan continue betting on an increasingly uncertain US victory? Why should Japan's Self-Defense Forces pledge support to a power increasingly unable to secure the Western Pacific?

So many questions remain unanswered, while Japan's military is preparing for such a crisis by organizing maneuvers south of the Ryukyu (in the Nansei Islands) for the first time.[38] That said, as long as China remains under a single, nationalist, and dominating party and threatens Taiwan, it is hard to see Japan exiting the alliance. Rather the Quad option will continue to be explored and promoted, even if it means giving it a much stronger military dimension than has been the case thus far.

CONCLUSION

Many Chinese words and deeds point to a desire to seize the Senkaku: this is presented as simply reparation for the damage China suffered when it was weak and humiliated. However, are the Diaoyu worth a war that would not only engage Japanese forces but also probably draw in the United States? That is the crux of the matter.

Beijing's claim is supported by many Chinese, on the mainland, in Hong Kong, and even in Taiwan, at least in so-called blue circles, that is, those close to the KMT. Most of them support Beijing's more muscular policy, marked by the multiple incursions discussed earlier. In August 2012, some Hong Kong activists even managed to land on one of the islands of the archipelago before Japan's coast guard apprehended them. Can these challenges to Tokyo's effective sovereignty go further?

China is aware of the risks of any landing attempt because of the US and Japanese red lines. Can the argument mentioned above be reversed: for Beijing too, "is the game worth the candle"? Perhaps not, unless Tokyo shows signs of hesitation or weakness, which is unlikely in the years to come. Because for the Japanese too the certitude is great that the Senkaku legitimately belong to them.

Consequently, quite possibly the war of attrition initiated by China around these unimportant islands has other goals. One, it enables acting as a lever to exert pressure and try to divide, and thus weaken, Japan's political class, above all the LDP. Two, it contributes to extending the maritime domain and ADIZ claimed and gradually dominated by China and thus rendering more vulnerable, in the event of war against Taiwan, Japanese and US advanced military deployment established in the Ryukyu.[39]

Notes

1. Ma focused part of his doctoral thesis in law at Harvard University (1981) on this question: "Legal Problems of Seabed Boundary Delimitation in the East China Sea," *Occasional Papers/Reprints Series in Contemporary Asian Studies*, No. 3, 1984 (62), https://digitalcommons.law.umaryland.edu/cgi/viewcontent.cgi?referer=https://en.wikipedia.org/&httpsredir=1&article=1061&context=mscas.

2. Cited by China's Foreign Ministry, "Set aside dispute and pursue joint development," Undated, https://www.fmprc.gov.cn/mfa_eng/ziliao_665539/3602_665543/3604_665547/t18023.shtml.

3. Alessio Patalano, "A Gathering Storm: China's 'Attrition' Strategy for the Senkaku/Diaoyu Islands," *RUSI Newsbrief*, August 2020, Vol. 40, No. 7, https://rusi.org/publication/rusi-newsbrief/chinese-attrition-strategy-senkaku.

4. Michael E. O'Hanlon, *The Senkaku Paradox: Risking Great Power War Over Small Stakes*, Washington, DC: Brookings Institution Press, 2019.

5. White Paper, "Dioayu Dao Is China's Inherent Territory," Information Office of the State Council of the People's Republic of China, September 25, 2012, http://www.china.org.cn/government/whitepaper/node_7168681.htm.

6. Cf. Jean-Pierre Cabestan, "Who Does the Diaoyus Belong to?" *China Perspectives*, No. 37, September–October 1996, pp. 45–49.

7. Robert C. Watts, "Origins of a 'Ragged Edge'—The U.S. Ambiguity on Senkaku Sovereignty," *Naval War College Review*, Vol. 72, No. 3, Summer 2019, https://digital-commons.usnwc.edu/cgi/viewcontent.cgi?article=8045&context=nwc-review.

8. For an analysis of the agreement, cf. https://www.loc.gov/law/foreign-news/article/japan-taiwan-landmark-fishing-agreement/.

9. White Paper, "Dioayu Dao, an Inherent Territory of China," September 25, 2012, http://www.china.org.cn/government/whitepaper/2012-09/25/content_26628107.htm.

10. However, the declaration signed during Hu's Japan visit has never been formally challenged. It is the fourth bilateral "political document" approved by both

countries, along with the 1972 declaration of recognition, the 1978 peace and friend-ship treaty, and the 1998 joint declaration. Its application was simply shelved. Cf. "China-Japan Joint Statement on All-round Promotion of Strategic Relationship of Mutual Benefit," Chinese Foreign Ministry, May 22, 2008, https://www.fmprc.gov.cn /mfa_eng/wjdt_665385/2649_665393/t458431.shtml.

11. Another country implicated is Russia, whose incursions' number is relatively stable (268 in FY2019 and 258 in FY2020), "Scrambles Through FY2019," *Japan Defense Focus*, No. 124, June 2020, https://www.mod.go.jp/en/jdf/no124/activities .html#article02; "Statistics on Scrambles through FY2020," *Japan Defense Focus*, No. 136, 6/8, https://www.mod.go.jp/en/jdf/no136/pageindices/index6.html#page =7; JASDF (Japan Air Self-Defense Force), Undated, https://www.mod.go.jp/asdf/ English_page/roles/role03/index.html.

12. "Japan's Air Defense Force Jet Scrambles Increase in 1st Half of FY2022," *NHK News*, October 14, 2022, https://www3.nhk.or.jp/nhkworld/en/news/20221014 _25/.

13. "Japan PM Abe Warns China of Force over Islands Landing," *BBC*, April 23, 2013, https://www.bbc.com/news/world-asia-22260140.

14. "Clinton Says Disputed Islands Part of Japan-US Pact: Maehara," *AFP*, September 24, 2010, https://www.energy-daily.com/reports/Clinton_says_disputed _islands_part_of_Japan-US_pact_Maehara_999.html; "Obama Says Disputed Islands within Scope of U.S.-Japan Security Treaty," *Reuters*, April 23, 2014, https://www .reuters.com/article/us-japan-usa-obama-interview-idUSBREA3L1YD20140422.

15. "Japan, China Launch Maritime-Aerial Communication Mechanism," *The Mainichi*, June 8, 2018, https://mainichi.jp/english/articles/20180608/p2a/00m/0na /002000c.

16. "Japan, China to Skirt Mentioning Senkakus in Communication Mechanism," *Kyodo*, May 7, 2018, https://english.kyodonews.net/news/2018/05/01ff06eacb3a -update1-japan-china-to-skirt-mentioning-senkakus-in-communication-mechanism .html.

17. Zhang Tuosheng, "Building Trust between China and Japan, Lessons Learned from Bilateral Interactions in the East China Sea," *SIPRI Policy Brief*, February 2015, https://www.sipri.org/sites/default/files/files/misc/SIPRIPB1502c.pdf, cited and analyzed by Mathieu Duchâtel, "China's Policy in the East China Sea: The Role of Crisis Management Mechanism Negotiations with Japan (2008–2015)," *China Perspectives*, 2016/3, pp. 13–21.

18. The Chinese statement referred to "four political documents" the two sides signed including, without citing it, the May 2008 agreement, "Chinese Premier Calls for Efforts to Advance Ties with Japan," The State Council Information Office, People's Republic of China, October 29, 2018, http://english.scio.gov.cn/m/topnews /2018-10/29/content_68828479.htm.

19. "Prime Minister Abe Visits China," Japanese Ministry of Foreign Affairs, Octo-ber 26, 2018, https://www.mofa.go.jp/a_o/c_m1/cn/page3e_000958.html.

20. "Japan-China Summit and Dinner," Japanese Ministry of Foreign Affairs, June 27, 2019, https://www.mofa.go.jp/a_o/c_m1/cn/page3e_001046.html.

21. "Xi, Abe Reach 10-Point Consensus to Promote Bilateral Relations," *Xinhua*, June 28, 2019, http://www.xinhuanet.com/english/2019-06/28/c_138179432.htm.

22. 2020 Defense of Japan, *Defense White Paper Digest*, https://defense.info/wp -content/uploads/2020/08/DOJ2020_Digest_EN.pdf; the following White Papers have reiterated this statement, cf. Defense of Japan 2022, *Defense White Paper Digest*, https://www.mod.go.jp/en/publ/w_paper/wp2022/DOJ2022_Digest_EN.pdf.

23. "Japan Coast Guard Says Chinese Vessels Sail Near Disputed East China Sea Islands," *Reuters*, October 11, 2020, https://www.reuters.com/article/us-japan-china -navy-idUSKBN26W0B9.

24. Liu Zhen, "China-Japan Relations: Defence Chiefs Discuss East China Sea Tensions," *South China Morning Post* (*SCMP*), December 14, 2020, https://www .scmp.com/news/china/diplomacy/article/3113918/china-japan-relations-defence -chiefs-discuss-east-china-sea.

25. Tetsuo Kotani, "The Maritime Security Implications of the New U.S.-Japan Guidelines," *Asia Maritime Transparency Initiative*, April 30, 2015, https://amti.csis .org/the-maritime-security-implications-of-the-new-u-s-japan-guidelines/.

26. Brochure, Japan Coast Guard, 2022, https://www.kaiho.mlit.go.jp/e/pdf/r04 _panfu_en.pdf.

27. Nao Arakawa and Will Colson, "The Japan Coast Guard: Resourcing and Responsibility," *Asia Maritime Transparency Initiative*, April 1, 2015, https://amti .csis.org/the-japan-coast-guard-resourcing-and-responsibility/.

28. Edmund J. Burke, Timothy R. Heath, Jeffrey W. Hornung, Logan Ma, Lyle J. Morris, and Michael S. Chase, *China's Military Activities in the East China Sea, Implications for Japan' Self-Air Defense Forces*, Washington, DC: Rand, 2018, https: //www.rand.org/content/dam/rand/pubs/research_reports/RR2500/RR2574/RAND _RR2574.pdf.

29. Brochure, Japan Coast Guard, 2020, https://www.kaiho.mlit.go.jp/e/image /2020_brochureofJCG.pdf.

30. "Remote Control: Japan's Evolving Senkakus Strategy," July 29, 2020, https:// amti.csis.org/remote-control-japans-evolving-senkakus-strategy/.

31. Seth Robson, "Air Force Ospreys Make First Landing on Japanese Destroyer to Start Keen Sword Drills," *Stars and Stripes*, October 27, 2020, https://www.stripes .com/news/pacific/air-force-ospreys-make-first-landing-on-japanese-destroyer-to -start-keen-sword-drills-1.650048; Laura Zhou, "American Troops Could Be Sent to 'Defend the Senkaku Islands,' US Commander Says," *SCMP*, October 27, 2020, https://www.scmp.com/news/china/diplomacy/article/3107291/american-troops -could-be-sent-defend-senkaku-islands-us.

32. "Biden Says US-Japan Defence Treaty Applies to Disputed Senkaku Islands," *Financial Times*, November 12, 2020, https://www.ft.com/content/3aec3bbd-a86d -4eef-9cf4-4b5e8f190013.

33. "Readout of President Joseph R. Biden Jr. Call with Prime Minister Yoshihide Suga of Japan," January 27, 2021, TheWhiteHouse.gov, https://www.whitehouse.gov/ briefing-room/statements-releases/2021/01/27/readout-of-president-joseph-r-biden-jr -call-with-prime-minister-yoshihide-suga-of-japan/.

34. U.S.–Japan Joint Leaders' Statement: "U.S.–Japan Global Partnership For a New Era," April 3, 2021, TheWhiteHouse.gov, https://www.whitehouse.gov/briefing -room/statements-releases/2021/04/16/u-s-japan-joint-leaders-statement-u-s-japan -global-partnership-for-a-new-era/.

35. Seth Robson And Hana Kusumoto, "Biden Doubles Down on Pledge to Defend Senkakus in Call with Japan's New Leader," *Stars and Stripes*, October 5, 2021, https://www.stripes.com/theaters/asia_pacific/2021-10-05/joe-biden-fumio -kishida-senkakus-japan-china-north-korea-3131972.html#:~:text=Kishida%20told %20reporters%20Tuesday%20that%20Biden%20conveyed%20a,pandemic%2C %20climate%20change%20and%20nuclear%20weapons%2C%20he%20.

36. Michael E. O'Hanlon, *The Senkaku Paradox: Risking Great Power War Over Small Stakes*, Washington, DC: Brookings Institution Press, 2019.

37. Grant Newham, "Why Japan May Cede the Senkakus to China," *Asia Times*, August 12, 2020, https://asiatimes.com/2020/08/why-japan-may-cede-the-senkakus -to-china/.

38. "Taiwan Contingency Looms Large," *Yomiuri Shimbun*, November 20, 2020, https://www.pressreader.com/japan/the-japan-news-by-the-yomiuri-shimbun /20201120/281831466275333.

39. Minnie Chan, "Chinese Series Highlights PLA Pilots' Efforts to Protect Air Defence Identification Zone," *SCMP*, October 7, 2022, https://www.scmp.com/news/ china/military/article/3194999/chinese-series-highlights-pla-pilots-efforts-protect-air.

6

Border Tensions and Risks of a China–India War

We have already noted the two countries' old border dispute, still unresolved, and the rise in tensions along the Line of Actual Control (LAC) starting from 2017 and rising since 2020 (cf. chapter 1). The dispute inherited from the British Raj era covers a 3,488 km border divided into three sectors: the western one between Ladakh and Aksai Chin, the central one (Uttarakhand, Himachal Pradesh west of Nepal, Sikkim in the east), and the eastern sector (Arunachal Pradesh). India has never recognized China's annexation of Aksai Chin (38 000 km2). For its part, Beijing has always deemed worthless the MacMahon line which since the 1914 Simla conference separates what India calls Arunachal Pradesh (90,000 km2) from Tibet and which it considers to be South Tibet (the Republic of China government denounced the convention signed then). In the early 1950s, Aksai Chin was integrated into Tibet, and China built a strategic road between Lhasa and Kashgar in Xinjiang, completed in 1957.

In 1959, as Beijing–New Delhi tensions rose, Zhou Enlai offered Nehru an exchange that would have roughly confirmed the LAC and a 40 km demilitarized zone on either side of it, but the latter rejected it. The 1962 war was to freeze this situation, with the PLA withdrawing from Arunachal Pradesh after it had imparted what Chinese propaganda then called a "lesson" to India (about 1,400 Indians dead, 700 Chinese). Meanwhile, China extended its control over all of Aksai Chin, up to the Karakorum Pass and Pangong Lake, which was in the news in 2020. To complicate matters, in 1963 Pakistan ceded to China the Trans-Himalayan Shaksgam Valley or Karakorum Strip, claimed by India like the rest of northern Kashmir. Moreover, as we will see, the LAC is far from having been precisely delineated, a source of recurrent tensions between Beijing and Delhi.

Between 1988 and 1993, as the two sides sought to improve relations, they negotiated confidence-building measures that led to "strict compliance" with the LAC, a reduction in troops stationed on both sides, and prior notification of military maneuvers. In 1996, they agreed that "neither side shall use its military capability against the other" and signed a protocol to prevent any incursion, including aerial. In 2003, India for the first time recognized in writing that Tibet belonged to China: while this was only indirectly linked to the border question, it contributed to boosting mutual confidence. In 2012–2013, the two sides went further, deciding to spell out the LAC, and setting up consultation and coordination mechanisms to ensure "peace and tranquility" along it. This progress did not end border incidents such as in 2013, just before Li Keqiang's India visit, and 2014 when Xi was in New Delhi. These incidents fueled multiple speculations both on the lack of coordination between China's political and military authorities and, which is more probable, on Beijing's duplicity and the firmness it intended to signal New Delhi. But these incidents remained peaceful and were solved after a meeting between flag officers stationed on the LAC.[1]

RECENT RISE IN BORDER TENSIONS

Since 2017, India has observed and made public an increase in Chinese incursions. After a relative decline in 2018, they have resumed, amounting to 1,035 between 2016 and 2019.[2] More importantly, like in the South or East China Sea, Beijing is seeking to change the status quo in its favor.[3]

In June 2017, the crisis was caused by the PLA's road construction on the Doklam plateau, an area disputed by China and Bhutan and which borders Sikkim. China and Bhutan had reached agreements in 1988 and 1998 to maintain the status quo in the area pending a border accord. In 2012, China and India agreed on the principle that the final fixing of the point where the three countries' borders meet could only be decided with mutual agreement. Bhutan's Protector, India, immediately sent troops to force the Chinese to stop work and evacuate this plateau. A tense seventy-two-day faceoff followed after which the PLA withdrew from Doklam.[4] For Delhi, this area is strategic, facilitating access to the "chicken's neck," the narrow Siliguri corridor in southern Sikkim and which connects West Bengal to northeast India. Consequently, at New Delhi's request, Thimphu has refused the territories exchange proposed by Beijing between Doklam and a region located in the country's east.

Beijing then preferred to concede so as not to vitiate ties with the Modi government. But the following year, the PLA boosted its numbers and presence around the Doklam plateau, confirming China's desire to eventually seize the advantage over India in the Himalayan region, particularly in Nepal and in Bhutan.[5] In June 2020, at a conference of the Global Environmental

Facility, an intergovernmental organization financing projects in developing countries, Beijing announced for the first time that the Sakteng Wildlife
Sanctuary (300 km2), located in eastern Bhutan, was also a disputed area on
the agenda of bilateral talks.[6] In October 2020, China inaugurated a newly
built village near Doklam in an area, according to a US institute's satellite
images, also claimed by Bhutan (Beijing of course questions this claim).[7] In
May 2021 it emerged that China had since 2015 built several villages in the
areas Bhutan claims, before any agreement relating to a possible exchange of
territories, once again highlighting its fait accompli policy.[8]

In such circumstances, the question is how much longer Bhutan can resist,
under Indian pressure, establishing diplomatic relations with China, with
which trade has rapidly developed in recent years: Thimphu's caution during
the 2017 crisis and its modest protests in 2020 point to a desire for normalization. In January 2023, Bhutan and China held a fresh round of talks in
Kunming (Yunnan) on the border issue and reached a "positive consensus,"
promising a rapid implementation of an unknown 2021 agreement establishing a "three-step road map" to resolve the dispute.[9] But without India's
nod of approval, both Bhutan-China normalization and border agreement
seems unlikely.

What is of interest here is the modus operandi Xi's China has adopted,
a strategy of fait accompli, which some call "salami" (salami slicing), also
practiced in the South China Sea or elsewhere. In 2017, China made a tactical
retreat following a rapid Indian intervention the PLA had not expected. But
this crisis heralded others, especially as the PLA certainly intended to "take
revenge" for the momentary setback, and try again to change the status quo.

In 2020, during the crisis that occurred in a disputed Galwan Valley area
between Ladakh-Kashmir and Aksai Chin, at 5,000 meters above sea level, a
more serious line was crossed. On June 15, things turned violent. For the first
time since 1975, there were deaths on the LAC: twenty on the Indian side,
four on the Chinese side (forty-three going by some sources).[10] Others were
reportedly taken prisoner and later released or exchanged. Difficult, to date,
to know all the facts, particularly if this confrontation had been meticulously
planned, which in Indian soldiers' eyes, whose intelligence services were
caught out, is beyond doubt.[11] In Beijing's version, its troops responded to an
ambush and an Indian attack with "steel tubes, clubs and stones"; the higher
Indian casualties due to inadequate medical support.

As noted, since 1996 both sides' troops along the LAC have been instructed
to avoid the use of firearms in faceoffs or altercations. They have complied.
But that did not stop them from challenging each other and fighting with bare
hands and then with studded sticks and clubs, over a disagreement on the
precise LAC. The initial fighting actually took place in May in the Galwan
Valley by Pangong Lake: 72 Indians were reportedly injured in a clash with

fists and stone-throwing between 250 Indian and Chinese soldiers, but no deaths were reported.[12]

In India's view, the PLA again sought to challenge the status quo on the ground. China's view is that it "has always exercised its sovereignty over the Galwan Valley area," which India deems "exaggerated and untenable."

The serious immediate cause of the crisis was India's construction of a more modern road in the LAC's immediate vicinity. In China's view, this put its troops in a vulnerable situation on the LAC's other side and thus it denounced the project in May 2020. The tardy Indian modernization effort aimed to catch up with China, which had for several years improved roads and multiplied infrastructures on its side. Sino–India disagreements over the actual LAC also fueled the crisis. However, the deeper reasons could be threefold: (1) the separation in October 2019 of Ladakh from Jammu and Kashmir state and transformation of the two regions into "union territories," thus stripping their autonomy, provoking a strong reaction from China ally Pakistan which also claims Kashmir; (2) the vocal reactivation by some Indian nationalist politicians, including Home Minister Amit Shah, of the claim on Aksai Chin and its being part of Ladakh; and (3) China's hostility to Indo–US strategic rapprochement, the limits of which it is seeking to test. The COVID-19 crisis would also have goaded China to react vigorously.

Since June 2020, military officials from both sides along the border as well as diplomats have made several attempts at de-escalation. In September, Russia tried if not to play mediator, to facilitate a way out of the crisis, on the sidelines of the meeting, held in Moscow, of the Shanghai Cooperation Organization, which India had joined in 2017. But tensions remained high and in the following months, other incidents took place there, and on the Sikkim and Arunachal Pradesh borders. This led on both sides to a stronger massing of troops and armaments near the LAC, especially in its western part but also along central and eastern sections.[13] However, the incidents mainly occurred in Ladakh. Indian Special Frontier Forces (SFF), including many Tibetans, began in August to occupy strategic positions in the Galwan Valley south of Panglong Lake, helping better monitor Chinese military deployment.[14] On August 30 and then on September 7, 2020, exchanges of fire, probably warning shots, were reported in the area but with no casualties.[15] Indian soldiers would have fired the first shots in order to block Chinese troops' progress, and the second by the latter, extending the faceoff south of the lake. In early September, two Tibetans from the SFF blew up on a mine on the Pangong shore and one of them died.[16]

It transpired that in November 2020 China had used phonic or ultrasonic weapons to retake two Indian-occupied heights since the beginning of the crisis: by releasing electromagnetic waves at the foot of these heights, the PLA would have forced Indian soldiers, most sick with vomiting, to withdraw.[17] Were the two developments related? Perhaps, but it is impossible to confirm. In early 2021, there were signs of tensions easing. In January, Beijing announced the withdrawal of 10,000 LAC soldiers.[18] A month later, the two sides agreed on withdrawal of troops, tanks, and artillery from Pangong Lake and transforming it into a kind of "buffer zone."[19] By July 2022, sixteen series of bilateral "Corps Commander Level meetings" had taken place and in September, it was announced by both sides that troops had "disengaged at the border."[20] But the numbers of troops massed in Ladakh and Tibet are still in several tens of thousands (probably 40,000 on the Chinese side against 60,000 before).[21] While China now seems to retrospectively prefer minimizing the crisis, for India nothing is settled and its impact on bilateral relations continues in 2023 to be felt. The absence of any bilateral meeting or even a handshake between Xi Jinping and Modi at the September 2022 SCO summit speaks volumes about the difficulties for both sides to de-escalate and resume more normal relations. Their short courtesy meeting at the G20 meeting in Bali in November 2022 has not really eased the relationship. On December 9, another border clash took place in the Tawang area (in Danzhong for the Chinese) of Arunachal Pradesh, at the same location as a previous faceoff that had taken place in October 2021, soldiers of both sides suffering minor injuries. What apparently caused the incident was the PLA attempt to dismantle construction built by the Indian military in a contested grassland, the Dogoer mountain pass. The PLA was "compelled to return to their post" according to Indian Defense Ministry. But more incidents are likely to take place in the future.[22]

Consequently, it is obvious that no progress on the border issue has been made and domestic pressure on Modi from the opposition Congress Party, which has accused him of having lost 1,000 square kilometers of land to China in the Himalayas, also complicates any improvement in bilateral relations, despite similar, if not identical views, on the war in Ukraine.

What does this crisis teach? Again, Beijing resorted to coercion, violence, and fait accompli without using firearms, at least at the confrontation's beginning. Thus, the PLA has pushed the limits of gray zone tactics and operations a little further. This development has increased war risks. But in the present circumstances and the foreseeable future, is an armed conflict between China and India conceivable?

RISKS OF SINO–INDIAN WAR

Sino–Indian relations have evolved greatly since the 1962 war. Bilateral relations featuring a mix of economic cooperation, diplomatic convergences, and strategic competition, have on the whole improved and deepened. Summit visits have multiplied, among the recent years, the most significant being the two-day tête-à-tête between Xi and Modi in Wuhan in 2018, specifically to settle or rather bury the Doklam crisis. Bilateral trade has grown exponentially, with a large Indian deficit (reaching $65 billion in 2021). While trade decreased in 2020 ($78 billion against $86 billion in 2019), it bounced back, despite the border crisis, in 2021 to $128 billion including $96 billion Indian imports, making Beijing again New Delhi's leading trade partner ahead of Washington. The two countries played a leading role in forming the BRICS (Brazil, Russia, India, China, and South Africa) in 2009–2010, a new group of major emerging countries which, despite their differences, share the desire to differentiate themselves from the North. Moreover, since 1998, India is nuclear-armed, forcing the two sides to think twice before embarking on a real war.

But counterarguments abound. First, Pakistan's emergence immediately thereafter as a nuclear power failed to end incidents and even armed conflicts with India, the most serious having been the 1999 Kargil war, along their de facto border, the Line of Control (LOC). Moreover, multiple faceoffs and skirmishes have taken place in the area, especially since 2016. While Beijing has deliberately remained tight-lipped about recent Sino–Indian border incidents, Chinese experts are more concerned. Above all, among Indian elites and public opinion, the June 2020 confrontation caused a decisive turning point in the relationship, leading the Modi government to significantly reassess its China policy and move closer to, if not align with the United States.[23] India has imposed a number of sanctions against China, for example banning first 59, then more than 200 Chinese applications including TikTok as also Huawei and ZTE from 5G. For its part, the Trump Administration lent India strong support, treating it as a quasi-ally, and accusing China of violating international commitments.[24] The Biden Administration has continued the US support for India on the border issue.[25]

More importantly, debates about war risks have developed with an unprecedented and sometimes worrying vigor.

In China, the media was quickly unleashed against "Indian nationalist forces," accusing them of not respecting the 1959 LAC (which noteworthy as that of 1962 is more unfavorable to India), and threatening a second "lesson" if they continue provoking the PLA, repeating accusations made during the Doklam confrontation.[26] Some Chinese experts blame such nationalists for inciting Indian forces to mount provocations.[27] The same propaganda sought to demonstrate Indian forces' inferiority by pointing out, for example, the deficiencies of their logistics and inability to maintain a significant troops number at high altitude during the winter: most of the twenty Indian soldiers who died in the Galwan Valley on June 15, 2020, were said to have frozen to death as they were not evacuated in time. Prior to the Moscow meeting, while deploring its powerlessness to "control the narrative" on the crisis, *Global Times* claimed that if an armed conflict erupted on the border, Chinese victory would be quick: "Indian troops would be completely annihilated."[28]

Shortly before the June 2020 clashes, while acknowledging the strategic dilemma in which the two countries were locked and its direct influence on the border dispute, Chinese experts were optimistic. Some hoped that growing economic and cultural relations as well as the concept dear to Xi of "community of shared destiny for mankind" could facilitate cooperation on security issues.[29] But in reality, while advocating flexibility, other Chinese analysts were complaining about India's lack of cooperation and its constant encroachments on the border, calling for a "strengthening of control over disputed areas" (*jia dadui zhengyi diqu of guankong lidu*).[30] An interesting assertion as it indirectly recognizes the legitimacy of the PLA's fait accomplis.

After the June crisis, Chinese South Asia specialists joined the pessimists' camp, noting the incompatibility between the Modi government's power play and Xi's "community of shared destiny for mankind" project: the two countries have entered a "confrontation" and "decoupling" period, and the risks of armed incidents and even large-scale war, not only on the border but also in the South China Sea, will undeniably increase.[31] India was thus warned against trying to meddle in the maritime disputes China was engaged east of the Strait of Malacca. "It does not concern you," they could have written.

After the 2020 incidents, China's media and experts sought to discourage India from any armed reaction, reminding it of who was the dominant military power in Asia. Thus, the strategic rapprochement with the United States or the supply of modern armaments, such as French Rafales, would be useless if armed conflict erupted on the border: the war, a new "lesson," would necessarily be short and decisive, humiliating India again and probably more decisively than in 1962.[32]

In India, pessimism has grown as experts see in the recent clashes the results of Indian forces' unreadiness for the PLA's new strategy, which China has exploited to seize several disputed LAC points. In India's view, the PLA has changed its modus operandi from April 2020: whereas previously it tested Indian reaction to any advance beyond the LAC and then withdrew after negotiations between the military officials on the ground, now it holds its positions. Most likely decided at the highest echelons and consistent with the strategy adopted in the South China Sea, this policy of fait accompli places the Modi government in a difficult dilemma: react militarily and be responsible of a difficult-to-control escalation; or else accept the new situation and make a mobilized public believe the PLA had withdrawn from "Indian territory." A third option would be to quickly seize territories beyond the LAC so as to trade them for Chinese-occupied areas. But the PLA would be ready for such tactics. And generally, it is difficult to reverse completed and successful faits accomplis.[33]

This new situation forced Indian forces to modify their own doctrine and strategy: instead of preparing for a 1962-style ground invasion, they must better guard against any Chinese exploitation of gray zone tactics on the Himalayan border. The LAC troops' rapid reaction capacity is key to any future containment of such encroachments, which appear peaceful but have led to violent clashes.[34] However, such evolution in Indian strategy is likely to be partial, its Army continuing to count on numbers rather than on mobility.

Clearly, despite repeated de-escalation efforts, now is not the time for compromise. Sino–US tensions adds to the rigidity of both sides' stands.[35] India has made it clear that it was facing the most serious crisis in relations with China since 1962.[36] And the similar stand that both countries have adopted in 2022 on the Russian aggression of Ukraine—they have abstained to vote a resolution condemning this act—has not helped them mend their relationship and solve the border issue.

That said, it would be wrong to exaggerate Sino–Indian war risks. As previously mentioned, their nuclear status has fundamentally changed the situation compared to 1962, forcing them to more carefully weigh any military escalation. Chinese experts are also aware of this.[37] Moreover, China is not Pakistan: a Kargil-type limited confrontation would be the kind of trap into which the Modi government should not fall. It knows that as do many Indian analysts.[38] Reignited by India with Pakistan, China, and now Nepal, the geographical map war bears little relation to any real war.[39] Chinese authorities might be fond of what some hawks close to Modi call the 4 Ds: "deception, denial, distortion and disinformation."[40] Nevertheless, it is striking how quickly the two diplomacies resumed bilateral talks and control of the situation. In a joint statement on September 10, 2020, the two foreign ministers reaffirmed their desire for disengagement and dialogue, particularly asking troops to maintain "an appropriate distance."[41] Obviously, on the ground, we are still far from a return to previous status quo and probably it will never really be restored. But communication channels between soldiers are much more developed than earlier. Both sides display a desire to contain the territorial disputes within acceptable limits.

A final consideration for India: the limits of US support. On the diplomatic level, it has been straightforward, but if war erupts, what support could Washington give? Still heavily dependent on Russia for armaments, Indian forces could see their elbow room rapidly diminish if Moscow gave in to Beijing's demands for an embargo. These are many strategic constraints that Chinese specialists have not failed to point out.[42]

China too has no interest in engaging in even a limited war with India. Certainly, the PLA could then demonstrate its new capabilities. It would also give Beijing an opportunity to more clearly remind New Delhi and other capitals who is now the "boss" in Asia. But what would such a conflict's objectives be? By using gray zone tactics and successive faits accomplis, can't China get what it wants: counter India's territorial and strategic ambitions and impose on it a definitive solution to festering border dispute based on Zhou Enlai's 1959 proposals and the current LAC? Moreover, China has no interest in embarking on an offensive that would harm it diplomatically, the 2020 crisis having shown how international public opinion leaned toward India, without even trying to understand the Chinese position. Of course, China's international image is no longer a priority for Xi. But India is not the West and any war between the two Asian giants would shift China's fight with the outside world to the South-South terrain where Xi intends continuing scoring points. These arguments cannot prevent a war or a "lesson" if such is China's ambition. But they will certainly come into play.

CONCLUSION

The PLA might continue pushing its advantage where it wants, with Indian forces seeking to prevent any future fait accompli. More troop buildup on both sides of the LAC is arguably not temporary. It helps China better display to India its capabilities and resolve. But China will not be able to prevent India from continuing its modernization effort in the Himalayas and catch up in military infrastructure terms. For all these reasons, while some incidents are possible and even probable, it is difficult to envisage any real Sino–Indian war. This is also most foreign observers' conclusion.[43]

Finally, does the 2020 crisis provide lessons for both sides? Will it be able to promote, if not a demilitarization of the LAC areas, a more predictable modus operandi between the PLA and Indian forces? Still too early to tell. But the soldiers who have fallen on both sides will not have died in vain if such mechanisms are adopted.

Notes

1. Richard M. Rossow, Joseph S. Bermudez Jr., and Kriti Upadhyaya, "A Frozen Line in the Himalayas," *CSIS Brief*, August 2020, https://csis-website-prod.s3.amazonaws.com/s3fs-public/publication/200817_Rossow_HimalayasBrief_web.pdf,

2. Government of India, Ministry of Defence, Lok Sabha, Unstarred question No. 1577, "Transgression in Indian Territory by China," November 27, 2019,

Parliament of India Lok Sabha House of the People, http://loksabhaph.nic.in/
Questions/QResult15.aspx?qref=7965&lsno=17.

3. For India's interpretation of the 2017 crisis, cf. Committee on External Affairs,
"Sino-India Relations Including Doklam, Border Situation and Cooperation in
International Organisations," September 2018, http://164.100.47.193/lsscommittee/
External%20Affairs/16_External_Affairs_22.pdf.

4. Richard M. Rossow, Joseph S. Bermudez Jr., and Kriti Upadhyaya, "A Frozen
Line in the Himalayas," *CSIS Brief*, August 2020, https://www.scribd.com/document
/473270747/CSIS-Brief-A-Frozen-Line-in-the-Himalayas.

5. Joel Wuthnow, Satu Limaye, and Nilanthi Samaranayake, "Doklam, One Year
Later: China's Long Game In The Himalayas," *War on the Rocks*, June 7, 2018,
https://warontherocks.com/2018/06/doklam-one-year-later-chinas-long-game-in-the
-himalayas/.

6. Anita Joshua, "Beijing Now Bullies Bhutan," July 6, 2020, *The Telegraph*, https:
//www.telegraphindia.com/world/beijing-now-bullies-bhutan/cid/1785446.

7. Steven Lee Myers, "Beijing Takes its South China Sea Strategy to the Himalayas," *The New York Times*, November 27, 2020, https://www.nytimes.com/2020
/11/27/world/asia/china-bhutan-india-border.html. Fan Lingzhi, Bai Yunyi, "Pangda
Village Hyped by Indian Media as in Bhutan is Chinese Territory, Satellite Images,
Documents Show," *Global Times*, November 23, 2020, https://www.globaltimes.cn/
content/1207785.shtml.

8. Robbie Barnett, "China Is Building Entire Villages in Another Country's Territory," *Foreign Policy*, May 7, 2021, https://foreignpolicy.com/2021/05/07/china
-bhutan-border-villages-security-forces/.

9. Kunal Purohit, "India's Alarm Spikes as China and Bhutan Move Closer to
Resolving Border Feud," *South China Morning Post (SCMP)*, January 25, 2023,
https://www.scmp.com/week-asia/politics/article/3207973/neighbourhood-watch
-indias-alarm-spikes-china-bhutan-move-closer-resolving-border-feud.

10. "China Suffered 43 Casualties during Face-Off with India in Ladakh: Report,"
India Today, June 16, 2020, https://www.indiatoday.in/india/story/india-china-face
-off-ladakh-lac-chinese-casualties-pla-1689714-2020-06-16. The official number of
Chinese casualties remained secret until February 2021. Then Indian sources revealed
that another sixty Chinese soldiers had been injured. Mimi Lau, "China-India Border
Clash in June Left Four Chinese Dead, One Injured, Report Reveals," *SCMP*, February 19, 2021, https://www.scmp.com/news/china/diplomacy/article/3122320/china
-india-border-clash-june-left-four-chinese-dead-one.

11. Cf. The interview of Gautam Bambawale, former ambassador to China, in
The Hindu, June 21, 2020, https://www.thehindu.com/opinion/interview/for-minor
-tactical-gains-on-the-ground-china-has-strategically-lost-india-says-former-indian
-ambassador-to-china/article31884054.ece.

12. Sukanya Roy, "All You Need to Know about India-China Stand-Off in
Ladakh," *Business Standard*, May 28, 2020, https://www.business-standard.com/
podcast/current-affairs/all-you-need-to-know-about-india-china-stand-off-in-ladakh
-120052701358_1.html.

13. At the start of the 2020 crisis, there were 70,000 Chinese troops along the border and 250,000 in the entire PLA Western Theater (Tibet and Xinjiang included); Indian troops massed south of the LAC were estimated at 225,000. Minnie Chan, "China-India dispute highlights both sides' growing military presence at border," *SCMP*, June 4, 2020, https://www.scmp.com/news/china/military/article/3087494/china-india-dispute-highlights-both-sides-growing-military.

14. Brahma Chellaney, "China Is Paying a High Price for Provoking India," *Project Syndicate*, September 23, 2020, https://www.project-syndicate.org/commentary/china-expansionism-meets-indian-resistance-in-himalayas-by-brahma-chellaney-2020-09?barrier=accesspaylog.

15. Vijaita Singh, "LAC standoff | Officials Confirm Two Incidents of Firing at South Bank of Pangong Tso," *The Hindu*, September 11, 2020, https://www.thehindu.com/news/national/lac-standoff-officials-confirm-two-incidents-of-firing-at-south-bank-of-pangong-tso/article32576781.ece.

16. Rupam Jain and Devjyot Ghoshal, "Tibetan Soldier's Death Near Tense India-China Border Sheds Light on Covert Unit," *Reuters*, September 16, 2020, https://www.reuters.com/article/india-china-tibet-idUSKBN25T2H5.

17. "Zhongguo jucheng yong lai duifu Yinjun de weibo wuqi shi he shenqi" (What kind of artifact is the microwave weapon that China allegedly used to deal with the Indian army?), *Lianhe Zaobao*, November 16, 2020, https://www.zaobao.com.sg/realtime/china/story20201116-1101404. There are reports that similar weapons have been used by China and Cuba against US embassies in Beijing and Havana, respectively.

18. Minnie Chan, "China Pulls 10,000 Troops from India Border, Source Says," *SCMP*, January 12, 2021, https://www.scmp.com/news/china/military/article/3117419/china-pulls-10000-troops-india-border-source-says.

19. Kunal Purohit, "China-India Border Dispute: Was New Delhi's Pull-Out from Pangong Tso Lake a Mistake?" *SCMP*, April 26, 2021, https://www.scmp.com/week-asia/politics/article/3131031/china-india-border-dispute-was-new-delhis-pull-out-pangong-tso.

20. "Indian, Chinese Troops Disengaging from Disputed Himalayan Border," *PressTV*, September 8, 2022, https://www.presstv.ir/Detail/2022/09/08/688876/India-China-border; "Chinese, Indian Troops Disengage at Border," *Xinhua, Ecns.cn*, September 29, 2022, http://www.ecns.cn/news/2022-09-29/detail-ihcepfvq8470638.shtml.

21. Manjeet Negi, "60,000 Chinese Troops Deployed Near Indian Border, Indian Army also Enhances Troops in Ladakh," *India Today*, January 3, 2022, https://www.indiatoday.in/india/story/india-china-army-pla-border-standoff-eastern-ladakh-1895545-2022-01-03.

22. Hemant Adlakha, "The Tawang Clash: The View from China," *The Diplomat*, December 17, 2022, https://thediplomat.com/2022/12/the-tawang-clash-the-view-from-china/; John Reed, "Indian Opposition Presses Narendra Modi on China Border Clashes," *Financial Times*, December 22, 2022, https://www.ft.com/content/ec9f9ec0-5b3f-4b94-9b4d-1930a30874af.

23. Aman Thakker, "Sino-Indian Border Clashes: Implications for U.S.-India Ties," *CSIS Commentary*, July 16, 2020, https://www.csis.org/analysis/sino-indian-border-clashes-implications-us-india-ties.

24. Rajeswari Pillai Rajagopalan, "This Time the US Is Taking India's Side Against China," *The Diplomat*, July 23, 2020, https://thediplomat.com/2020/07/this-time-the-us-is-taking-indias-side-against-china/.

25. Dylan Donnelly, "Joe Biden Blasts China's 'Attempts to Intimidate' India in Stark Warning to Beijing," *Express*, February 4, 2021, https://www.express.co.uk/news/world/1393216/Joe-Biden-news-India-China-Ladakh-border-LAC-military-conflict-latest-ont.

26. "Shelun: Yingdu 'Zhongguo bu hui dongshou' de wupan feichang weixian" (Editorial: India's misjudgment on 'China that won't fight' is extremely dangerous), *Huanqiu shibao* (Global Times), August 25, 2017, https://opinion.huanqiu.com/article/9CaKrnK4T3u.

27. Interview with Liu Zongyi, "Yindu zi yiwei ba zhun le Zhongguo de mai, suoyi gan yu duoduo biren" (India believes it has made a good diagnosis of China's problems and therefore dares to become aggressive), *Guancha* (The Observer), September 21, 2020, https://www.guancha.cn/liuzongyi/2020_09_21_565802_s.shtml.

28. "Talks with India Come with War Preparedness: Global Times editorial," *Global Times*, September 9, 2020, https://www.globaltimes.cn/content/1200560.shtml.

29. Zhang Li, "Yi dai yi lu beijing xia Zhongyin anquan kunjin de bianhua ji yingdui" (Changes in the Sino-Indian Strategic Dilemma Under the Belt and Road Initiative and Responses to It), *Nanya yanjiu* (South Asia Studies), No. 3, March 3, 2020, pp. 59–91.

30. Zeng Hao, "ZhongYin bianjie zhengduan jiejue fangfa de lishi huigu yu xiaoguo bijiao" (Historical Review of Sino-Indian Border Dispute Resolution Methods and Comparison of Their Effectiveness), *Nanya yanjiu* (South Asia Studies), No. 4, April 4, 2019, pp. 60–84.

31. Yang Siling, "Jialewan hegu liuxue chongtu: Yindu de weixian youxi ji qidui ZhongYin guanxi de yingxiang" (Bloody conflict in the Galwan Valley: India's dangerous game and its influence on China-India relations), *Yunmeng xuekan* (Yunmeng Review, Hunan), Vol. 41, No. 5, September 2020, pp. 1–10.

32. "Talks with India Come with War Preparedness," op. cit.

33. Christopher Clary and Vipin Narang, "India's Pangong Pickle: New Delhi's Options after Its Clash with China," *War on the Rocks*, July 2, 2020, http://cis.mit.edu/publications/analysis-opinion/2020/indias-pangong-pickle-new-delhis-options-after-its-clash-china.

34. Arzan Tarapore, "Rethinking the Defense Doctrine," *The Hindu*, September 10, 2020, https://www.thehindu.com/opinion/op-ed/rethinking-the-defence-doctrine/article32566102.ece?homepage=true.

35. Bhat Burhan, "Voices From the Himalayas Amid Tensions Along the China-India Border," *The Diplomat*, September 22, 2020, https://thediplomat.com/2020/09/voices-from-the-himalayas-amid-tensions-along-the-china-india-border/.

36. Indian External Affairs Minister Dr S. Jaishankar's statement, "Most Serious Situation after 1962: External Affairs Minister Dr S Jaishankar on India-China Border Clash" *WION*, August 27, 2020, https://www.wionews.com/india-news/most-serious -situation-after-1962-external-affairs-minister-dr-s-jaishankar-on-india-china-border -clash-323427.

37. "Duihua Lin Minwang: ZhongYin hui fasheng da guimo junshi chongtu?" (Dialogue with Lin Minwang: Will a large-scale armed conflict between China and India take place?), *Sohu.com*, September 30, 2020, https://www.sohu.com/a/421817724 _433398.

38. Stanly Johny, "A Game of Chess in the Himalayas," *The Hindu*, September 12, 2020, https://www.thehindu.com/opinion/lead/a-game-of-chess-in-the-himalayas /article32584483.ece.

39. Ambassador M. K. Bhadrakumar, "War of the Maps in South Asia," *Rediff.com*, August 8, 2020, https://www.rediff.com/news/column/war-of-the-maps-in-south-asia /20200808.htm.

40. Col. Pradeep Jaidka, "Deception, Denial, Distortion and Disinformation (D4) by China," *Vivekananda International Foundation*, November 17, 2020, https: //www.vifindia.org/article/2020/november/17/deception-denial-distortion-and -disinformation-d4-by-china. Jaidka is a former Indian military intelligence officer.

41. Chinese side: Ministry of Foreign Affairs, "The Chinese and Indian Foreign Ministers Issue a Joint Press Statement and Both Sides Reach Five-point Consensus," September 11, 2020, https://www.fmprc.gov.cn/mfa_eng/gjhdq_665435/2675 _665437/2711_663426/2713_663430/202009/t20200913_513463.html; Indian side: Ministry of External Affairs, "Joint Press Statement - Meeting of External Affairs Minister and the Foreign Minister of China," September 10, 2020, https://mea.gov.in/ press-releases.htm?dtl/32962/Joint_Press_Statement__Meeting_of_External_Affairs _Minister_and_the_Foreign_Minister_of_China_September_10_2020.

42. Lou Chunhao, "Yindu bie wang le wuban he chengneng de lishi jiaoxun" (India should not forget the historical lessons of its misjudgments and capabilities), *Huanqiu shibao* (Global Times), September 10, 2020, https://opinion.huanqiu.com/article /3zp03QsPyNE.

43. Interview with French India specialist Jean-Luc Racine, November 30, 2020; cf. also Roger Cliff, "A New U.S. Strategy for the Indo-Pacific," *National Bureau for Asian Research*, Special Report No. 86, June 2020, p. 28.

7

Which Armed Conflicts Might China Engage In?

This chapter considers under what circumstances China would go to war. Could it not be tempted or forced, under the pressure of circumstances, to embark on what is known as a military operation abroad (MOA)? The very MOA notion is somewhat of a catchall: it can range from evacuating civilians from a conflict zone to formal engagement against a state or non-state actor.[1]

A gray zone tactics-adept concerned with staying below any war threshold, China will probably continue to favor non-lethal and legal MOA under public international law, modeled on those it has already conducted far from its borders to protect its interests or its nationals. As shall be noted, Beijing has acquired experience in this regard. The globalization of China's economy has led an increasing number of companies to set up abroad, following the government's advice to "get out" of the country (*zouchuqu*), exposing them to new risks. It has also led millions of Chinese nationals to emigrate, including to countries in the South where their safety is far from always assured. It is estimated that one million have settled in Africa, but this figure must be treated with caution and has probably decreased recently. Managing the globalization-induced risks requires considering various types of MOAs, probably more ambitious as also more dangerous than those carried out so far.

China organizing MOAs in the future forcing it to exceed, more or less openly, the armed engagement threshold cannot be ruled out. This could take the form of a PLA intervention in the national territory's immediate vicinity so as to strengthen its security. Such military operation would undoubtedly be limited and could aim to neutralize actions undermining internal stability. There are all the Islamist groups in Central or South Asia (Afghanistan, Pakistan) which seek to hurt Chinese authority on their own soil or by infiltrating in Xinjiang. But such MOAs could target other cross-border threats, for example from Burma and some of its minorities.

To answer these questions, it is necessary to present both the warning signs of such interventions and PLA's preparations to strengthen its projection capacities. Finally, I will consider the various future MOA scenarios.

WARNING SIGNS

Many relatively recent developments suggest the PLA is preparing for future MOAs. Paradoxically it is far from China's borders that initial MOAs have taken place, most often under UN aegis, in coordination with the international community. Posing limited risks, these MOAs let the PLA improve its projection and logistical capabilities while demonstrating its desire to contribute in a consensual manner to global security. Discussed and perhaps already prepared, the PLA's MOAs in China's immediate vicinity, however, remain largely in the planning stage. While some have already taken place, these operations remain particularly discreet and limited, as they could potentially turn out to be controversial and fraught with difficult-to-control risks.

The PLA's MOAs Far from National Territory

The PLA's first real MOA was its participation, from December 2008, in anti-piracy operations in the Gulf of Aden. Decided after Japan announced its participation, this decision was well received in the West and in the region, most observers seeing it as signaling China's desire to better integrate into the international community. However, PLA vessels have not been part of any common system, such as the European-led Operation Atalanta or NATO's Operation Ocean Shield. They have operated in parallel in a specific area, minimally communicating and coordinating with other navies present, especially those from countries engaged outside the coalition (South Korea, India, Japan, and Russia). Moreover, and importantly for this study, the PLA has been highly cautious in its interceptions, avoiding capturing the pirates, always leaning toward show of force rather than use of force and only resorting gradually to its embarked special forces. But its 15,000 sailors and commandos deployed in the area since 2008 have learned a lot from this experience in terms of long rotations at sea, logistical supplies, and rapid interventions.[2] This is how China's Navy became familiar with the region, especially the Djibouti port where it often called before establishing a base there.

The second MOA was the successful evacuation in March 2011 of some 36,000 Chinese nationals from Libya. That operation was only partly military, having been organized in haste, lacking preparation and visibility: the Chinese embassy in Tripoli had estimated the number at just 10,000. Most of the Chinese stranded there during Gaddafi's fall left either on civilian ships, Greek especially, chartered by their government, or by road to Egypt. The frigate *Xuzhou*, present in the Gulf of Aden, managed to arrive in the Mediterranean in time to escort those ships, ensuring greater security. But the PLA's role was limited. Only a minority of Chinese (about 1,700) were evacuated on four PLA transport planes (Il-76) which could land in Tripoli after a stopover in Khartoum, then politically close to Beijing. However, this was the first time China's Navy and Air Force had participated in an evacuation operation far from home.[3]

The second evacuation took place in March 2015 in Yemen while the country was torn apart by a continuing civil war. There, the number of Chinese evacuated through the port of Aden was much lower: 571. But unlike Libya, it was the PLA Navy engaged in the fight against piracy in the Gulf of Aden that carried out this operation, later evacuating 225 nationals from other countries to Djibouti. The mission's other feature was its greater danger: the fighting had moved closer to Aden when the first Chinese frigate arrived. Again, it was the PLA presence in the area that made the operation possible.[4]

The fourth known development was obviously the establishment of a PLA logistics base in Djibouti. Decided in 2013, approved by Djibouti's government two years later, it was inaugurated on August 1, 2017, the ninetieth anniversary of PLA's founding. It now has around 2,000 military personnel, including marine troops and special forces battalions who train regularly in Djibouti's desert. Chinese authorities had for long denied any intention to have military bases abroad, symbols they deemed of "Western imperialism." But the Belt and Road Initiative's launch, the need to better protect interests and nationals abroad, growing PLA participation in UN peacekeeping operations (PKOs), particularly in Africa, Beijing's desire to contribute more to African security and finally its concern to better protect its maritime communication channels persuaded Xi to take the plunge and the PLA to establish a foothold in Djibouti.[5]

The Djibouti "logistics" base's official mission is threefold: combating piracy, humanitarian action, and assisting PLA soldiers taking part in PKOs. In reality, since 2016, piracy has almost disappeared from the Gulf of Aden. Since its establishment, the Chinese base has participated in few humanitarian missions. It has been increasingly used as a rotation as well as rest and recuperation point for the Chinese peacekeepers in Africa or the Middle East. Yet its role is much more to familiarize itself with managing a PLA contingent stationed overseas and forge relations with other countries' armed deployments; also to learn from them and more generally to improve Chinese military intelligence in the area; finally, it is to prepare the PLA to quickly intervene in a local or regional theater if necessary. But the low number of soldiers deployed or readily available limits any such mission's scale (cf. infra).[6]

For now, it is unclear whether China will establish more military bases abroad. The PLA now manages satellite control stations in Namibia and Argentina, thus strengthening its defensive and offensive capabilities in the space domain. However, these are not bases, properly speaking.[7]

As for future bases, there is talk of Gwadar in Pakistan where the PLA already enjoys logistical facilities. Since 2019, there is the Ream naval base in southern Cambodia where the PLA is said to have acquired exclusive access rights and the Dara Sakor airstrip located nearby. Americans mention a dozen potential locations, in Asia (Burma, United Arab Emirates, Indonesia, Thailand, Sri Lanka), in Africa (Angola, Equatorial Guinea, Kenya, Namibia, Seychelles, Tanzania), or in the Pacific (Solomon, Vanuatu).[8] But overall, it is logistical advantages or more specifically "strategic support points" (*haiwai zhanluë zhidian*) that China is seeking. And for that, China does not necessarily have to build new military bases. Secure facilities allowing PLA vessels to stop over, resupply, and crew to rest suffice. Meanwhile, facilitating access rights to PLA ships, the many ports built around the world by Chinese state-owned enterprises such as COSCO or China Merchants, could offer the logistical benefits it seeks. This without having to permanently maintain, as in Djibouti, an overseas military contingent nor undertaking highly secured and expensive installations. This dual strategy does not mean more overseas Chinese military bases will not be built in the future, especially in areas where the PLA will seek force projection, that is, where Chinese economic interests are focused.[9] But for now, the first option is preferred.[10]

This leads to another harbinger: active PLA participation in UN PKOs. Although China is the permanent member of the UN Security Council with the highest number of peacekeepers, the figures remain modest: while over thirty years, some 40,000 PLA soldiers took part in twenty-five PKOs, around 2,600 of them were in 2020 divided into six missions.[11] Bangladesh contributed to PKOs in the same year more than 6,600 blue helmets.[12] Moreover, in each peacekeeping mission, PLA contingents constitute only a small part of the peacekeepers deployed.[13] But in the absence of wars, these operations constitute an irreplaceable learning ground for the PLA. Hence China's interest in participating and committing combat forces in PKOs since 2012, particularly in Mali (about 400 officers and soldiers) and South Sudan (more than 1,000); previously, it preferred sending police, doctors, and engineering personnel there. Moreover, PLA's participation in the South Sudan PKO is also intended to protect major Chinese oil interests.[14] Admittedly, and this is important to note for this study, Chinese blue helmets tend to avoid taking risks: any death of one of them—twenty between 1993 and 2022[15]—receives a great deal of media attention in China and sometimes provokes negative reactions on social networks, showing how much Chinese society has become unaccustomed to any armed conflict.[16] But the PLA is taking advantage of such missions to gradually improve its logistical capabilities. For instance, in 2017, for the first time China deployed a helicopter unit to Sudan as part of the African Union-UN led PKO in Darfur (UNAMID). Two years later, in September 2019, also for the first time, Chinese peacekeepers and their equipment were sent directly to the Democratic Republic of the Congo by a PLA transport plane (Y-20).[17] China has invested heavily diplomatically and financially in such UN missions, and this investment has increased after 2012: since 2016 it has been the second largest contributor to the PKO budget (more than 15% in 2020–2021), behind the United States (28%) but now ahead of Japan (8.5%).[18] In addition, in 2017 it registered with the UN a "standby force" of 8,000 Chinese peacekeepers. It has also used these operations to improve operational and force projection capabilities.

Similarly, China decided in 2014–2015 to take part in the fight against the Ebola crisis in West Africa. Coordinated by the World Health Organization, then headed by Margaret Chan, a former Hong Kong Health Secretary who became known for her anti-SARS efforts in 2003, the anti-Ebola campaign was actually directed by the United States (Liberia), Britain (Sierra Leone), and France (Guinea Conakry). But, as a "responsible great power," China was keen to contribute. While some of the Chinese medical teams sent to Sierra Leone and Liberia were civilians, most were from the PLA, especially from the Academy of Military Sciences. This experience taught the PLA much regarding rapid deployment of medical personnel and equipment, rapid construction of field hospitals as well as epidemic management in remote and difficult environments.[19] China and the PLA were to draw on lessons from this during the COVID-19 crisis five years later, but it also helps strengthen the medical and health support capacities for any future PLA external operation.

More generally, the PLA's participation in humanitarian missions organized by the international community following natural disasters contributes to strengthening its overall capacities. Between 2012 and 2018, China participated in nine such missions in the Asia-Pacific, Africa, and Middle East.[20]

PLA Activities in China's Immediate Vicinity

PLA activities in China's immediate vicinity are still rare and not very well-known. For the most part, they are not really MOAs and are concentrated in Central, Western, and Southeast Asia.

Since the Shanghai Cooperation Organization (SCO) was founded in 2001, the PLA has regularly trained with the armies of other member states, including Russia, Kazakhstan, Kyrgyzstan, and Tajikistan. While these exercises indirectly contributed to strengthening the security of China's western borders against Islamist terrorism, they did not lead to joint overseas operations in Central Asia or Afghanistan. Although it did not prevent the continuation of these maneuvers, the SCO's admission of India and Pakistan in 2017 nevertheless contributed to constraining the organization, forcing Beijing to strengthen bilateral security cooperation.

The deterioration in Afghanistan's military situation after the US pullout started in 2014 and the desire to enhance security in Xinjiang led China to deepen such cooperation with neighboring countries.[21] Thus, in 2016, it created, with Afghanistan, Pakistan, and Tajikistan, a quadrilateral anti-terrorist mechanism intended to boost its border security. Meanwhile the PLA was establishing a base in Tajikistan, not far from Afghanistan's border. Chinese People's Armed Police personnel are also stationed there.[22] Beijing has thus far denied the base's existence. However, several reports suggest that the PLA was conducting anti-terrorist operations from there in northern Afghanistan, at least until the total withdrawal of US military in August 2021. The recently reinforced military force located in Xinjiang near the Wakhan corridor could also have been taking part in them. Chinese sources also indicate that Beijing financed the construction in 2018 of an Afghan base in this corridor. Despite the denials from both sides, it is likely that this base facilitates organization of joint military operations on Afghan soil.[23] Stemming any infiltration of Uyghur or Islamist militants into Xinjiang is a likely mission of this base. For obvious reasons, Beijing remains discreet about the desire to secure its borders and probably also its territory's "near abroad."[24] Even before complete US withdrawal from Afghanistan in 2021, this securing of borders was coupled with China's quest for a modus vivendi with the Taliban. And since then, while China has largely sealed off its border with Afghanistan, its cooperation with the Taliban has remained more necessary than ever.[25]

After the terrorist attack on its embassy in Bishkek in August 2016, China also strengthened security cooperation with Kyrgyzstan. The attack, which left the driver of a vehicle loaded with explosives dead and injured three others, was allegedly sponsored according to Beijing by the East Turkestan Islamic Movement (ETIM), which is active in Xinjiang and figures since 2002 on the UN terrorist groups list (although the United States dropped it from its own list in November 2020). Rising insecurity in Kyrgyzstan sparked debate among Chinese experts on whether to send a PLA detachment there. However, Beijing quickly opted for a more cautious strategy: on the one hand, strengthening security cooperation with Kyrgyzstan, marked especially by increased joint exercises between the Kyrgyz national guard and the Chinese armed police; and on the other, using private firms to ensure the security of Chinese companies and businessmen in the country.[26]

Such large-scale use of private security companies remains the preferred mode for Chinese security in the countries involved in the BRI.[27] Any change in this modus operandi will depend in part on strengthening the PLA's projection capabilities.[28]

There is the same caution along the border between China and Southeast Asian countries. After drug traffickers diverted two Chinese transport vessels on the Mekong (Lancang in Chinese) in northern Thailand, leaving thirteen crew members dead in October 2011, China persuaded the three other riparian countries (Burma, Laos, and Thailand) two months later to organize joint river patrols. These are conducted by Chinese public security forces in Yunnan and their counterparts in neighboring states.[29] These more or less monthly patrols have continued: the 98th took place in October 2020 and the 122nd in October 2022. They involve limited numbers: for example, conducted over four days in August 2019, the 85th patrol was made up of seven vessels, including two Chinese, and 140 security officers.[30] Despite Vietnam's reservations about them, these patrols have enabled China to strengthen security along its border areas and boost influence over its neighbors. However, to date the PLA is not associated with these operations.

STRENGTHENING PLA PROJECTION CAPABILITIES AND FUTURE MOA SCENARIOS

Two particularly nationalist films, *Wolf Warrior 2 (Zhanlang er)* and *Operation Red Sea (Honghai xingdong)*, have staged possible Chinese armed interventions far from its territory. The first, 2017 film depicts a kind of Chinese Rambo who manages to evacuate from an imaginary African country plagued by civil war and threatened by Western mercenaries, several Chinese and African nationals working in a Chinese factory, in coordination with the local Chinese embassy and a PLA frigate stationed offshore. Interestingly, the film shows the vessel's commander hesitating to intervene in the internal conflict, anxious to comply with international norms. Finally, faced with the emergency and in order to avoid a massacre, he orders a missile salvo neutralizing the enemy camp and allowing the evacuation of the Chinese and African workers who take refuge in a UN camp. As is known, *Wolf Warrior 2* inspired the expression "wolf warrior diplomacy" (cf. chapter 2).[31]

The second, a 2019 film, includes multiple adventures and twists and is more official. It mainly shows how a Chinese marine commando, deployed in a country which is undoubtedly Yemen from a PLA fleet vessel patrolling the Gulf of Aden, frees compatriots taken hostage by terrorists. It ends with a warning to the United States that is not directly related to the story: five PLA vessels intercept three US ships and order them to leave "Chinese waters" immediately. While directly alluding to the South China Sea tensions, it does not say, however, whether the US Navy complied. But it is as if Beijing is signaling what it intends for the future. Mostly, the film highlights PLA elite units' new capacities, or rather the desired capacities for projection and intervention.

A third movie, not least nationalist and titled *Home Coming* (*Wanlu Guitu*), was made based on the Libyan experience. Taking place in an imaginary country called Numea and released at the end of September 2022, it emphasizes the role of Chinese diplomats rather than the role of the military in the protection of nationals abroad.

PLA: Projection Capabilities of an Expeditionary Force

Power projection capacities are still largely lacking and therefore limit any PLA MOA conducted far away from the national territory.[32] It was not until 2009, on the occasion of an exercise, that the PLA was able to demonstrate its ability to rapidly transport a division-sized force over long distances within the country's borders. Some experts say the PLA Navy can deploy a three-ship intervention force for seven to eight months to Africa's eastern shores. But the force would find it difficult to conduct an armed operation at such a distance from China for more than two weeks. It will only be by 2035 that the PLA can organize such operations more easily. Establishing larger means of air transport can help it. But it will remain difficult to carry out any prolonged armed operations. Finally, despite the 2015 reorganization, the chain of command for such an MOA is far from clear: most likely all the units assigned to such an intervention force will be placed under the immediate direction of the Party's Central Military Commission (CMC).[33]

However, the PLA has already established a three-phase development plan for projection capabilities. This was revealed in 2019 in an article by Liu Jiasheng, an official of the CMC's transport and projection office.[34] In the short term, that is, perhaps by 2025, the PLA will have to be ready to wage a limited war in the maritime domain on China's periphery. To reach this objective, it will therefore have to strengthen maritime and air transport means. In the medium term or by 2035, the PLA will have to be prepared for a limited war overseas to protect its interests in any BRI partner country. In the long term or around 2050, the PLA will have to focus on acquiring "global projection" capabilities, helped by bases abroad as well as its air and space assets (Beitou navigation system): the goal will be to be ready to rapidly deploy forces anywhere worldwide.

The articulation between this plan and the security guarantees Xi intends to adopt in coordination with China's BRI partner countries is noteworthy. It is for China extending its "strategic depth": the PLA will protect these states first if necessary, even if it entails prior installation of "strategic platforms with a military vocation." This prospect worries the United States especially.

In order to have an intervention force—previously called expeditionary force—the PLA knows it needs boosting in six specific areas: amphibious assault, naval power projection, air power projection and transport, long-range precision strikes, global logistics, and what Americans include under the acronym C4ISR (*command, control, communications, computers, intelligence, surveillance and reconnaissance*). Its most modern cruisers (055), destroyers (Luyang III 052B), and amphibious landing helicopter docks (075) constitute the mainstays. The PLA's regular exercises with the Russian armed forces help it progress, giving it the opportunity to deploy large numbers of personnel and equipment beyond China's borders. China's military is also learning from Russia on MOA, such as being able to quickly deploy a brigade-sized force. For example, during the Vostok-2018 maneuvers (September 2018), the Russians conveyed to the Chinese the experience gained in Syria shortly earlier.[35]

But the PLA's intervention force development requires constituting a marine troops corps much larger than at present. This objective has been briefly noted in the chapter on Taiwan (cf. chapter 3). In fact, Taiwan and many other potential MOAs require similar capabilities acquisition.

With eight brigades in 2020, which comprises around 40,000 men (compared to 10,000 in 2015), the Chinese marine troops are expected to reach a workforce of 100,000 officers and soldiers. PLA might realize this goal by 2025. For now, three brigades are truly operational and another three have achieved initial operational capability.[36] These PLA Navy troops have seen their exercises and thus their potential missions diversify: it is no longer just a question of regaining control of an island or a reef but being able to operate in greatly diverse theaters, featuring different terrain (mountain, desert) and climate configurations. The PLA's obvious model is the United States. Experts believe that by 2035 the PLA will be able to deploy to the Middle East over a six-month period (with fifteen-day rotations) six amphibious task forces the size of a US Marine expeditionary unit (2,600 sailors and soldiers).[37]

Possible MOAs

Although substantial, this new capability will however force the PLA to focus for the foreseeable future on protecting its economic interests, infrastructure, and nationals abroad as well as maritime communication routes. It can only consider specific operations limited in time and space. Just for context, it will not have before 2035, and perhaps 2050, the capacity to conduct an MOA of the French Serval operation type (in Mali in 2013).

To date, the most probable—or rather the least improbable—hypothesis of a large-scale PLA MOA abroad remains an intervention in North Korea.[38] Kim Jong-un's regime is not about to collapse; far from it. But the long and turbulent history that both unites and opposes the two countries favors such a hypothesis. In the event the regime implodes or a military crisis erupts between the two Koreas, it is difficult to see China remaining passive. Ensuring the North Korean nuclear weapons' security would be a priority. Preventing refugees from flooding into Manchuria would also be a key concern. Consequently, even more than in 1950, Beijing's interest is to keep the peninsula divided into two states around the 38th parallel and US and South Korean forces away from the Yalu, the river which separates North Korea and China. It is difficult to envisage what form such intervention would take and what its objective would be: sending the PLA or the Armed Police to maintain stability in the north and the status quo with the south while waiting for a definitive solution would be the most likely scenario. China would be able to rely on the 1961 Sino–North Korean Treaty of Friendship, Cooperation and Mutual Assistance to justify its intervention. But to reinforce such action's legitimacy, it could also seek to obtain the UN's green light. Chinese experts remain discreet on this subject. Nevertheless, the regular organization of combined PLA maneuvers near the North Korean border by the Northern Theater Command, for example when tension rises in the peninsula, signal potential engagement if a crisis erupts.[39]

An MOA in Afghanistan in the event a lasting cross-border threat looms cannot be ruled out, either. However, it will necessarily be local and rapid, as China will want to avoid finding itself even partly responsible for securing the country, a task no great power has so far managed to achieve.

Briefly mentioned in the introduction to this chapter, an MOA in the Burma border areas in order to restore order and stability could prove necessary if the Burmese government remains unable to control the situation there and to disarm rebel groups. In 2017, Xi pledged to help Burma ensure peace in the border areas between the two countries. The deteriorated relations between the Burmese military authorities and the minorities since the February 1, 2021, coup could increase such an intervention's likelihood, especially to protect the Kyaukpyu pipeline, a significant feature of China's BRI.[40] However, multiple diplomatic and political obstacles to such an intervention can be imagined. Moreover, such an MOA is not necessarily in Beijing's interests. Actually, many observers suspect it favors, or at least tolerates, Chinese arms sales to various Burmese rebel groups (especially the Kachin's Arakan Army, the Ta'ang Liberation Army of Palaung, Kokang and Wa State) in order to acquire an additional means of pressuring the Naypyitaw regime.[41] Other reports attest to China's difficulties in controlling the flow of military equipment across the Sino–Burmese border. The Chinese security forces' priority remains to avoid refugees flooding into the national territory in the event of unrest in Burma's peripheral areas.[42] This is a more serious risk since the 2021 military coup.

This leads into the last potential scenario as of this writing: an MOA intended to evacuate Chinese nationals from a country that has descended into instability or civil war. But unlike previous evacuations, this one may have to take place in a non-friendly environment, that is to say with lethal force. As noted, the PLA already has the means to carry out such an operation. But the decision to undertake one and its success will be a real test for the PLA.

CONCLUSION

MOAs are a new stage for the APL.[43] It is gradually familiarizing itself with them, starting with the easiest, least risky, and thus least deadly ones. But it is likely that as a great power concerned with defending its interests and its nationals, China will be forced to consider more dangerous MOAs, near its borders or, more probably, far from them.

For obvious reasons, this test is much easier to pass than an attack on Taiwan or an attempt to seize the Senkaku or even an islet in the South China Sea. It does not present the same risks nor diplomatic-strategic consequences. On the contrary, if Beijing takes all the necessary legal precautions, it is the type of MOA activity that is likely to win support among the Chinese people as well as the international community while advantageously demonstrating the PLA's new projection and combat capabilities. Hence it is logically more probable. But that does not mean they have more chance of being undertaken, as the objectives indicated above are loaded with nationalist passions and thus more widely supported by the authorities as well as Chinese society.

Obviously, MOAs away from China's sphere of influence take us away from the Thucydides Trap, this book's raison d'être. However, they are relevant because the PLA lacks combat experience and therefore needs to prove itself where it is possible and easier before embarking on an operation that is much more complex and dangerous.

Notes

1. Julian Fernandez and Jean-Baptiste Jeangène Vilmer, eds., *Les opérations extérieures de la France* (France's foreign operations), Paris: CNRS Editions, 2020, pp. 14–19. The Chinese Defense Ministry prefers to use the concept of "overseas military operations," which is broader since it includes joint exercises, peacekeeping and escort missions, cf. Ministry of National Defense, People's Republic of China, News, Overseas Operations, http://eng.mod.gov.cn/news/node_48721.htm (accessed on November 1, 2022).

2. Andrew S. Erickson and Austin M. Strange, "No Substitute for Experience: Chinese Antipiracy Operation in the Gulf of Aden," *CMSI Red Books*, 11–2013, Newport, RI: U.S. Naval War College Digital Common, https://digital-commons.usnwc.edu/cgi/viewcontent.cgi?article=1009&context=cmsi-red-books; Jérôme Henry, "China's Military Deployments in the Gulf of Aden: Anti-Piracy and Beyond," *Note de l'IFRI*, Asie. Visions 89, November 2016, https://www.ifri.org/en/publications/notes-de-lifri/asie-visions/chinas-military-deployments-gulf-aden-anti-piracy-and.

3. Gabe Collins and Andrew S. Erickson, "Implications of China's Military Evacuation of Citizens from Libya," *China Brief*, Vol. 11, No. 4, March 11, 2011, https://jamestown.org/program/implications-of-chinas-military-evacuation-of-citizens-from-libya/; Jonas Parello-Plesner and Mathieu Duchâtel, "International Rescue: Beijing's Mass Evacuation from Libya," in "China's Strong Arm: Protecting Citizens and Assets Abroad," *Adelphi Series*, Vol. 54, 2014, No. 451, pp. 107–24.

4. Nathan Beauchamp-Mustafaga, "PLA Navy Used for First Time in Naval Evacuation from Yemen Conflict," *China Brief*, Vol. 15, No. 7, April 3, 2015, https://jamestown.org/program/pla-navy-used-for-first-time-in-naval-evacuation-from-yemen-conflict/.

5. Cf. my article, "China's Military Base in Djibouti: A Microcosm of China's Growing Competition with the United States and New Bipolarity," *Journal of Contemporary China*, Vol. 29, No. 125, September 2020, pp. 731–47.

6. Joel Wuthnow, "The PLA Beyond Asia: China's Growing Military Presence in the Red Sea Region," *Strategic Forum*, January 2020, https://www.ndu.edu/Portals/68/Documents/stratforum/SF-303.pdf.

7. Mark Stokes et al., "China's Space and Counterspace Capabilities and Activities," *Project 2049* and *Pointe Bello*, March 30, 2020, pp. 91–92, 94, cited in *2020 Report to Congress of the U.S.-China Economic and Security Review Commission*, Washington, DC: U.S. Government Publishing Office, December 2020, https://www.uscc.gov/sites/default/files/2020-12/2020_Annual_Report_to_Congress.pdf, p. 403.

8. *Military and Security Developments involving the People's Republic of China 2020*, Annual Report to Congress, Washington, DC: Office of the Secretary of Defense, August 21, 2020, p. 129.

9. Then Chinese Foreign Minister Wang Yi's statement, March 9, 2016, cited by Tom Bayes, *China's Growing Security Role in Africa: Views from West Africa, Implications for Europe*, Brussels, Berlin: Konrad Adenauer Stiftung, MERICS, 2020, p. 64.

10. *2020 Report to Congress*, op. cit., pp. 400–4. Cf. also Nadège Roland, ed., *Securing the Belt and Road Initiative. China's Evolving Military Engagement Along the Silk Road*, Washington, DC: National Bureau of Asian Research, NBR Special Report No. 80, September 2019, https://www.nbr.org/wp-content/uploads/pdfs/publications/sr80_securing_the_belt_and_road_sep2019.pdf.

11. "Full Text: China's Armed Forces: 30 Years of UN Peacekeeping Operations," *Xinhua*, September 18, 2020, http://www.xinhuanet.com/english/2020-09/18/c_139376725.htm.

12. "Contribution of Uniformed Personnel to UN by Country and Personnel Type: Experts on Mission, Formed Police Units, Individual Police, Staff Officer, and Troops

As of: 31/03/2021," https://peacekeeping.un.org/sites/default/files/05-country_and
_post_36_mar2021.pdf.

13. "United Nations Peacekeeping, Troops and Police Contributors, Country contributions by mission and personnel type (as of June 30, 2022) China," https://peacekeeping.un.org/en/troop-and-police-contributors (accessed on November 1, 2022).

14. Jonas Parello-Plesner and Mathieu Duchâtel, "China in Deep in the Oil-rich Sudans," in "China's Strong Arm: Protecting Citizens and Assets Abroad," *Adelphi Series*, Vol. 54, 2014, No. 451, pp. 125–44.

15. "United Nations Peacekeeping, Fatalities (as of August 31, 2022), China," https://peacekeeping.un.org/en/fatalities (accessed on November 1, 2022).

16. Cf. my articles "China's Involvement in Africa's Security: The Case of China's Participation in the UN Mission to Stabilize Mali," *The China Quarterly*, No. 235, September 2018, pp. 713–34; and "China's Evolving Role as a UN Peacekeeper in Mali," *USIP Special Report* 432 (Washington, DC: USIP, September 2018), 4, https://www.usip.org/sites/default/files/2018-09/sr432-chinas-evolving-role-as-a-un-peacekeeper-in-mali.pdf.

17. *2020 Report to Congress*, op. cit., p. 411.

18. United Nations Peacekeeping, How we are funded, https://peacekeeping.un.org/en/how-we-are-funded (accessed on November 1, 2022).

19. Cf. my article "China's Response to the 2014–16 Ebola Crisis: Enhancing Africa's Soft Security Under Sino-US Competition," *China Information*, Vol. 31, No. 1, pp. 3–24.

20. "Full Text: China's National Defense in the New Era," *Xinhua*, July 24, 2019, http://www.xinhuanet.com/english/2019-07/24/c_138253389.htm.

21. For an analysis of pre-2016 cooperation, Jonas Parello-Plesner and Mathieu Duchâtel, "China's 'AfPak' Hinterland," in "China's Strong Arm: Protecting Citizens and Assets Abroad," *Adelphi Series*, Vol. 54, 2014, No. 451, pp. 67–90.

22. *Military and Security Developments Involving the People's Republic of China*, November 3, 2021, US Department of Defense, p. 127; Sergey Sukhankin, "The Security Component of the BRI in Central Asia, Part Two: China's (Para)Military Efforts to Promote Security in Tajikistan and Kyrgyzstan," *China Brief*, Vol. 20, No. 14, August 12, 2020, https://jamestown.org/program/the-security-component-of-the-bri-in-central-asia-part-two-chinas-paramilitary-efforts-to-promote-security-in-tajikistan-and-kyrgyzstan/.

23. "Zhongguo zizhu Afuhan jian junshi jidi fankong? Meimei you xie danyou" (Is China funding the construction of an anti-terrorist military base in Afghanistan? US media has some concerns), *Huanqiu shibao* (Global Times) January 10, 2018, https://mil.huanqiu.com/article/9CaKrnK6ioj; Minnie Chan, "China Is Helping Afghanistan Set Up Mountain Brigade to Fight Terrorism," *South China Morning Post* (*SCMP*), August 28, 2018, https://www.scmp.com/news/china/diplomacy-defence/article/2161745/china-building-training-camp-afghanistan-fight.

24. Gerry Shih, "In Central Asia's Forbidding Highlands, a Quiet Newcomer: Chinese Troops," *Washington Post*, February 18, 2019, quoted by *2020 Report to Congress*, op. cit., p. 403. "Tajikistan: Secret Chinese Base Becomes Slightly Less

Secret," Eurasianet, September 23, 2020, https://eurasianet.org/tajikistan-secret
-chinese-base-becomes-slightly-less-secret; Dirk van der Kley, "China's Security
Activities in Tajikistan and Afghanistan's Wakhan Corridor in Roland," *Securing the
Belt and Road Initiative*, op. cit., pp. 71–90.

25. Raffaello Pantucci, "China Is Doomed to Play a Significant Role in Afghanistan," *Foreign Policy*, July 31, 2022, https://foreignpolicy.com/2022/07/31/sinostan
-china-afghanistan-relations-taliban-history/.

26. Sukhankin, "The Security Component of the BRI in Central Asia," op. cit.

27. Sergey Sukhankin, "The Security Component of the BRI in Central Asia,
Part One: Chinese and Regional Perspectives on Security in Central Asia," *China
Brief*, Vol. 20, No. 12, July 15, 2020, https://jamestown.org/program/the-security
-component-of-the-bri-in-central-asia-part-one-chinese-and-regional-perspectives-on
-security-in-central-asia/.

28. Alessandro Arduino, "China's Private Security Companies: The Evolution of a
New Security Actor," in Roland, ed., *Securing the Belt and Road Initiative*, op. cit.,
pp. 91–103.

29. Jonas Parello-Plesner and Mathieu Duchâtel, "Murder on the Mekong: The
Long Arm of Chinese Law," in "China's Strong Arm: Protecting Citizens and Assets
Abroad," *Adelphi Series*, Vol. 54, 2014, No. 451, pp. 91–106.

30. "85th Joint Patrol on Mekong River Completed," Xinhua, August 24,
2019, http://en.people.cn/n3/2019/0824/c90000-9608894.html; "98th joint patrol on
Mekong River completed," *Xinhua*, October 24, 2020, http://www.xinhuanet.com/
english/2020-10/24/c_139464313.htm.

31. On "wolf warrior diplomacy," cf. the speech of Vice Foreign Le Yucheng, who
compares it to the "China threat" syndrome, *Guanchazhe* (Observer), December 5,
2020, https://m.guancha.cn/politics/2020_12_05_573594.shtml?s=fwrphbios.

32. Kirsten Gunness, "The Dawn of a PLA Expeditionary Force?" in Roland,
Securing the Belt and Road Initiative, op. cit., pp. 33–46.

33. *2019 Report to Congress of the U.S.-China Economic and Security Review
Commission*, Washington, DC, U.S. Government Publishing Office, November 2019,
https://www.uscc.gov/sites/default/files/2019-11/2019%20Annual%20Report%20to
%20Congress.pdf, p. 326.

34. Kevin McCauley, "China's Logistic Support to Expeditionary Operations,"
Testimony before the U.S.-China Economic and Security Review Commission,
"China's Military Power Projection and U.S. National Interests," February 20, 2020,
https://www.uscc.gov/sites/default/files/McCauley_Written%20Testimony_0.pdf;
2020 Report to Congress, op. cit., p. 391.

35. *2019 Report to Congress of the U.S.-China Economic and Security Review
Commission*, Washington, DC, U.S. Government Publishing Office, November 2019,
https://www.uscc.gov/sites/default/files/2019-11/2019%20Annual%20Report%20to
%20Congress.pdf, p. 326.

36. Sebastian Roblin, "China's Marine Corps had double in size since 2017, and it
would be a key part of any attempt to invade Taiwan," *Insider*, August 15, 2022, https:
//www.businessinsider.com/chinas-growing-marine-corps-would-be-vital-to-taiwan

-invasion-2022-8. *Military and Security Developments Involving the People's Republic of China 2022*, op. cit., pp. 56–57.

37. Dennis J. Blasko and Roderick Lee, "The Chinese Navy's Marine Corps: Chain-of-Command Reforms and Evolving Training," *China Brief*, February 15, 2019; *China Military Online*, "PLA Marine Corps Conducts Massive Groundbreaking Maneuvers," March 16, 2018; *Military and Security Developments involving the People's Republic of China 2021*, op. cit., pp. 52–53.

38. This is also the Pentagon's view, cf. *2020 Report to Congress*, p. 108.

39. Cf: 2013, "Meimei cheng jiefangjun shangzhouri zai ZhongChao bianjing shidan yanxi" (US media said the People's Liberation Army conducted live ammunition drills on China-North Korea border), *Xinlang junshi* (Sina Military), April 9, 2013, http://mil.news.sina.com.cn/2013-04-09/1007721023.html.

40. John Walsh, "Why Are Chinese Troops Assembling on the Myanmar Border," *EastAsiaForum*, July 3, 2021, https://www.eastasiaforum.org/2021/07/03/why-are-chinese-troops-assembling-on-the-myanmar-border/.

41. "China's Weapon Supply to Terrorists in Myanmar Reignites India's Fear of Another Insurgency in North-East: EFSAS," *ANI*, July 25, 2020, https://in.news.yahoo.com/amphtml/chinas-weapon-supply-terrorists-myanmar-ignites-indias-fear-014154882.html; Bertil Lintner, "Myanmar's Wa Hold the Key to War and Peace Ethnic Armed Group Has Leveraged Ties to China to Avoid Conflict and Build a Prosperous Nationalist State," *Asia Times*, September 6, 2019, https://asiatimes.com/2019/09/myanmars-wa-hold-the-key-to-war-and-peace/?utm_source=The%20Daily%20Report&utm_campaign=081b55a690-EMAIL_CAMPAIGN_2019_09_06_09_27&utm_medium=email&utm_term=0_1f8bca137f-081b55a690-31599241.

42. *China's Role in Myanmar's Internal Conflicts*, United States Institute of Peace, September 14, 2018, https://www.usip.org/publications/2018/09/chinas-role-myanmars-internal-conflicts.

43. Phillip C. Saunders, Arthur S. Ding, Andrew Scobell, Andrew N. D. Yang, and Joel Wuthnow, eds., *Chairman Xi Remakes the PLA: Assessing China's Military Reforms*, Washington, DC, National Defense University Press, 2019, pp. 723–25.

Conclusion

WAR OR PEACE TOMORROW?

War tomorrow? How many times has this question been raised! The danger of China engaging in armed conflict, especially with the United States, continues to rise. Obviously the two great powers have no monopoly on war risks. As in the old Cold War era, peripheral wars between non-nuclear states or a nuclear state and a non-nuclear state remain more likely. The 2020 Armenia–Azerbaijan conflict and the Russian invasion of Ukraine in 2022 being the most recent illustrations. However, the growing rivalry between rising power China and established and, in some respects, declining power United States is also fraught with multiple armed confrontation risks. This duel is not lacking in motives and thus potential conflict theaters in China's vicinity: Taiwan, the South China Sea, the Senkaku, but also the Korean peninsula, and more broadly the control of the first, then the second chain of islands as well as the Malacca Strait which restricts China's access to the oceans. But the Sino–US strategic rivalry is global: it is about world leadership.

As we have shown, despite its promotion of multipolarity, China clearly has the ambition to supplant the United States and become the world's leading great power. In this sense, Rush Doshi is right: China has a grand strategy, a long game.[1] But where I disagree with him is that this long game may not always remain peaceful, and as a result can rapidly be disrupted and may prevent China from realizing its objective. As Taylor Fravel's earlier work and, to some extent, this book, have demonstrated, to solve territorial disputes, China has been reluctant to use force.[2] Yet it is clear that under Xi Jinping, China has been more prone to take risks, to push the envelope, and to go further in the use of gray zone tactics and operations. And there is no guarantee that these tactics will not provoke military crises and even wars.

In this new duel, the duel of the twenty-first century, who will win? China or the United States?

This book does not claim to directly answer this fundamental question. It focuses on war risks today and in the foreseeable future. I sought in the preceding chapters to show that war is probably not imminent, not even for tomorrow but that risks of military incidents and crises, particularly between China and the United States, have clearly risen. "Improbable war, impossible peace": as before 1989 and the fall of the Berlin Wall, Raymond Aron's words continue to ring true. In this conclusion, I will try to provide several answers to the question formulated above: between these two great powers, will there be a winner? Are we really dealing, as Graham Allison and others suggest, with a power transition? Could the new bipolarity that has emerged in the last ten to fifteen years not remain asymmetric and therefore continue giving the United States the advantage? Finally, what lessons should the United States and its allies draw from China's growing ambitions, the new bipolarity that has taken shape and the increased risk of a Beijing–Washington military crisis?

WAR WILL LIKELY NOT ERUPT TOMORROW

First, I wanted to alert readers to the fact that war risks involving China are increasing daily. Nationalist passion, increasingly numerous and sophisticated military means, irredentist unification project with Taiwan, dominating the South China Sea, recovering the Senkaku, and even adjustment to its advantage along the provisional border with India, all these factors point in the same direction: Xi's China is more willing to take risks than earlier to achieve these goals because it has the will and the means, even if it puts it in direct confrontation with the United States.

Passion and ammunition are obviously united, especially on China's side, whose military aims for parity with US armed forces by 2035 and a superiority that would allow it to defeat them by 2050. However, on both sides, and indeed on all sides, particularly in Japan, Taiwan, and India, we hear the "sound of boots" or, in less metaphorical language, a strengthening of defense efforts and concern to be better prepared for possible conflict. More importantly, the United States has shown it does not intend to "let go," in other words, to let China overtake it militarily and technologically.

Fortunately, confrontation or strategic rivalry does not automatically mean armed conflict. Like General Lucien Poirier, one of France's best-known nuclear strategists, "I believe in the rationalizing virtue of the atom."[3] That the United States, China, but also India and Russia are nuclear powers forces them to think twice before engaging in direct military confrontation among themselves. Like earlier, this reality remains paradoxically a factor for peace and thus keeps them, and us, away from the Thucydides's Trap.[4] We saw it, at our expense, during Moscow's annexation of Crimea in 2014 and even more after it invaded Ukraine in 2022: while Washington and other NATO capitals have provided much military and financial help to Kyiv, they have clearly refrained from getting directly involved in the conflict. As during the Cold War, it is a proxy war because nuclear powers cannot directly go to war against each other without risking its nuclearization. And a too-direct US or NATO involvement in this conflict would risk triggering, as Putin has already threatened, a recourse to nuclear weapons by Russia.

As General Poirier noted, let us not forget the atom's equalizing power. It thus imposes itself on the two great powers that interest us here: it also obliges Washington to show caution. The main risk in the future would be Beijing's decision to "sanctuarize" Taiwan, or even the Senkaku or the entire South China Sea: any US intervention in these contested territories would provoke a nuclear response from the PLA. To date, such a threat remains unlikely as it would raise the stakes and give the last two territorial disputes disproportionate importance. But it can't be entirely ruled out if a PLA military adventure against Taiwan—blockade or targeted attacks—goes awry.

Another development has rendered any future war between great powers very different: its cyber and space dimensions. As noted, cyber warfare has long since begun without having been declared. Both Chinese and Americans are preparing to destroy the adversary's space and cyber assets even before hostilities begin. But will they carry out their threats? In fact, a new form of Mutual Assured Destruction (MAD), that is, deterrence, has taken shape in this domain. Will it persuade states mastering these new weapons to engage in negotiations to control their development and effects? Too early to say. Billions of people's daily dependence on space and cybernetic means of communication is likely to make military decision-makers think twice before embarking on such a war. A new reality that also contributes to thwarting the Thucydides Trap.

But hasn't China shown that it need not come to that? We have seen how it has become adept at gray zone tactics, believing that their extensive use is the best way to assert territorial claims and defend security interests. And how much it thinks it can thus exert effective pressure on countries which, from its viewpoint, contest its claims and undermine its security.

This strategic choice also highlights Chinese decision-makers' propensity to avoid taking too many risks, or rather to precisely manage any new risk-taking. Staying below the war threshold seems a constant guideline. Clearly, some confrontations can provoke incidents, even military crises. Nonetheless, thus far, nothing contradicts Xi's China prioritizing gray zone tactics. Vis-à-vis Taiwan, this strategy continues to be combined with a united front policy intended to gradually win over elites and then the island society to the cause of unification and the "one country, two systems" formula.

The reason for this strategic choice is twofold. On the one hand, the PLA has not been engaged in a real war since its 1979 border conflict with Vietnam, which was more than forty years ago. Unlike the US armed forces, which since the early 1990s have been almost constantly at war, the PLA lacks combat experience. It is acutely aware of this.[5] In order to gradually acquire such experience, it is better for it to test new capacities through occasional MOAs, first non-lethal then more risky, near or far from national territory.

In other words, the CCP leadership cannot afford to throw the PLA into a conflict whose outcome would be uncertain and consequences multiple and far reaching. Any failure would have considerable domestic and international repercussions. It could weaken the leadership team in place, cause economic difficulties, lead to unrest, favor political evolution, and thus endanger the regime. It would undermine China's "prestige," one of the three essential power components, along with wealth and strength, according to Raymond Aron, among others. Failure would also risk compromising its "national renaissance" project and thereby its ambition to supplant the United States.

But would a success or a partial success in a war against Taiwan make China stronger and more secure? As shown above (cf. chapter 3), the Russian invasion of Ukraine has had so many international strategic as well as economic consequences that the Chinese authorities have been assessing in detail. It is likely that any attempted PLA annexation of Taiwan would put China in the doghouse for a long time. Beijing has for some time tried hard to reduce its dependence on the West, and to decouple with it in strategic sectors of its economy. It is also clear that it is improving its preparedness for any Western sanctions and ostracism. Nonetheless, the price to pay would remain very high, especially if the United States and its Asian and European allies continue to narrow their differences and consolidate their strategic posture vis-à-vis China's ambitions. In other words, the war in Ukraine has led the Chinese leadership to think deeper before embarking on a military operation against Taiwan.

Finally, would growing economic difficulties and domestic challenges persuade Xi or his successor, as a diversion or to unify the Chinese society around the CCP, to go to war against Taiwan? In my view, the regime's stability and perpetuation remain the CCP's priorities, ahead of any unification with Taiwan. Consequently, as I have written elsewhere, faced with internal problems, the CCP's strategic culture tells it to focus on resolving them rather than embarking on external operations.[6] This inexperience of war is thus a factor for peace or at least imposes some limits on any future PLA armed engagement.

On the other hand, this strategic choice favoring gray zone tactics and operations also to some extent reflects the Chinese society's state of mind. It has become unused to war. Nationalist and even warlike passion in China sometimes seems limitless and invincible. Xi-promoted "wolf warrior diplomacy" is its international acme. Nevertheless, as noted (cf. chapters 7 and 5), internal reactions to any Chinese blue helmet's death in Africa (four in recent years) or any PLA soldier killed in operation (as on the Indian border in 2020) have shown how ill-prepared Chinese society is for a conflict which would necessarily bring back numerous coffins to national soil. In fact, steeped in propaganda films and techno-military programs, Chinese nationalists often have an unreal, even playful vision of war. However, unlike electronic games which offer several lives, wars take the only life each fighter has. And despite Beijing's pro-Russian propaganda, the war in Ukraine has vividly reminded the Chinese society of the disastrous human and material consequences of any real war. In this context, the Chinese diplomats' aggressive tweets appear as so many psychological compensations for the authorities' hesitations to embark on a real war.

Meanwhile, by pushing its advantage by neither totally peaceful nor totally bellicose means, China has, without necessarily wishing it, almost mechanically led targeted states to react and adapt their strategies. Proving Kenneth Waltz's balance of power theses, the main result has been a stronger US engagement with its official and de facto allies, especially Japan, Taiwan, and the Philippines. There has also been a realignment of strategic postures among capitals that do not have formal security agreements with Washington: Hanoi and New Delhi of course, but also to some extent, Singapore, Kuala Lumpur, and Jakarta. There has also been the Quad's strengthening (Australia, United States, India, and Japan) and its gradual transformation, if not into Asian NATO as the Chinese government claims, at least into a strategic-military coordination structure, to Beijing's chagrin. Finally, in September 2021, the Biden Administration launched the AUKUS Pact with Australia and the United Kingdom, providing the former nuclear submarines and strengthening the US's strategic posture vis-à-vis China.

This strategic realignment has created a new balance of power which is also likely to ward off war risks. China's Navy has now become the world's largest navy, but if in the event of a conflict around Taiwan or in the South China Sea, the US, Japanese, Taiwanese, even Australian and Indian navies are engaged, the balance of forces would largely favor the United States and the official or de facto US allies. The reaffirmation or extension of US security guarantees also helps ward off war prospects. Although any incident or even military crisis cannot be ruled out, this is true for Japan, Taiwan, and the Philippines.

What about other countries? The diplomatic-strategic rapprochement between the United States and Vietnam or India does not offer any additional security guarantees to them. The same holds for Malaysia or Indonesia, which are to varying degrees embroiled in territorial or maritime disputes with

China. However, is it in Beijing's interest to take advantage of this to wage war on them? We have seen (cf. chapter 4) how much ASEAN and the prospects for adopting and implementing a code of conduct in the South China Sea contribute to restricting China's options. An armed offensive, a "lesson" as Beijing propaganda likes to call it, to a neighbor deemed to be too reckless or rash is not impossible. But there is also here a proportionality issue, which China is more aware of than is often believed. Beijing has many levers that can increase, if necessary, the pressure on a recalcitrant neighbor without having to cross the war threshold. Although the risks of gray zone operations turning to conflict cannot be totally ruled out, why would China abandon a strategy that has so far paid off? In other words, "winning without fighting" remains Chinese authorities' main guideline.

RISKS OR ARMED INCIDENTS AND MILITARY CRISES

Many arguments developed in this book reveal a real increase in the risk of armed incidents and even military crises, including between China and the United States. The more frequent frictions between the PLA Navy and the US Seventh Fleet in the South China Sea and Chinese coastguard incursions into the waters surrounding the Senkaku, and especially recent rise in PLA Air Force intrusions in Taiwan's ADIZ will sooner or later lead to an incident and a crisis that will have to be managed. As noted, Beijing and Washington, and more specifically the PLA and the Pentagon or INDOPACOM already have communication channels and mechanisms to resolve such crises. But it is not certain that in case of crisis these mechanisms will be activated. Moreover, on the Chinese side, and even the US side, provoking an incident to test the adversary's reactions cannot be ruled out. A non-premeditated incident, that is, resulting from a commander's or pilot's action, such as that of the EP-3 in 2001, is more likely to be resolved relatively quickly by diplomats. But a deliberate incident like the harassment of the *USS Decatur* in 2018 or probably also the clubbing attack on Indian soldiers on the border in June 2020, is much more difficult to resolve. That the first type of incident has given way to the second is worrying, as it reflects a clear desire for greater risk-taking. Such risk-taking, a military translation of China's power assertion, which we have witnessed since 2008 and perhaps even 2006, has been more evident since the 2017 19th Party Congress.[7] While bearing in mind Robert Jervis's advice on the gap between the real degree of centralization of the decision and the perception that one can have of it, this tendency seems undeniable.[8] As a good student of Kenneth Waltz, enjoying a more favorable balance of power, China thinks it can go further.

The *Decatur* commander's quick reaction helped avoid a collision, showing how much effort the US side was making in 2018 to prevent any escalation. There is greater and more lasting caution on Japan's part, refusing to open fire on Chinese coast guards or fighter planes, which violate its sovereignty around the Senkaku a little more every day. Rather similar behavior among Taiwanese authorities who seek at all costs to avoid any incident that would likely inflame passions on the continent and therefore ignite a clash.

However, the obvious increase in PLA's provocations has led the United States since the end of the Trump presidency to in turn consider greater risk-taking.[9] The aim of this US hardening is to try and persuade Xi to return to a less aggressive and above all less destabilizing behavior. But isn't it precisely Beijing's ambition to challenge the status quo and gradually weaken the sovereignty and security of Taiwan, the South China Sea islands it does not control, and the Senkaku?

Of these three objectives, Taiwan is now the most pressing. For reasons I have already explained, the other objectives can wait, as the current strategy already helps China strengthen its hand. Rumors were rife in China in 2021 that Xi had planned to forcibly take the democratic and de facto independent island in 2022, just before the 20th Party Congress. This has not happened but for some time among the US military, dire predictions of a war against Taiwan before the end of the current decade have multiplied.[10] Xi's power consolidation at this CCP Congress may boost his temptation to "solve" by violent means the "Taiwan issue" and as a result appear both as the great "reunifier" of the Chinese nation and the father of its rejuvenation. In any event, he has promoted at the 20th CCP Congress in October 2022 the right persons at the CMC to conduct such an operation, if he decides to act. These include its new vice president, general He Weidong, former commander of the Eastern War Zone, who organized Taiwan's "blockage rehearsal" after Nancy Pelosi's visit in August 2022, and the new chief of the general staff, general Liu Zhenli, the former commander of the PLA ground forces and a war hero involved in the 1986 border clashes with Vietnam.

What form will action on Taiwan take? The PLA is not yet ready to launch a frontal action (cf. chapter 3). China also does not want to be held responsible for sparking a third world war against the United States and its allies, even if it takes care to avoid nuclearizing it. As I have already hinted, Xi has no interest in embarking on an adventure which could, if it fails, destabilize him and even endanger the CCP's monopoly power. But he has pledged to reunify with Taiwan, otherwise China cannot, in his eyes, regain its greatness. He therefore needs to scare the Taiwanese, as they are so attached to their identity and their state—the Republic of China on Taiwan—and remain reluctant to any unification with the People's Republic of China. Will he deliberately provoke a military crisis, for example a partial and temporary blockage, in the strait to force the DPP Taiwanese government to endorse the so-called 1992 consensus, that there is one China, and later open unification talks? Will he raise the stakes, especially if after 2024 the DPP stays in power, in an attempt to persuade the Biden Administration to "twist the arm" of Tsai Ing-wen's successor and her party and coerce them into endorsing this "consensus"? The temptation, of course, is great. But for the reasons presented in chapter 3, chances of such a strategy succeeding are limited in the foreseeable future. For one thing, any US arm twisting of the Taiwanese authorities would violate the "Six Assurances." For another, being ready for a war in the Strait by 2027 does not mean that the PLA will act against Taiwan that year.[11]

However, intensified PLA intimidation contributes to arousing in Taiwan as in the United States debates on the island's long-term future.[12] It is clearly aimed at making the Taiwanese aware of the hard reality that there is no other outcome for them but a reunification with the mainland. This is a crucial pillar of Beijing's psychological war against Taiwan, the United States, and anyone in the world that believes otherwise. For now, such intimidation has increased the likelihood of a Cross-Strait and as a result a Sino–US military crisis. It has been a wake-up call for a Taiwanese society that had remained for too long carefree of the security challenges that it has been facing. Now Taiwan is really getting serious about its military defense and the conventional deterrence that it must put into place. And it is even harder for the United States to cave in as it would signal the end of *Pax Americana* in the Indo-Pacific region. On the contrary, everything indicates that the US military is getting ready for a showdown. Isn't it the best deterrence against any military adventure? For these reasons, as Kevin Rudd and others, I believe that a war in the Taiwan Strait remains avoidable.[13]

SINO-US STRUGGLE FOR WORLD LEADERSHIP: HOW WILL IT END?

There is now consensus in Washington on what has become of Xi's China: the main threat to US leadership. Can the United States maintain this leadership without seeking to contain and even weaken Chinese power in one way or another?

We thus return to Thucydides's Trap, this book's starting point and main inspiration. The fight between the two main powers now for world leadership is not only military in nature. It is global. On the economic front, it is likely that China will seize the top spot from the United States around 2030, even if its economic slowdown may postpone this development. But each country's gross GDP does not reveal the whole reality.[14] Moreover, beyond the COVID-19 crisis, the Chinese economy's growing difficulties, particularly its depressed housing sector, private sector, and job market, as well as its risks of becoming mired in the "middle income trap" have increased. In science and technology, the United States as a more open and attractive country is likely to remain the leader, despite China's massive investment in research and development. Actually, China's progress in this area has been partial and sometimes overstated.[15] This has obvious implications for China's defense industrial base which is not without vulnerabilities.[16] In addition, the partial decoupling decided by the Trump Administration and deepened by Biden, in a number of high-tech sectors, such as the semi-conductors, is intended to prevent the United States losing the lead it still enjoys in these areas. Politically and ideologically, each side believes it can win, but the United States remains more universalist and messianic than China, forced to adopt a position that I would describe as "defensive-aggressive" to justify repression of opponents, the harsh assimilation of minorities, particularly in Xinjiang and Tibet, the taming of Hong Kong, and continuation of a one-party dictatorship.

Finally, it is doubtful that China can supplant the United States militarily even by 2050. It will then undoubtedly have the world's largest military in terms of numbers of ships, aircraft, and conventional missiles, forcing the United States to adopt an asymmetric defense strategy in the Western Pacific. Moreover, it is clear that the US military is facing a number of well-known challenges.[17] But backed by a more vibrant defense industrial platform, US armed forces are likely to remain more global, advanced, and sophisticated.

The United States can also continue relying on Asian allies and partners as well as on the Five Eyes (Australia, Canada, United States, New Zealand, and United Kingdom) which, in the new strategic context, have strong reasons to remain faithful to it. The contrast between the perception of the Trump presidency among them (Japan, Taiwan, India, and Vietnam especially) and among NATO members highlights this inescapable reality. Whereas China has no allies and hardly any strategic partners who would be ready to come to its aid if a conflict erupted: even Russia, which supplies it with armaments, has not made this commitment.

In other words, the United States is far from having withdrawn and has a good chance of remaining in a favorable position vis-à-vis China. To use Susan Strange's theory, in its four dimensions (security, production, financial system, and knowledge), US "structural power" will continue outweighing Chinese power.[18] We are thus witnessing not a power transition, but rather the establishment of a new bipolarity, characterized by, in my opinion, a durable asymmetry.[19] For its part, China is persuaded, or more exactly has persuaded itself of the opposite. The duel or confrontation is thus destined to continue, probably without precipitating the two great powers into the Thucydides Trap.

TOWARD A NEW KIND OF COLD WAR AND ITS CONSEQUENCES FOR THE WESTERN PACIFIC

In reality, Sino–US strategic rivalry is likely to remain largely peaceful while fostering a new Cold War quite different from the first.[20] And this for several reasons.

In the economic domain, despite a partial but persistent decoupling desired on both sides, the interdependencies and thus common interests are too numerous. Both sides' business lobbies are pressing for their activities to not be too affected by strategic tensions. China's state capitalism—the Party empire lording it over all economic actors—can lend them some advantages in this regard. However, US businesses have never been able to prevent their president from declaring war if he deemed it to be in the national interest. Moreover, China needs globalization to succeed, although it has been seeking since 2020 to reduce external dependence. Relying on the new asymmetry that has emerged, China is using the economic weapon to influence partners and to neutralize any hostile measures they may take. It does not need to start a war.

Meanwhile, technological competition and consequent measures taken by the United States and its allies and by China to better protect themselves in this area can only harden further. Such competition is reminiscent of the Soviet era but now it is much broader, affecting all technologies—military, civilian, or dual, since it is getting harder and harder to disentangle these various types of technologies.

Finally, two of the new Cold War features make it resemble the old one: spying and ideological competition. Espionage has evolved, making great use of cyberspace, with Chinese services quickly learning from the US National Security Agency (NSA). It may be argued that such activity, relying on a greater variety of technical and human means and affecting a wider spectrum of scientific and technological fields, is more intense than in the Soviet era. The growing distrust of Chinese students studying and researching in the hard sciences in US universities reflects this.

Initially fueled by the CCP inside China, the new Cold War's ideological dimension has now spread to the United States and to the whole democratic world. Beijing's interest is to avoid any internationalization of this ideological conflict by wrapping itself in the most conservative Confucianism without abandoning a Marxism to which Xi is particularly attached.[21] Clearly, while claiming to have sinicized Marxism, Xi's China has not only stuck to the Soviet model but also reinforced it. It incessantly attacks what it calls "Western democracy" and, like the Soviet Union before, only promotes economic and social rights to the detriment of civil and political rights. This ideological confrontation should not be underestimated. It is quite likely that a democratic China will also seek to dethrone the United States. But a bit like the British-American rivalry in the late nineteenth century, such competition would leave much more room for cooperation. Like Randall Schweller and others, I think this ideological rivalry has largely fueled the current confrontation and, among other things, the impossibility of finding an acceptable solution on both sides of the strait to the Taiwan issue.

Can China win this new type of Cold War? Despite its undeniable economic successes and the diplomatic advances it has made in the region and more broadly among developing countries, probably not.

However, China's emergence and PLA modernization have favored a new balance of power in East Asia and the whole Asia-Pacific, which is gradually reducing US maneuverability and in the longer term may force its allies to find a modus vivendi with China. We are not there yet. But that is probably Beijing's calculation. Hence it is important that the international community, albeit lacking influence on China's internal regime, mobilize to change its external behavior in a direction that serves its interests and removes war risk. This evolution depends on everyone, especially every democratic nation, and above all the United States and its allies.

THE ROLE OF THE UNITED STATES AND ITS ALLIES

The Chinese leadership's international behavior, and especially its decision to go to war, does not only depend on Xi and his inner circle of confidants. It also depends on the United States and its allies.

The good news is that since he came into office, contrary to his predecessor, Joe Biden has given priority to improving relations with US allies both in Asia and in Europe. The growing tensions in the Taiwan Strait as well as the war in Ukraine have contributed to strengthening this strategic solidarity. Japan, South Korea, and the Philippines have responded positively to this initiative, particularly getting better prepared than before for any Taiwan contingency, in coordination with the US military. China is now part of the NATO agenda and the possibilities for US–European Union coordination of their policy toward this country have increased, making it possible to exert more influence on China.

It is clear that the Europeans will remain unable to weigh in, except in the economic and financial fields, on the global power balance in the Indo-Pacific. And this even when the main EU member states, primarily Germany and France, to which it would be desirable to add Britain, act in concert and adopt in their own ways, an Indo-Pacific strategy.[22] If the Europeans want to influence the Asia-Pacific strategic situation, they have no choice but to do so with the United States and its regional partners, especially Japan, India, Australia, and Taiwan.[23]

Yet the only power able to deter China from starting a war, particularly against Taiwan, is the United States. Contrary to what Beijing had hoped, the Biden Administration has not reset its China policy but strengthened the posture introduced by the two previous presidents (Obama and Trump) and made it more systematic and consistent. In many respects, its objective is not to contain China for the sake of doing so, but to counter China's growing power to prevent it from achieving regional hegemony in the Indo-Pacific and later supplant the United States everywhere.[24] It seems that the Biden Administration has adopted some of the recommendations made by Elbridge Colby and others in applying a "strategy of denial" on China.[25] While not totally lifting its strategic ambiguity, the Biden Administration has introduced more clarity about its commitment to Taiwan's security and more broadly the US defense perimeter in the Indo-Pacific. It is also crafting a much more credible "anti-hegemonic coalition" around China, together with Japan, AUKUS, and the Quad, in particular. The priority given to China as opposed to Russia follows also Colby's recommendation.

"Si vis pacem, para bellum": if you want peace, prepare for war. The old Roman adage appears to have been taken up more decisively than ever by the Biden Administration as the best way to deter China from starting a war, and especially attempting a military adventure against Taiwan.

Yet the US government would be well advised to avoid escalation and show "resolute restraint" in case of Chinese provocation, following the recommendations of Michael O'Hanlon and others.[26] It should also rely more on economic pressure and diplomacy, together with its allies, to defend its security as well as the security of its allies and partners. It seems that the Biden Administration has started adopting this strategy, for example when the PLA conducted an unprecedented military exercise in the Taiwan Strait in August 2022 or even after the Chinese spy balloon saga in February 2023. Moreover, as the PLA modernizes and get stronger, the US military has no choice but to adopt an asymmetric defense and deterrence strategy.

Moreover, better preparing for war does not mean that the United States or its allies should abandon their engagement policy with China. This policy must continue on all subjects on which it is possible to cooperate: climate change, health issues such as COVID-19, educational and cultural exchanges as well as non-proliferation (Iranian and North Korean cases especially). And on the economic front, cooperation and exchanges should continue to deepen in all the non-sensitive sectors.[27] But it is essential for the United States and its allies to make this commitment more selective, more conditional, that is, to constantly adjust it according to Beijing's behavior, and in light of any possible openings or concessions.

We must also keep in mind that this engagement policy does not aim to change China's political system as that would be unrealistic in the foreseeable future. Unfortunately, not enough Chinese people are willing to put pressure on their government and take risks to democratize their country.[28] This does not mean the United States and its allies should abandon promoting their values and denouncing the CCP-promoted authoritarian model. Quite the contrary. For both moral and strategic reasons, it is in their interest to intensify the fight for respect for human rights and to condemn more firmly, using more often targeted sanctions, Beijing's policy in Xinjiang, in Hong Kong, or with regard to the regime's opponents.

The United States and its allies must also insist more steadfastly that China respects international norms. The law of the sea and especially the 2016 arbitration decision on the South China Sea are the norms on which they should insist in priority. In order to be credible, it is indispensable that the United States ratifies the UNCLOS and aligns itself with the majority of the international community on this matter.

For this reason, it is important that the US Navy and other allied navies continue to sail in the South China Sea as well as in the Taiwan Strait. While the United States FONOPs may be more intrusive that its allied navies' passages, it should be noted that more Asian (Japan, India) and European nations (as France, Britain, and Germany) have joined this type of operations, sending a clear signal to Beijing.

It is also in the United States and its allies' interest that China's economy and society keep realizing greater prosperity. However, is it in their interest to help strengthen Chinese power and its influence over them? Hence it is necessary to both the United States and its Asian as well as European allies to propose stronger and more sustainable alternatives to the BRI. For the same reason, the United States and its allies must strengthen their screening of any Chinese investment or project on their respective territories. More broadly, in order to increase their bargaining power against China, it is necessary for them to reduce their economic dependence on this country in strategic sectors.

Such a task won't be easy as all these countries' economies have become highly dependent on the Chinese market. And a complete decoupling or isolation of the Chinese economy remains totally unrealistic. Yet there is a need for the United States and its allies to be better placed to hedge against the China risk.

In that respect, a deeper coordination between the United States and its allies is to be hoped for. In view of the unilateral decisions regarding semiconductors made by the Biden Administration in October 2022, it won't always be easy. Nonetheless, this coordination is necessary if the United States wants to prevent some of its allies, especially European ones, from being tempted by adopting a position of equidistance between Washington and Beijing. Such risks may be decreasing as China becomes more aggressive. Yet this temptation is always there, ready to be exploited any time by Beijing to drive a wedge between the United States and its allies and weaken its major rival.

In sum, realism and firmness with China are the best strategy for defending our interests and values, to help mitigate war risks between the new great power and the United States or its neighbors and to persuade its leadership to gradually accept international norms and perhaps one day democratize.

Notes

1. Rush Doshi, *The Long Game: China's Grand Strategy to Displace American Order*, New York: Oxford University Press, 2021.

2. Taylor Fravel, *Strong Borders, Secure Nation: Cooperation and Conflict in China's Territorial Disputes*, Princeton: Princeton University Press, 2008.

3. "Lucien Poirier: 'je crois en la vertu rationalisante de l'atome' (Lucien Poirier: "I believe in the rationalizing virtue of atom), *Le Monde*, May 27, 2006, https://www.lemonde.fr/planete/article/2006/05/27/lucien-poirier-je-crois-en-la-vertu -rationalisante-de-l-atome_776774_3244.html. Lucien Poirier was my professor of international strategy at the University of Paris 1 in 1978–1979. He died in 2013, aged ninety-four.

4. Steve Chan, *Thucydides's Trap? Historical Interpretation, Logic of Inquiry, and the Future of Sino-American Relations*, Ann Arbor: University of Michigan Press, 2020. Cf. also Alexander Vuving, "Great Power Competition: Lessons from the Past, Implications for the Future," Daniel K. Inouye Asia-Pacific Center for Security Studies (APCSS), September 2, 2020, https://apcss.org/wp-content/uploads/2020/09/02 -Vuving-25thA.pdf.

5. Minnie Chan, "China Military: 'Leaders' Lack of Combat Experience' a Drag on Modernisation Drive," *South China Morning Post* (*SCMP*), November 30, 2020, https://www.scmp.com/news/china/military/article/3111922/china-military-leaders -lack-combat-experience-drag.

6. *China Tomorrow: Democracy or Dictatorship?* Lanham, MD: Rowman & Littlefield, 2019.

7. Susan L. Shirk, *Overreach: How China Derailed Its Peaceful Rise*, Oxford University Press, 2022.

8. On China's foreign and security policy decision-making, cf. my article, "China Foreign and Security Policy Institutions and Decision-Making under Xi Jinping," *The British Journal of Politics and International Relations*, Vol. 23, No. 2, 2021, pp. 319–36.

9. Remarks by Lisa Curtis, member, National Security Council, "Global China: Assessing China's Growing Regional Influence and Strategy," Washington, DC, July 29, 2020, https://www.brookings.edu/wp-content/uploads/2020/08/fp_20200729_ global_china_transcript.pdf; cf. also Gabriel B. Collins and Andrew S. Erickson, *Hold*

The Line through 2035: A Strategy to Offset China's Revisionist Actions and Sustain a Rules-Based Order in the Asia-Pacific, Houston, TX: Baker Institute for Public Policy, Rice University, November 12, 2020, https://www.bakerinstitute.org/media/ files/files/1e07d836/ces-pub-asiapacific-111120.pdf.

10. In March 2021, Admiral Aquilino, the Commander of the US INDOPACIFIC Command, said that about a possible war against Taiwan: "This problem is much closer to us than most think, and we have to take this on," quoted by Rebecca Kheel, "Top Admiral: Possibility China Tries to Invade Taiwan 'Closer to Us Than Most Think,'" *The Hill*, March 23, 2021, https://thehill.com/policy/defense/544556-top -admiral-possibility-china-tries-to-invade-taiwan-closer-to-us-than-most/.

11. Iain Marlow, "'Sloppy' US Talk on China's Threat Worries Some Skeptical Experts," *Bloomberg*, November 4, 2022, https://www.bloomberg.com/news/ articles/2022-11-03/-sloppy-talk-on-china-threat-by-us-is-decried-by-some-skeptical -experts.

12. Neil Ferguson, "A Taiwan Crisis May Mark the End of the American Empire," *Bloomberg*, March 22, 2021, https://www.bloomberg.com/opinion/articles/2021 -03-21/neil-ferguson-ataiwan-crisis-may-end-the-american-empire?sref=ojq9DljU; Michael O'Hanlon, "An Asymmetric Defense of Taiwan," *The National Interest*, April 28, 2021, https://www.brookings.edu/blog/order-from-chaos/2021/04/28/an -asymmetric-defense-of-taiwan/; Charles L. Glaser, "Washington Is Avoiding the Tough Question on Taiwan and China," *Foreign Affairs*, 28 April 2021, https://www .foreignaffairs.com/articles/asia/2021-04-28/washington-avoiding-tough-question -taiwan-and-china.

13. Kevin Rudd, *The Avoidable War. The Dangers of a Catastrophic Conflict between the US and Xi Jinping's China*, New York: Public Affairs, 2022.

14. Sean Kenji Starrs, "American Economic Power Hasn't Declined—It Globalized! Summoning the Data and Taking Globalization Seriously," *International Studies Quarterly*, Vol. 57, No. 4, December 2013, pp. 817–30, and *American Power Globalized: Rethinking National Power in the Age of Globalization*, Oxford: Oxford University Press (forthcoming).

15. Cf. the report, titled *China-US Strategic Competition in Technology: Analysis and Prospects* in Chinese, produced by a Peking University think tank in January 2022 but rapidly censored. This report acknowledges that China still lags the United States in key technologies—particularly high-end semiconductors, operating systems and software, and aerospace. It has been archived here: https://uscnpm.org/2022/02 /06/pku-iiss-2022-report-tech-competition/.

16. Cortney Weinbaum, Caolionn O'Connell, et al., *Assessing Systemic Strengths and Vulnerabilities of China's Defense Industrial Base, With a Repeatable Methodology for Other Countries*, Washington, DC: Rand Corporation, 2022, https://www.rand .org/pubs/research_reports/RRA930-1.html.

17. GAO, "Challenges Facing the DOD in Strategic Competition with China," *National Security Snapshot*, February 2022, https://www.gao.gov/assets/gao-22 -105448.pdf.

18. Susan Strange, *States and Markets*, London: Pinter Publishers Limited, 1988.

19. Øystein Tunsjø, *The Return of Bipolarity in World Politics: China, the United States and Geostructural Realism*, New York: Columbia University Press, 2018.

20. Michael McFaul, "Cold War Lessons and Fallacies for US-China Relations Today," *The Washington Quarterly*, Vol. 43, No. 4, Winter 2021, pp. 7–39. For a more critical view with which I disagree, cf. Thomas J. Christensen, "There Will Not Be a New Cold War: The Limits of US Chinese Competition," *Foreign Affairs*, March 24, 2021, https://www.foreignaffairs.com/print/node/1127274.

21. Jie Dalei, "Six Principles to Guide China's Policy Towards the United States," *Carnegie-Tsinghua Center for Global Policy*, December 3, 2020, https://carnegietsinghua.org/2020/12/03/six-principles-to-guide-china-s-policy-toward-united-states-pub-83293.

22. François Godement and Gudrun Wacker, "France and Germany Together: Promoting a European China Policy," *Policy Paper*, Institut Montaigne, November 25, 2020, https://www.institutmontaigne.org/en/publications/promoting-european-china-policy-france-and-germany-together.

23. Cf. my own take on this issue, "France's Ambitious Indo-Pacific Goals for its EU Presidency," *Insights*, GMF, February 8, 2022, https://www.gmfus.org/news/frances-ambitious-indo-pacific-goals-its-eu-presidency.

24. *The White House, National Security Strategy, October 2022*, The White House, Washington DC, October 12, 2022, https://www.whitehouse.gov/wp-content/uploads/2022/10/Biden-Harris-Administrations-National-Security-Strategy-10.2022.pdf.

25. Elbridge A. Colby, *The Strategy of Denial, American Defense in an Age of Great Power Conflict*, New Haven, CT: Yale University Press, 2021.

26. Michael O'Hanlon, *The Art of War in an Age of Peace: U.S. Grand Strategy and Resolute Restraint*, New Haven, CT: Yale University Press, 2021.

27. Ryan Hass, Patricia M. Kim, and Jeffrey A. Bader, "A Course Correction In America's China Policy," Global China, *Policy Brief*, November 2022, https://www.brookings.edu/wp-content/uploads/2022/11/FP_20221103_america_china_policy.pdf.

28. Cf. *China Tomorrow: Democracy or Dictatorship?* op. cit.

Index

About the Author

Jean-Pierre Cabestan is Emeritus Senior Researcher at the French Center for Scientific Research, Paris, and Emeritus Professor of Political Science, Department of Government and International Studies at Hong Kong Baptist University. He is also associate researcher at the Asia Centre, Paris and at the French Centre for Research on Contemporary China, Hong Kong. His main themes of research are Chinese politics and law, China's foreign and security policies, China–Africa relations, China–Taiwan relations, and Taiwanese politics. His most recent publications are *China Tomorrow: Democracy or Dictatorship?*, Lanham, MD: Rowman & Littlefield, 2019 and *Demain la Chine: guerre ou paix?* (China Tomorrow: War or Peace?), Paris, Gallimard, 2021.

9 781538 169896